Constructing
"Race" and "Ethnicity"
in America

Constructing "Race" and "Ethnicity" in America

Category-Making in Public Policy and Administration

Dvora Yanow

M.E. Sharpe
Armonk, New York
London, England

Library of Congress Cataloging-in-Publication Data

Yanow, Dvora
  Constructing "race" and "ethnicity" in America : category-making in public policy and
administration / by Dvora Yanow.
    p. cm.
  Includes bibliographical references and index.
  ISBN 0-7656-0800-6 (hc: alk. paper) ISBN 0-7656-0801-4 (pbk.: alk. paper)
    1. Group identity—United States. 2. Race. 3. Ethnicity. I. Title.

HM753.Y36 2002
305.8′00973—dc21

                                                            2002024500

Printed in the United States of America

The paper used in this publication meets the minimum requirements of
American National Standard for Information Sciences
Permanence of Paper for Printed Library Materials,
ANSI Z 39.48-1984.

BM (c)   10   9   8   7   6   5   4   3   2   1
BM (p)   10   9   8   7   6   5   4   3   2   1

Table of Contents

Two men were walking along the river. One said to the other,
"Look how happy the fish are as they swim in the river!"
The other said, "You are not a fish.
How do you know whether the fish are happy?"
The first replied, "You are not me. How do you know
whether I know what the fish think?"
                    —*Chinese fable (from Minow 1990, p. 227)*

Similarly the Russian radical Alexander Herzen observed
that we classify creatures by zoological types,
according to the characteristics and habits
that are most frequently to be found conjoined.
Thus, one of the defining attributes of fish
is their liability to live in water,
hence, despite the existence of flying fish,
we do not say of fish in general
that their nature or essence—
the "true" end for which they were created—
is to fly, since most fish fail to achieve this
and do not display the slightest tendency in this direction.
          —*Isaiah Berlin,* Four Essays on Liberty *(quoted in Gray 1996)*

to explore and to celebrate the similarities
which join us in the human community,
and the differences between us which make us
fascinating to each other;
to reveal "the other" in ourselves …;
to provoke laughter and tears,
to excite, to startle, to shock …
              —*Jeanne Cannizzo and David Parry (1994, p. 45)*

From this promiscuous breed
has risen
that race now called
Americans.
                    —*Crèvecoeur (quoted in Jefferson 1999, p. E2)*

Preface

What do we mean in the United States today when we use the terms "race" and "ethnicity"? What do we mean, and what do we understand, when we use the standard set of five race-ethnic categories: White, Black, Asian-American, Native American, Hispanic/Latino/a (or their variant forms)?

It has become commonplace in the academy—among the social sciences in particular, from anthropology, sociology, and ethnic studies to some fields of political science, especially political theory—to speak of "race" and "ethnicity" and their specific categories (e.g., "African-American," "Asian-American," "Native American") as socially constructed concepts. That is, they are perceived and understood to be human inventions, created to impose some sense of order on the surrounding social world, often for political purposes. This means that they are variable, rather than fixed and stable. Indeed, a historical view of groups and individuals considered "White" on some occasions and "Black" on others shows this to be the case.

And yet, in many areas of the contemporary administration of public policies, both concepts and categories are used in precisely the opposite way—as if they *were* fixed, stable, and scientifically grounded in the human social world, as if they did correspond to some naturally occurring reality. This book explores this seeming conundrum: why it is that social and biological scientists' current understanding of race and ethnicity has not made inroads into policy and administrative practices. In analyzing several of these practices, it becomes clear that the answer lies in the practices themselves: the ways in which race, ethnicity, and their categories are used in policy and administrative arenas undergird and sustain a public perception of them as "scientifically" factual.

In many areas of the contemporary administration of public policies, we ask others or are asked ourselves for identification by race-ethnic makeup. Policy and administrative uses of the five standard race-ethnic terms now most commonly occurring create categories of Americans for political purposes, and such ongoing, commonplace, everyday usage sustains them—or introduces opportunities for change. The widespread use of "race" and "ethnicity" and their terms evokes their societal importance and centrality in the United States today for the crafting of individual identity. This contemporary discourse creates, maintains, and reifies concepts and categories of race and ethnicity that have no empirical grounding either in the natural world or in any accepted scientific field studying that human world.

American "ethnogenesis"—the creation of the "peoples" of the United States—is thereby achieved through the use of these two kinds of demographic categories—"racial" and "ethnic." Contemporary race-ethnic discourse is marked by the interweaving of two sets of meanings concerning personal and political identity: the concepts of race and ethnicity themselves, and their specific attendant categories. Such ethnogenesis is accomplished in large measure without explicit attention: category making is a mode of implicit reasoning. But this implicit reasoning leads to explicit actions— both in the realm of individual identity practices and in the crafting of social policies and their implementation. Policy and administrative practices sustain the reification of a set of categorical relationships that, were we but explicitly cognizant of them, many would likely disown. It is my hope in this book to begin to make some of these silences in public discourse speak.

"Race-ethnic" identity is complex and multifaceted. Part of that complexity is that although *race* and *ethnicity* are often used to refer to different things, they are also used interchangeably. For this reason I use "race-ethnic" in this book as a single referent for both. This lack of terminological clarity is part of the subject of my argument. To draw attention to their artifactual character, as distinct from the "scientific" character in which spirit they are commonly used, I should put quotation marks around "race" and "ethnicity" consistently throughout the book. I have not done so for editorial reasons, but I invite the reader to envision them marked in this way.

Chapter 1 outlines the cognitive ideas and associated practices embedded in the concept of "categories" and their construction. What do we do when we categorize, and how can category names or labels shape thought and action?

The rest of the book then asks, why these particular categories? That is, according to what characteristics is today's population being divided? Why are these the characteristics being used, rather than others? And, importantly, what characteristics are being left out? On what are these categories silent? What public discourse is encouraged by this form of categorization, and what discourse is being discouraged? What are some of the implications of contemporary American race-ethnic discourse for public policy and administration, and vice versa? The book is, then, about contemporary practices of categorizing and their implications for race-ethnic identity and race-ethnicity– related policies.

Much of the work on American races and ethnicities, whether in ethnic studies or in one of the academic disciplines from which it draws, focuses on a single group or, at most, on relations between two groups, and in that case predominantly, still, on "Blacks" and "Whites." With the exception of the handful of books on mixed race,[1] most such studies begin with a priori definitions of "race" and "ethnicity," often relying in this on anthropological texts. I have sought to begin from the other end, in the world of practice, to see how the concepts are being used in everyday life and from there to determine what "senses-in-use" Americans have been making of the terms. This practice- or act-based orientation has led me to the world of public policies and their administrative implementation, and in particular to two federal data collection agencies—the U.S. Census Bureau, which makes the most extensive use of the concepts and their affiliated categories, and the Equal Employment Opportunity Commission (EEOC), which monitors race and ethnicity in employment—and to the schools, hospitals, police departments, and other local agencies that collect and use these categories for various state, federal, and local programmatic purposes. I also turned to one sector of social science research—that concerned with workplace diversity—to see how academic researchers were using the concepts and categories.

Focusing on the meanings made by various policy and organizational actors in the creation and enactment of public policies, rather than on a priori academic or dictionary definitions, constitutes an interpretive approach to policy and organizational analysis.[2] It is a reading of meanings in use, in action, in practice—an inductive reading from human act to human meaning, rather than a deductive examination beginning with conceptual definitions to see how they are applied. Methodologically, such an approach requires an attention to the artifacts created by human actors—language, objects, acts—that embody those meanings (Yanow 2000a). In this case, these artifacts are: the words and linguistic structure of the categories, the census and other questionnaires as objects vested with policy meaning, and the acts of asking for identification and of self-identifying.

I need first to establish, for the argument, that the concepts of race and ethnicity are not reflections of the naturally occurring human world—they are not given by nature—and are not supported by sense-based observations alone. Rather, the categories we use today for American race-ethnic groups (as for all such) are social constructions created by humans to bring order and sense to human experience. While this is more of a commonplace in contemporary anthropology and biology, and becoming more accepted in legal studies and in ethnic studies—and so to academics, it might seem unnecessary to reiterate this argument—it is still not common sense in public policy and administration or among much of the public, to judge from my graduate students' reactions at the beginning of our seminars on this subject. In fact, part of my argument here is that the concepts and categories are treated in contemporary American policy and administrative practices as if they *were* scientifically grounded, with attendant implications. This is seen most clearly in OMB Directive No. 15 and the U.S. Census, the subjects of chapters 2 and 3. The 1990 census questions treated race and ethnicity separately, yet the categories made available for answers clearly show that race and ethnicity *in use* are treated as if they mean the same three things: color, culture, and country of origin. Changes to Census 2000 have not altered this usage, although they address some aspects of it.

An examination of other administrative and policy enactments of race-ethnicity and the categories further demonstrates their logical fallacies and inadequacies as scientific categories. Chapter 4 compares Census Bureau data collection policies with those of the EEOC and other agencies. This comparative analysis raises questions about who gets to choose and assign an individual's identity: the individual or the agency administrator. "Passing"—living a public life that is at odds with the race-ethnic identity ascribed by society—is one way in which individuals resist assigned identities, although the concept itself depends on a perception of the categories as fixed and stable. Chapter 5 explores the implications of such contemporary race-ethnic discourse for administrative practices in local agencies as they collect data for state and federal purposes and seek to use them for their own program planning. In chapter 6 these issues are reflected in an analysis of published research on what has been called workplace cultural diversity and its management, showing ways in which social scientists as researchers, writers, consultants, and journal editors contribute to ethnogenic processes. Recording the field data from these sites leads, at times, to a certain repetitiveness in these chapters, as similar data are found in disparate sites. And yet it is important, I think, to see the wealth of these primary data in order to grasp the full extent and implication of these several practices. These layerings of data constitute a "thick description" (Geertz 1973) of processes of ethnogenesis through category usage in race-ethnic policy and administrative practices.

The categories are used in these several policy and administrative contexts in much the same ways: as if they were grounded in science, given by nature, fixed, and immutable. This analysis points to several inadequacies in the embedded logic of race-ethnic category construction. The distinctions that the categories imply and impose do not hold up to individuals' experiences. For one, more and more individuals find themselves not fitting into single race-ethnic categories as propounded in American policies and administrative practices. They claim membership in multiple categories, or they don't fit into any at all. While Census 2000 provided for such multiplicity, other agency practices do not (yet). These individuals are categorical "surplus" or "leftovers," and they are saying so in ever increasing numbers and in ever louder voices. This means the categories are no longer (if they ever were) functionally exhaustive. The implications for administrative practices are that programmatic and personnel choices are being made on the basis of categorical assumptions of internal homogeneity that are misleading, resulting in administrative policies and practices that are destined to mismatch their intended and desired results. College admissions programs, for example, intended to implement policies on behalf of underrepresented groups, often exclude them because those groups—Hmong, for example—are categorized broadly, for example, as Asian-Americans, and "Asian-Americans" are overrepresented among college and university populations, on the whole. In actual practice, then, the uses of the terms "race" and "ethnicity" and of the categories are anything but standard. The commonsense understanding of race, ethnicity, and their categories as scientifically regular and objective cannot be sustained, based on actual human experience.

Why do we continue, then, as a collective to use these concepts and particular categories? In chapter 7, I argue that current American ethnogenesis allows the telling of three kinds of stories: national identity stories, group identity stories, and national origin stories. These storytelling practices are narrated and enacted through administrative apparatuses such as the census. Through these narratives we sustain and revise our collective sense of who "we" are as Americans and of what it means to be an American. At a greater remove from practice, it can be seen that individuals' stories no longer fit the conceptual story told by the categories. To the extent that this conceptual story has reflected a sense of national identity and citizenship, the lack of fit implies a shifting national story. This suggests that even before September 11, 2001, Americans may have reached a key point in redefining ourselves as a nation, reshaping our collective self-perception, including its encapsulation in these categories.

And yet, since the 1980 census, we have developed a greater reliance on these categories for social justice purposes, and for the sake of comparative counting to measure progress (or its lack), the categories have to be frozen in time. This may put a burden on implementing agencies that they can no longer support. The admixture of data collection purposes for redistributive and social-justice ends with individual and collective narrative purposes is not working well for either. The nation is engaged in a symbolic discourse on national identity—on what makes the "good" American—but the symbolic artifacts can no longer support the weight of the multiple meanings they have been asked to carry. These identity questions need to be discussed explicitly, publicly, and nationally. As I suggest in chapter 8, such discourse must include a reexamination of the purposes of and needs for data collection in regards to race-ethnicity. Only such an explicit public conversation can free our policy and administrative apparatuses from carrying, tacitly, a burden they are incapable of implementing.

States count. Almost any almanac gives figures for crop sizes by variety and region; for miles of asphalt roadways; for average rainfalls per annum; for rural, urban, and metropolitan population sizes. This book does not seek to explain why they count or create categories for doing so. Neither is it a history of the census or of "race science," although both of these figure in the discussion here. Nor is it a work of political theory, although it is informed by theoretical and philosophical arguments. It is, instead, a field study of public policy and administrative practices relative to the concepts of race and ethnicity. It seeks to discover how "race" and "ethnicity" work in practice and how language use—specifically, in the form of categories and categorizing—shapes and is shaped by those practices; and it seeks to suggest why they work that way and what might be entailed in changing those practices. It is, in this regard, both an illustration of how interpretive policy analysis might be done (i.e., one form it might take) and an example of what it brings to the analytic table. One idea it brings, in the context of race-ethnic studies to which it is here applied, is an appreciation for the complexity of categories as socially constructed entities: They take on an ontological status as objectively real, especially as they are invoked and used by the state and imputed with the aura of "science"; but as *social* constructions, they can be socially changed—with all the difficulties entailed in doing so, which requires unseating a reified concept.

I write here as an American—and I use the collective "we" when I want to point to what I see as a collective, national, American discourse. That is also part of the argument of this book: that our collective policy and administrative practices are creating and reflecting and sustaining a national identity story that coexists and struggles with, and at times transcends or is submerged by, other stories of subnational groups in which some of us, including myself, may claim membership. I ask my readers to interpret this "we" in reference to those moments when each of us—by filling out some form that asks for race-ethnic identification, for instance—plays a part in the collective (re)creating, or challenging, of American race-ethnic-genesis.

There is another reason for the "we" voice. This is a deeply personal piece of work, as others have been, but in different ways. The more I delved into this subject matter, the more I found echoes and explanations of my own lived experience as a child. This, too, accounts for my choice to use "we"—in an effort not to produce an antiseptic, arm's-length treatment of a subject that is so close to my own self-constitution. I fully recognize the ambiguities of referent inherent in this choice, as well as some readers' feeling that I am making inclusive statements that nevertheless leave them, or others, out. Like Haney López (1994, 3, n. 5), I believe the ambiguity and confusion may be useful. As he notes, "the anxiety induced by the indeterminacy of words like 'we' and 'our' demonstrates the complexity of socially mediated identities."

As an interpretive social scientist, I believe that our experiences—family, communal, educational, work-related—shape our understandings, of our selves, our surroundings, our readings. This includes, perforce, our understandings of race and ethnicity, and hence of what is written here. I have had many indications of this already, in readers' responses to this manuscript as it took shape and as I have used various parts of it in teaching. *De no ser notada*—not to call attention to oneself as different—is still an ingrained part of the reactions of many of us Americans to aspects of our contemporary race-ethnic discourse; but increasingly less so, I think. I hope this book will contribute to that process of turning what is still experienced by many as an Anglo-centric national identity narrative into a multi-centric one, in which all race-ethnic groups are valued equally, not just in categories, but in practices.

Notes

1. Root (1992) and Zack (1992, 1993, 1995) in social science; Scales-Trent (1995), Williams (1995), and others in more literary works.

2. Interpretive analysis is a developing approach within public policy analysis, drawing on early- to mid-twentieth-century philosophical work in hermeneutics, phenomenology, and some critical theory. See, for example, de Leon (1998), Edelman (1964, 1977), F. Fischer (1998), F. Fischer and Forester (1993), Fox (1990), Healy (1986), Jennings (1983, 1987), Maynard-Moody and Stull (1987), Roe (1994), Yanow (1993, 1995, 1996).

Acknowledgments

This book has been many years in the crafting—in some respects, I might even say, most of my life, as I can recall ruminating on racial and ethnic matters as a teenager. During its academic life, I have been aided and encouraged by many colleagues, students, friends, and family members, as the ideas branched out into ever newer areas. There were many paths that I wanted to pursue further, many additional sources of ideas left unexplored and unread. I had to call a temporary halt—or risk drowning in material. For it is an endless, enthralling, and infuriating subject, for all its intractability and injustice.

I began this work in reaction to the many questionnaires about race or ethnicity with which one is confronted in the United States in the last two decades of the twentieth century and into the twenty-first. My starting question was: Why can't people be more careful to use "race" and "ethnicity" properly instead of confusing them—instead of using "ethnicity" to refer to Blacks, for example, and "race" to refer to Hispanics? At a small conference of organizational culture researchers in February 1992, I overheard Davydd Greenwood talking about convening a group of Spanish and American anthropologists to discuss race and ethnicity and mentioned that I was writing on that subject. I sent him a copy of the conference paper that was the first expression of the ideas developed here and promptly received back enthusiastic and extensive comments and an invitation to the gathering the following spring. He also gently referred me to his and other work that suggested that the scientific underpinnings I (and others) assumed to underlie such a distinction did not hold. Davydd's encouragement has been ongoing, along with very material contributions in the form of detailed comments on subsequent papers and the evolving manuscript. Without his collegial support, I would have long ago given up the work in the face of my own fury and dismay at what I was learning. Davydd's co-convener of the conference, Carol Greenhouse, also offered encouragement, along with other conferees, among them Phyllis Chock, Josep Maria Comelles, and Dan Segal.

David Rosenhan also read that first paper and several of its subsequent revisions and responded with great verve. He made possible an extended affiliation as Visiting Scholar at Stanford Law School, which helped me feel like a scholar again. During part of that time, I was able to attend Stanford's Faculty Seminar on Comparative Race and Ethnicity, and my thinking was stimulated by many of the papers presented there.

The late Murray Edelman (1919–2001) was a continuing source of support for this and other work, reading and commenting on an earlier version of the manuscript and sending copies of his own work. Our e-mail exchanges during these last several years touched, among other things, on mysteries and Israel and Jewish matters. I miss his collegial friendship.

I also miss the lively intellectual engagement and friendship of two others who no longer walk among us. Helen Vogel Yanow (1921–1998), my mother, was a staunch supporter of all my work but took a particular interest in this project. As I once again worked through the newspaper clippings that constitute some of the data, I was very moved, over three years after her death, to find her handwriting on several of them, from Chicago to Orange County, calling my attention to one feature or another of the debate. In many ways, she acted as my research assistant on this book. And David Mackenzie Parry (1942–1995), a man of the theater, of folklore, and of folksong, taught me to appreciate "interpretation" in a new way, as he and his troupe wrote plays that enacted ideas about the Canadian race-ethnic "mosaic" in interpreting museum displays.

Martha Feldman read an earlier copy of the manuscript, and her attentive reading led me to rethink the structure of the book. An author could not have hoped for better reader-reviewers than Mary Hawkesworth and Steven Maynard-Moody. To them I owe the debt of supreme collegiality: each reviewed the final draft in record time, providing detailed commentary that has helped me to clarify my intended meanings.

I need to acknowledge an intellectual debt to Scott Noam Cook, whose suggestions helped to frame the first conference paper. Stella Nkomo and Ella Bell offered initial encouragement after reading the early papers, as did Hal Colebatch, who added his own particular take from "down under," and Ellen Pader, whose view of home occupancy codes brought another angle to the conversation. Mitch Allen's publisher's eye picked out the holes in an early draft of the manuscript, and his sharp questions helped me explicate what I was trying to say; and Peter Labella, also reading as only an editor can, offered the sort of response that keeps an author going at critical points. To Harry Briggs, my editor at M.E. Sharpe, I am indebted for encouragement, for close textual readings, for conference-time breakfasts and such, and for an ear attuned to sound and nuance. I could not have wished for a finer editor.

That the artifact you hold in your hands falls short of these readers' respective visions is no fault of theirs.

I am grateful to several former students, among them Mary Irving for research assistance in the preparation of an earlier version of chapter 2; Kevin Lynch for his very able research assistance in preparing the paper that served as the basis for chapter 6; and Renee Chin for providing assistance on a section of the preliminary research for that paper. Students in a Fall 1992 graduate seminar provided a most helpful check on, and thought-provoking discussion of, that research: John Espinoza, Karen Ueno, Luana Kiger, Macgreagor Wright, Rose Ugbah, Jennifer Cullen, Ed Stewart, and Greg Brown; and my understanding was also enriched by the comments of their classmates Karen Dundes, Leyne Ezray, Taha Fattah, Shawn Jackson, and Karen MacNamara. Chapter 5 grew out of stories told me by a number of public administrators, some of whom asked not to be identified. Not among the latter are students in my Winter 1996 graduate seminar, who shared my amazement at how race-ethnic categories are used in agency practices and whose research and insights drew my attention to yet other practices: Barry Kalar and Amy Brown on police departments, Juliet Shanks on mixed-race couples and their children, Lanamaria Smallwood on hospitals, and Sandra Oubre on schools. My thanks to them and to Charles Cook, Len Libresco, and Vit Novotny for their comments and to students in subsequent seminars for their responses to the evolving manuscript, including Tess O'Leary for her insights into adoption processes and placements and Zara Mirmalek for her historical work and her insightful reflections more broadly.

Parts of what became chapters 1 through 6 were presented at the Fifth National Symposium on Public Administration Theory, Chicago, April 9–10, 1992; the Western Political Science Association Annual Conferences in Pasadena, California, March 18–20, 1993, and in Portland, Oregon, March 16–17, 1995; "Democracy and Difference," a public conference convened by Carol Greenhouse and Davydd Greenwood at Indiana University, Bloomington, April 22–25, 1993; the American Society for Public Administration Annual Conference, San Francisco, July 19–21, 1993; and the American Political Science Association Annual Meeting, Washington, DC, September 2–5, 1993. I especially thank the members of the audience at Indiana University and my Spanish and American co-conferees for their lively responses to this work, and Joelle Bahloul of IU's Anthropology Department for her stimulating public comment on the paper. Earlier versions of material in some of these chapters have appeared as "American Ethnogenesis and the 1990 Census" in *Democracy and Ethnography*, ed. Carol J. Greenhouse (Albany: SUNY Press, 1998)—parts of chapters 1–4 here; "American Ethnogenesis and Public Administration," *Administration & Society* 27:4

(February 1996), 483–509—part of chapter 5; and "Public Policies as Identity Stories: American Race-Ethnic Discourse," in *Telling Tales: On Narrative and Evaluation*, ed. Tineke Abma, Advances in Program Evaluation, vol. 6 (Stamford, CT: JAI Press, 1999)—sections of chapter 7.

I have learned that this subject touches the lives of many people, in many different aspects of life; and I thank the many colleagues, students, and friends who, after the formal conference panels, during class breaks, and in other private moments, shared with me their personal stories of race-ethnic identities that confound easy categorization.

Part I
Laying the Groundwork:
Giving a(n) (Ac)Count

What do the U.S. Bureau of the Census, the U.S. Equal Employment Opportunity Commission, the U.S. Department of Housing and Urban Development, police departments, and schools have in common? Aside from being public agencies—and, as such, agents of the state—they all play a central role in counting the population of the United States, each for its own specific programmatic reasons. All of these agencies, along with others not listed here, use sets of categories for these counts; and in counting and reporting by these categories, they participate not only in classifying those they enumerate, but also in *giving an account*—that is, in telling a story about the people they categorize and count. Chapter 1 relates counting to naming in the process of making categories, and both to science and the establishment of identity.

U.S. federal policy has mandated, since the late 1970s, that race-ethnic data be counted. The Office of Management and Budget published Statistical Directive No. 15 in 1977, naming and defining the categories for tabulating these data. The directive was revised twenty years later, in time for Census 2000. Chapter 2 explores these names and definitions, as the ways in which the U.S. federal government "does" race-ethnicity in a "scientific" fashion.

1

Constructing Categories:
Naming, Counting, Science, and Identity

It is an anachronism to believe that our world
is more securely founded in knowledge
than one that is driven by pangolin power.
                              —*Mary Douglas (1975, p. xxi)*

Indeed, the very desire for guarantees
that our values are eternal and secure
in some objective heaven is perhaps only a craving
for the certainties of childhood
or the absolute values of our primitive past.
                              —*Isaiah Berlin,* Four Essays on Liberty
                                        (quoted in Gray 1996)

Let us begin with the first of two thought experiments. How many races are there in the United States? Name them.

If you answered five, you would be following common administrative practices between 1980 and 2000. The federal government, in the form of the Office of Management and Budget's (OMB) Statistical Policy Directive No. 15, identified—named and defined—for data collection purposes, beginning in 1980, five American racial or ethnic groups: White, Black, Hispanic, Asian or Pacific Islander, and American Indian or Alaskan Native. The 1990 U.S. Census, on its forms and in its data tabulations, made allowances for some additional variations on these five:

- An unspecified number of possibilities for American Indian, depending on the individual's principal tribal affiliation as indicated by him or her, and Eskimo and Aleut as possibilities for Alaskan Native;

- Twenty-five specific possibilities for Asian or Pacific Islander (API), plus the option of identifying another group;
- Two names for Black, Negro being the other (although there is only one box to check);
- Eleven possibilities for Hispanic, plus the option of naming some other one.

Discounting all the possibilities for choosing "Other" (other tribe, other API, other Hispanic, other race), that means the 1990 census provided specific possibilities for 41 different American race-ethnic groups. This is without itemizing the 119 federally recognized Native American tribes, plus untold numbers of others not (yet) recognized. According to one researcher, one mountainous province in North Vietnam alone reported being populated by as many as 16 ethnic groups in 1958, with over 100 for the whole country (Dang, n.d.); and although the Han ethnic group is dominant in China (at 91 percent of the population), there are 55 minority nationalities, including Manchu and Mongolian (Singer 1997). Even if only some members of these Vietnamese and Chinese groups immigrated to the United States, the American race-ethnic picture gets even more muddied. Indeed, with the 1997 revisions to OMB No. 15 and changes to Census 2000, the Census Bureau will report out 63 race-ethnic possibilities (Fan 1999).

Academic research suggests other possible answers. *Ethnic information sources of the United States* (Wasserman and Morgan 1976) identified 112 "ethnic peoples." This number does not include Blacks, American Indians, and Eskimos, for reasons the editors explain in their introduction.[1] The *Harvard Encyclopedia of American Ethnic Groups* (Thernstrom, Orlov, and Handlin 1980) lists 106 ethnic groups. The 1992 edition of *Ethnologue* (Grimes 1992) identified 191 American language groups (including, e.g., those speaking American Sign Language): 164 living, 26 extinct, and 1 a second language without mother-tongue speakers. Accepting language as one of the elements that constitutes an ethnic group, these sources yield a much larger picture of U.S. race-ethnicity than that defined by the federal government's five 1980 categories.

The second thought experiment is this. Imagine an employment questionnaire that begins by asking: "What is your race?" or "What is your cultural heritage?" and that for answers provides the following possibilities:

• Northeastern	• Southern
• Midwestern	• West Coast

or, perhaps, these possibilities:

• Downeasterner	• New Yorker
• Hoosier	• Appalachian
• Chicagoan	• Californian
• Texan	• Okie/Arkie
• Bostonian	• Southerner

These answers represent other possible category schemes for American race-ethnic identification, created and organized from a different vantage point from the one that has constructed the schema presently in use.

My intention with these two thought experiments is to suggest that there is nothing "natural" about how Americans think, talk, or practice the race-ethnic discourse most commonly in use in the United States today. We are making American race and ethnicity in everyday administrative practices and public policies, in acts and in the language used in carrying out those acts. This race-ethnic discourse—by which I mean both acts or practices and the language used in conducting them, in a mutually implicating fashion—constitutes the daily (re)creation of race-ethnic identities; in turn, this ethnogenesis sustains the specific race-ethnic categories created, invoked, and used.

Much of the collective, national knowledge about race and ethnicity is embedded in this category language and in the tacitly known rules for its use. The categories reflect a set of ideas about race-ethnicity, as do the various policy and administrative practices that create and use the concepts and categories. The concepts "race" and "ethnicity" as they are used in the United States, and the practices of naming and counting race-ethnic groups, reflect a set of ideas about identity. But although this knowledge is held conjointly in a society, much of it is known tacitly. As Polanyi (1966, p. 4) noted, "We can know more than we can tell." It is possible to begin to make at least some of this tacit knowledge explicit, and thereby begin to examine beliefs about race-ethnicity, by examining the practices in which this knowledge is used. It is in its use—in its enactments, including speech and writing—that tacit knowledge comes closer to the surface of explicitness and can be more readily, though not always easily, seen.[2]

Much ink has been spilled in attempting to define *a priori* what "race" and "ethnicity" are and are not.[3] As Goldberg (1992, p. 544) notes, most social science exploring the meaning of race has stipulated its definition in keeping with a sense of what the term *should* mean. What is of interest to me here, however, is how these concepts are used in actual practices, quite aside from normative usages or social scientists' definitional debates. How are the concepts of race and ethnicity understood by contemporary Americans, not as conceptually abstracted from a context of practice and daily life, but in their actual use as reflected in policy and administrative enactments? Call it "common sense" (Geertz 1983a), call it "folk wisdom" (Lakoff 1987), the definitions-in-use in public policies and administrative practices both reflect and shape human understanding of the meanings of these concepts.

This analytic approach rests on the distinction captured in the saying, "Do as I say, not as I do": thought and act are often discrepant. Asking people directly what they think about race-ethnicity is likely to elicit a set of espoused beliefs or values—whether because interview or survey participants often tell researchers what they think the latter wish to hear, or because they say what they think they ought and wish themselves to believe. By making a close "reading" of the categories constructed collectively, as a society, in and through public policy and administrative practices, I aim to make more explicit what those beliefs are, not as espoused, but as enacted.

It is the collective or social dimension of category and concept construction, learning, and knowing that I am after. Public policy and administrative practices reflect public knowledge at the same time that they shape it. Processes of category making in the public arena reflect and shape, maintain and change; both aspects are mutually interactive and inextricably intertwined. The OMB's revisions of its list of categories and the Census Bureau's revisions of its tabulation procedures are a product of numerous hearings, meetings, deliberations, testimonies, position papers, and so on. The new categories are, in short, *constructed* texts, not *authored* ones produced by some identifiable Ozian wizard behind a bureaucratic curtain.

Public Policy and Administrative Practices as Public Narratives

Pressman and Wildavsky (1973) maintained, in a view probably shared by many, that there is no point in legislating policies that cannot be implemented. This sentiment reflects an instrumental-rational approach to public policy (and perhaps a certain American pragmatism). And yet, many unimplementable pieces of legislation are, in fact, drafted and passed at all levels of government. One example of such seemingly unimplementable legislation may be found in several local governments in California's San Francisco Bay area—Hayward, Berkeley, Oakland, and Santa Cruz—as well as in Cambridge, Massachusetts, and Ann Arbor, Michigan. Each of these cities has declared itself a "nuclear free zone." Signs posted on their streets proclaim this status. Yet, these cities' governments are unable to stop the transshipment of nuclear materials across their borders: such shipping travels over federally funded highways, and federal law supersedes local law.

From an instrumental-rational point of view, such policy making is pointless, and any evaluation of it would only highlight that pointlessness. But sense does appear if we broaden our understanding of human action, including policy making, to include an expressive dimension. In this vein public policies can be seen as narratives or stories through which a polity's members express, to themselves and to one another, as well as to more distant publics, their collective identity and values.[4] Taylor (1988) defines expressive acts as those that have meaning for the people who engage in them. They are not only the instrumental, goal-oriented communication of information. Expressive behaviors, Taylor said, give voice to something within a repertoire of shared experience. Seen from an interpretive view, narrative is one such form of expressive act, created to give voice to human meaning.

Public policies are, in this sense, a collective narrative. They construct public, collective knowledge and identity as they link a memory of the past to the present, and possibly to some future as well. Through them, a polity, acting within a repertoire of shared experience, gives voice to its identity. Through public "policy-tales" (Schram and Neisser 1997; see also Buker 1987), members of the polity narrate publicly, to themselves and, at times, to others, who they are, as a polity, in terms of what they value (Yanow 1996, chap. 1). The nuclear-free cities case illustrates this. The policies were (and are) unimplementable, yet they were not exercises in futility (except from a perspective that sees public policies as solely instrumental endeavors); rather, they gave voice to each polity's collective sense of values, beliefs, feelings— to members' identity as a polity.

Identities are asserted by naming them. Each category scheme and the names it encompasses are a condensed articulation of an identity story. It is a group's collective story, but it also becomes the story of individual members of the group or the story against which they measure their own stories, fitting it or not. When the categories are created by the state, identity claims by individuals or groups may be subverted—or individuals and/or groups may feel their powers of, or rights to, self-definition being impinged upon. State-constructed category names channel the contestation of identity, thereby blurring the line between individual and collective self-affirmation through self-identification and the discriminating and sometimes discriminatory practices of other-identification (Greenhouse and Greenwood 1994, p. 9). There is a power in naming groups. The name evokes a common identity, and in so doing, it presumes a common interest. Yet the group name is needed in order to contest (and possibly refashion) that identity.

Collective identity narratives are typically on view in public displays or enactments: public policies, the implementory practices of administering those policies, discussions in public fora and the headlines and articles reporting on them. Although at some point of origin, parts of these may have had individual authors, by the time they work through legislative, organizational, and communal-societal processes, they have become collective efforts: "authored" texts become "constructed" texts. It is in these constructed texts that one can look to find collective identity stories.[5] Although public discourse and policy and administrative practices engage the substantive elements of the policy issue explicitly, the expanded story line is often known tacitly. It is communicated through the use of and interaction with policy and program artifacts (including language, physical objects, and acts) in a symbolic process, in which the communication is often tacit.

Public policy narratives sometimes feature another dimension. In the face of incommensurable values or beliefs, people often create a myth—a narrative, not an argument or explicit explanation, although not necessarily one with a fictionlike plot—which serves, at least temporarily, to suspend the tension between the incommensurables and allow action to proceed. Much like a bracket, it blocks further inquiry into the contradictions, forcing attention away from them and toward moving on. In the process, explicit public discourse on the incommensurability is rendered *verboten,* silenced. That does not mean, necessarily, that it does not take place. It may yet be conducted, albeit through tacit means. These include any form of human action—language, physical artifacts, acts—that represents, symbolically, the beliefs, feelings, values—the meanings—whose explicit discussion is forbidden or taboo (Yanow 1992a, 1996). Collective stories, whether or not they entail myth forms, are one such artifact through which what is meaningful to a polity may be symbolically communicated. The contest over American identity—the definition of the "good" American, a subject that is typically silenced from explicit public discourse—is being collectively and publicly played out, in part, in race-ethnic stories. These identity stories condense a more elaborate story line, which is communicated through the set of categories and the concepts.

This is a hermeneutic reading of public policies and their associated administrative practices, much as an anthropologist "reads" cultural displays: as "an ensemble of texts" that display and enact cultural meanings and that the anthropologist seeks to read over the shoulders, as it were, of those engaged with them (Geertz 1972; see also Bell 1997). Such a reading follows in the hermeneutic tradition of treating human acts and other nontextual artifacts as if they were texts ("text analogues," in Taylor's [1971] phrase; see also Ricoeur 1971) and applying to them analytic approaches developed for understanding the meaning of literal texts. As I am myself an American, I am, as it were, reading over my own shoulder, observing the culture in which I am participating, writing at times about "Americans" more distantly, at times including myself in the "we."

Categorizing

We make categories. As Stone (1988, p. 307) notes, "Categories are human mental constructs. . . . They are intellectual boundaries we put on the world in order to help us apprehend it and live in an orderly way. . . . [N]ature doesn't have categories; people do." Creating categories, in other words, is a human activity; the categories themselves are human artifacts, created in the process of living life.

Category making entails classifying a set of items according to qualities the classifier perceives in them as making them belong to one category rather than another. Categories highlight elements that are deemed to be similar within the boundaries they draw and different from elements beyond those boundaries. These perceptions of samenesses of things within categories and differences between things in different categories become the organizing principles or logic around which categories are built: something belongs in Category A because it shares "A-ness" and is not "not-A."

Category making and the classification of members of a category set are often everyday activities. Dishes and pots and pans are often grouped on cabinet shelves by shape and size, or color and style, or intended and customary usage, or some combination of these. Food is stocked in grocery stores by category: There are sections for fruits and vegetables, for breads, for dairy, for fish, for meats, for cans, for boxes, and so on; and within each category items are grouped by type: the dairy case contains milks, yogurts, cheeses, eggs. Books are located on library shelves by elaborate classification systems: the Dewey decimal system, the Library of Congress system, or (at home) one's own idiosyncratic alphabetical-and-subject system. States categorize and classify their citizens and residents in a wide range of areas: military service and rank, income and taxation levels, educational attainment, occupational and professional practices, and more (see Bowker and Star 1999 and Scott 1998 for other examples). Scientific theorizing often begins with the construction of categories or taxonomies, as variables are identified, defined, observed, classified, and counted. Unlike cooking or shopping or book shelving or agency administration, however, categorizing is rarely the focus of human activity. Even in identifying variables, the researcher more commonly focuses, at least initially, on the research question and the patterns of action within the realm of research, rather than on taxonomic characteristics. Categorizing is something that takes place more typically while one is attending to some other focus of attention. It is, in other words, embedded in a practice: in a set of activities together with the particular language and tools, spaces, or other objects used in that endeavor.

Category making, then, entails naming. The biblical book of Genesis relates

how God brought Adam all the animals to name *according to their kinds*—
that is, to name them by category. This is read in Western traditions as a mark
of humanity: none of the animals has the power to name. It is also read as a
mark of divinity: God, too, named and categorized—heaven and dry land;
day and night; fruit trees and vegetables; creatures of the air, sea, and land.
In many religious or cultural traditions, knowing the name of something or
someone is understood as giving the "knower" control over that thing or
person. Again, the Bible provides an example. In the book of Exodus, Moses
asks God what name the people Israel might use to call on God; in many
religions, knowing the right name is deemed important in compelling God to
answer one's prayers. Some groups give people multiple names, some for
use outside the house and among non–family members, others only known
to and used by family members. For example, anthropologist Sergei Kan
(1995), in speaking of a Tlingit woman who adopted him into her clan as her
younger brother (and named him after that brother, who died shortly after Kan
arrived in Sitka), calls her by her Tlingit name when speaking of her familiarity with traditional rituals and "Mrs. Young" when speaking of her as "a very
devout Orthodox Christian." I grew up calling my grandmother's brother
"Uncle Meshalter," learning only as an adult that that was a contraction of
his given name (Moshe) and the Yiddish word meaning "the Older." He was
sickly as an infant, so "*alter*" was added to his name to fool the Angel of
Death: the angel would come looking for an infant but find only "an older
one" in the crib.

Categorizing and classifying often lead to or are undertaken for the purpose of counting, especially in the realms of scientific and state administrative endeavors, and counting has a similar power to naming. Knowing how
many elements there are in a class of items, or how many classes there are in
a category set, implies intimate knowledge of the entity being classified, and
that knowledge can be used to affect or influence or control it. Knowing that
there are "ten million alcoholics in the United States" (Gusfield 1981, p. 55)
conveys a certain factual standing, and the magnitude of that number is enough
to compel serious public attention and shape public policy in respect of treatments or "cures" or other actions. Counting and categorizing often work
together, especially when counting entails a choice to count something "as"
one thing or another—that is, judging it as belonging to this category rather
than to that one. Building taxonomies—naming and counting—is one of the
practices undertaken in doing science; and this association lends a "scientific" quality to category making.[6]

In naming things and people, categories assert claims about their identity.
Although these identity claims do not reflect the whole of something or
someone's character, restricted as they are to those aspects of the categorized

elements that are highlighted by categorical logic and classificatory principles, they often come to be seen as the essence of the classified element. Naming a category asserts its importance; counting its members further underscores this. A set of category names encapsulates a story about the identities of its members. Enumerating category membership enacts the conceptual logic according to which the category set was created and narrates the identity claims it entails. This is especially the case when such category making is or reflects a public, collective activity—such as when the state creates, defines, and invokes a set of categories to itemize its population.

In analyzing American usages of race-ethnic categories in contemporary public policy and administrative practices, several characteristics became evident.

The Conceptual Logic Embedded in Category Construction

Category names comprise sets whose members share the features with respect to which they are the same and different. The so-called basic food groups, for example, share "foodness"; as elementary and high school students learn through exercises and tests, "meat, fruits, vegetables, grains, and books" would be an illogical category set, because books—while perhaps providing food for the mind and nourishing the soul—are neither protein, carbohydrate, nor fat and (usually) do not feed the body.

A category and its contents are internally undifferentiated: they constitute a single unit, a whole. They are portrayed, perceived, and treated as clearly distinct from all other categories and their contents in the category set. "Meat" and its contents (beef, lamb; steak, stew) is at once a single unit whose members share "meatness" and an entity distinct from "milk" and other "non-meatness" categories. The categories in a set are not treated as points on a continuum: they are portrayed and treated as if they were entirely distinct, discrete, and discontinuous.[7]

When a single category is treated (poultry, "White"), the similarities of its elements (chicken, turkey, duck, Guinea hen; Italian, Irish, Polish, German) appear more salient than their differences from elements of other categories. When a set of categories is examined (meat, poultry, cheese; White, Black, Native American), it is the differences that become more central. Classifying—assigning an element to one category or another within a set—entails an interpretive choice—a judgment—based on the relative importance of certain features over others.[8]

At the same time that they foreground the features with respect to which they are the same and different, categories blind us (by definition, not by moral failure) to other features that nonetheless remain present in the categorized elements. Meat, eggs, and yogurt are all animal "products," although this similarity is occluded by a set of category names organized from a different point of view (e.g., meat and dairy cases in a supermarket). As Edelman (1995, p. 130) noted: "While one connotation may be dominant in a particular context, the others remain latent or subconscious. . . ." The conceptual logic of category making implies that the differences between category set members are sharp (onions, carrots, broccoli), when from another viewpoint they may be only minor gradations of difference (vegetables).[9] Categories within a set are held together by the tension of this implicit, sharp (sometimes oppositional) differentiation: each depends upon its set members for continued existence.

The highlighting of some features ("foodness"; race, as a source of identity) lends them, on the surface, an importance denied to the occluded features ("animalness"; occupation, talents, birth order). The ideal version of the highlighted feature(s) for each category in the set becomes the prototype (Lakoff 1987) or what phenomenology would term the "typification" (Berger and Luckmann 1966) for that category. It often comes to be seen as the essence or the Platonic ideal that is the norm (or "normal" case) against which other elements in the category are assessed. The presumedly fixed, unchanging stability attributed to category sets and their membership derives from the sense that categories capture the essential attributes of the things they classify.

There is another mode of classifying that exists alongside the prototype mode, in which categorizing judgments appear to be more mechanical, less evaluative. In this mode, a set of rules has been worked out, and their application to the new element is carried out by rule matching rather than prototype norming. One example of this would be the sorting of mail in an office mailroom: the rule could be by alphabetical order of addressee's last name or by building floor (in ascending or descending order) or by department, and slotting or stacking would proceed accordingly. Although such categorizing also privileges one feature over others, there is less ambiguity in each feature: Yanow begins with a Y, the Department of Public Administration at Cal State Hayward is on the fourth floor, and it is not the Philosophy Department (also on the fourth floor, but next door).

Bowker and Star (1999, pp. 61–64), drawing on the work of linguist John R. Taylor, identify this more mechanical, binary distinction system as Aristotelian. To the extent that the prototype system harks back to notions of Platonic ideals, ancient debates between two schools of thought are here recapitulated in contemporary classification practices. In many cases, principles of classification cannot be delimited to one or two elements, and features are perceived differently by different people (Are meat, eggs, and cheese members of a single category set or not?); hence, the Aristotelian-prototype distinction breaks down. In most of the race-ethnic practices explored here, prototype judgments are the most common, despite efforts to develop a more binary-type "slotting" system. In fact, many of the difficulties in these practices arise when seemingly binary systems do not fit the lived experiences of the people being classified. However, one of the cases discussed in chapter 5 is a classic example of mechanical slotting, and it "works" because it is a people-less application of rules (although I hope that the discussion here will raise questions about what it is working "for").

The acts of judgment entailed in classifying are masked by the uses of categories, particularly in scientific contexts, which more often than not treat (or appear to treat) categories as if they were commonsensical reflections of the natural world. This treatment is embedded in the process of socially constructing human realities: The creative act (and the judgment it entailed) is submerged over time and gradually forgotten; the social realities take on the character of fixed, stable, unchanging, objectively real entities—they come to seem as if they were always "that way,"[10] as if they were and are naturally occurring, rather than as humanly created "conceptual boxes" (the phrase is Kuhn's [1970, p. 5]) superimposed on what it is they purport to describe. This seeming naturalness is undergirded by the perception of categories as embodying the essential attributes of their members: essences have a fixed, stable quality.

These basic aspects of category construction and classification themselves entail certain other features that are central to category analysis, an interpretive research method intended to gain insight into the logic underlying the architecture of a category set.

Category errors. A set of category names or labels implies two sorts of things about the world of elements being categorized. First, they suggest that nothing has been left out: the categories are exhaustive; everything in the world of the category set has a place in one of the categories. Second, there is no overlap in category membership: the categories are discrete; no element fits into more than one category. Categories become problematic when either (or both) of these two principles is violated: when one or more elements do not fit in to an existing category within the set, or when an element fits into more than one category. These may be termed category "errors" or "mistakes," from the perspective of the logic embedded in the category set. The classic case, in American and other Western societies, is sex, widely thought to come in two versions: male and female. When an infant is born with "ambiguous" genitalia, physicians, in consultation with parents, assign the child to one of the two accepted sexes and, surgically, make the child conform to that decision (Fausto-Sterling 2000).[11]

A defining point of view. The claim that categories are socially constructed ways of knowing and seeing entails two properties. As "constructed" entities, they are not natural kinds existing in the world, but human creations superimposed upon that world. As "social" constructions, categories express the shared meaning of a group of people about what characteristics of a situation are most salient; they are not the product of a single individual's thought or creation. The logic according to which the category set is constructed and named reflects this shared meaning from the point of view of the group creating the categories, naming them, and classifying elements within them.

Tacit knowledge. Moreover, the cognitive organizing principles underlying category making are typically not made explicit, although this knowledge is known, usually tacitly, to members of the group (organization, society, community, tribe) creating and using the categories (and it is passed on, also usually tacitly, to new members, through various processes of socialization and acculturation). Members of an interpretive community have the ability to, and typically do, group objects into similarity sets without explicitly having to ask, or needing an answer to, "similar with respect to what?"[12] This tacit knowledge, while self-evident to group members, is often bizarre or incomprehensible to nonmembers. Jorge Luis Borges (1966, p. 108), for example, presents the following taxonomy of the animal world, attributing it to an ancient Chinese encyclopedia: ". . . animals are divided into

(a) those that belong to the Emperor
(b) embalmed ones
(c) those that are trained
(d) suckling pigs
(e) mermaids
(f) fabulous ones
(g) stray dogs
(h) those that are included in this classification
(i) those that tremble as if they were mad
(j) innumerable ones
(k) those drawn with a very fine camel's hair brush
(l) others
(m) those that have just broken a flower vase
(n) those that resemble flies from a distance."

This may seem a fantastic example of incomprehensible categories, but it is not much more extreme to an outsider than the real-world example noted by Lakoff (1987) that included "women," "fire," and "dangerous things" as three of its elements.[13] In these and other cases, category logic may be self-evident to members of the group that created them and unfathomable to others.

Marking. Tacit knowledge is present in a second way. Within a category, one element—the prototype or typification—may be considered the usual case, the norm, against which deviating—"marked"—cases are assessed. For example, woman doctor, Asian-American writer: "doctor" and "writer" are the unmarked cases, the "default values," so to speak, the expected norms.

Jokes sometimes depend on tensions between marked and unmarked speech, as in the 1980s story about the boy who, riding with his father, is injured and rushed to the hospital. The surgeon, hurrying into the operating room, stops short, saying, "I can't operate. That's my son." The supposed riddle rests on the unmarked "surgeon" being identified, finally, as the boy's mother, a marked—unanticipatedly female—surgeon. The unmarked case is often taken to be the more basic variety, the simpler version, and this at times connotes a "better" one: the marked case is different, not normal, which in current American culture often connotes an inferior version.[14]

Occluded features and silences. The highlighting of some features of sameness and difference and the deflecting of attention from other features (which themselves might be perceived as keys to sameness and difference from another perspective) point to a central element of category analysis. It needs to attend not only to what characteristics are being highlighted as the basis for category making, but also to the traits that are being obscured or occluded. In looking at a social—that is, collective—construction in the public sector, analysis needs to ask, Is category making contributing to silences in public discourse? In focusing on race-ethnic elements of individual identity as central to American identity-formation and social justice concerns, is public discourse systematically silent on, or silencing, some other important element?

Situated, local knowledge and change. Categories reflect a historical moment with its attendant sociopolitical "realities." Other individuals or groups may not share in the same set of meanings or perceptions of salience. Since categorizing is a human activity, categories reflect human perception and understanding at a particular point in time.[15] This means that categories are themselves not fixed; category names, boundaries, and what they refer to may well change over time. That does not mean that such change is easy. "Conventional categories are hard to dislodge, especially when they are parts of an integrated, mutually reinforcing network" (Edelman 1995, p. 145). Lived taxonomies at times cannot be changed without concomitant upheavals in social life.[16]

It is not just their set-ness—their embeddedness in a nest of interwoven conceptual relationships—that makes category change difficult. We tend to reify many categories, forgetting that they are social constructions, treating them as if they were fixed and as though they existed in nature. In particular, categories that are related to areas of scientific research are accorded the qualities commonly attributed to the subjects of physical and natural science: that they are externally observable and verifiable. Even in the face of a number of category "errors," category logic is hard to dislodge. Their reification as naturally occurring entities and their perceived and attributed essentialism accord categories a very strong believability.

In the policy arena, these reified categories often become the basis for political judgments and administrative action, forgetting their "as if" quality.[17] At times action is justified by appeal to these categories long after the original perceptions of the human world that launched their genesis have changed. When administrative actions are based on categories that no longer fit individuals' lived experiences, these actions are likely not to solve the problems to which they are addressed. Indeed, they may even be the source of new administrative and human problems.

Race-Ethnic Categorizing and the Persuasive Power of "Science"

As philosophers and sociologists of science have argued, the practice of science itself is a cultural enterprise (e.g., Harding 1991, Kuhn 1970, Latour 1987, Longino 1990). This includes the construction of taxonomies. As Kuhn (1970) noted, "Scientific fact and theory are not categorically separable" (p. 7). What this means in the context of "race" and "ethnicity" as aspects of human identity is that embedded in them, as well as in their attendant categories, is a theory about the world that they purport to reflect and describe. Their long history of use in primary, secondary, and university biology and anthropology classes lends them the status and power that are associated, in American society, with "Science."

The social reality is that the concepts have been treated and taught for much of the twentieth century as scientific facts. There is a long history of "race science" in the United States, with European antecedents. Most histories of American or Western race-ethnic thought begin their narrative in the period of eighteenth-century science, typically with Carolus Linnaeus's four-part classification system of 1735: Americanus, Afer or Africanus, Asiaticus, and Europaeus, all geographically based, to which he added a fifth, *monstrosus,* each with its associated physical and behavioral traits.

Blumenbach elaborated on these, producing a different five-part scheme by 1781 (Caucasian, Mongolian, Ethiopian, American, Malay, also with associated descriptions; W.H. Tucker 1994). Anthropology textbooks published as late as the 1970s, and still found on library shelves today, present a three-part classification system of "modern man" (Caucasoid, Mongoloid, Negroid) according to statistical averages of body shape, height, skull size, physiognomy (nose, eye, and lip shape in particular), hair texture, and skin "color" measured in great detail and mapped around the world (e.g., Beals and Hoijer 1965, p. 210; Bean 1935; Kroeber 1948; Sheldon with Stevens and W.B. Tucker 1970; see also Marks 1995 and W.H. Tucker 1994 for critical general histories and Litvin 1997 in the context of "diversity"). A 1982 *World Atlas* maps the world by eleven different combinations of skin tone and hair texture (cited in Spickard 1992, p. 22, n. 4).[18] In scanning this literature, anthropologist Stanley Garn (1968, p. 9) noted that various researchers had "found" between 2 and 200 "racial" groups.

The contemporary fact that biologists and anthropologists have, by and large, abandoned claiming the concepts and categories as scientifically grounded entities has not yet widely percolated through to public consciousness, in part due to this long association with science and the power of its ongoing status, in part due to the heritage of old ideas and the entrenchment of tradition, in part due to their perceived "scientific" taxonomic character, and in part because they support a political stance itself grounded in a moral position, an argument made extensively by critics of race and racism (see, e.g., Greenwood 1984).

These ongoing practices continue to lend the concepts and categories a scientific quality, and their scientific heritage continues to bolster their public perception as scientifically grounded entities. As Gusfield (1981, p. 28) put it, "Science, scientific pronouncements, technical programs, and technologies appear as supports to authority, and counterauthority, by giving to a program or policy the cast of being validated in nature, grounded in a neutral process by a method that assures both certainty and accuracy." Given its association as a scientific practice, categorizing brings this validation to race-ethnicity. Research in the last fifteen years has shown that humans are genetically much more similar to one another than they are marked by "race"-based differences (such differences are limited to less than 10 percent).[19] Nonetheless, their long association with science "colors" the way these concepts are presently treated in public discourse—including, as I will show in chapter 6, academic discourse in public policy and administration. Usage of the concepts of "race" and "ethnicity" and of the standard categories further reinforces a perception of them as natural, scientific entities, rather than as humanly created, social (arti)facts.[20]

Moreover, these practices and this reiterative process carry on their backs, as it were, in a metaphoric fashion, remnants of the meanings attached to the concepts in earlier times, moving them implicitly from their source contexts into their new applications.[21] Every time the concepts and categories are used, these implicit meanings are reinforced, as collective learning transmits tacit knowledge (Yanow 2000b). Part of this tacit knowledge concerns the ancient meanings of race-ethnicity.

Although many contemporary critics of American race science locate its roots in eighteenth- and/or nineteenth-century European practices, the underlying ideas appear to have even earlier origins. The ancient Greeks— Hippocrates (460–377 B.C.E.) is one source—explained the composition of the material world in terms of four basic elements: earth, air, fire, and water (each of them a particular combination of two primary qualities, a hot/cold dimension and a dry/moist dimension).[22] The elements correlated with bodily "humors," and human behavior was seen as being produced by the humor predominating in each individual's combination of the four:

Elements $\longrightarrow$	Humors $\longrightarrow$	Behaviors
earth	black bile	melancholy
air	blood	nobility, militancy, courage
fire	yellow bile	choleric, excitable
water	phlegm	passivity

The ancient theory was that the four humors, developed by inhaling elemental essences, combined in different proportions within each person, and the predominant humor produced the affiliated behavioral trait. The balance of these four, they believed, could be affected by two aspects: genealogy and environment. These two aspects continue to affect contemporary usages of race and ethnicity, along with an essentialism that derives from seeing humans as composed of material "essences" associated with particular behaviors.

Greek philosophy is the source of another aspect central to the Western heritage of race-ethnic understanding. The ancient Greek concept of perfection laid the groundwork for the hierarchy of species, which later Christian thinking elaborated into the Chain of Being—although the typical "tree" describing its offshoots reduces the four elemental-humoral-behavioral aspects to three races: Caucasoid (white), Mongoloid (yellow-brown), and Negroid (black; see Bean 1935, p. 86). The moral dimension seems to enter here, as these three are assigned biblical origins descending from Noah's three sons (Shem/Caucasoid; Ham/Negroid; Japhet/Mongoloid): the hierarchy of animal species, extended to a hierarchy of humans, attaches Christian moral judgment (and political argumentation) that derives its justification from biblical text, to the classifications. The attachment of a valuative hierarchy to the colors, justified in terms of the associated behaviors, provides the underpinnings of the four-part color scheme and its associated behavioral attributes that still shows up over 2,000 years later: the lazy, melancholy Black; the noble (red) "Savage" (Indian); the excitable (yellow) Asian; the placid White.

These taxonomic efforts to develop a hierarchical ranking of American race-ethnicities were intertwined with emerging nineteenth-century ideas of statistics as a science of measurement, used to measure and classify body parts in terms of size and shape according to categorical "norms" (the prototype form) and marked deviations from the norm, across continents and nationalities. This, in turn, joined the growing eugenics movement of the nineteenth to twentieth centuries, immigration policies, and tests for measuring intelligence. One of the central figures in statistics, Englishman Sir Francis Galton, was a leader in the eugenics movement, as was Francis A. Walker, a statistician and, as Superintendent of the Census Office, director of the 1870 and 1880 U.S. censuses (and later president of MIT; Anderson 1988; Haller 1963; Nobles 2000, p. 60, gives 1860 and 1870 as the dates of the censuses Walker administered, while Zuberi 2001, p. 25, lists 1870, 1880, and 1890). While his thinking was influenced by evolutionary theorist Herbert Spencer, who developed a hierarchy of cultural groups, Galton's own ideas influenced Karl Pearson, who developed a statistical measure to explain the stratification of humans in society (Tucker 1994). These ideas, in turn, entered the public policy arena in immigration legislation that linked eugenics—the building of a "beautiful" race—with restrictions on certain populations. Davydd Greenwood observes (correspondence, 1/2/2000) that parametric statistics draws on the notion of the Platonic ideal. As noted above, that notion marks one of the dominant approaches to categorizing, and particularly to categorizing race-ethnicities. The idea of ranking humans and their race-ethnic-influenced attributes extended statistics into psychology through the development of "intelligence" tests, particularly in the work of Lewis Terman (see Zuberi 2001 for a more extensive history).

In many respects, state efforts to name and count populations by race-ethnic identity markers still exhibit elements of this history. The Irish, Italian, Jewish, and other non–Anglo-Saxon, non–Protestant European immigrants identified as races in the 1800s to mid-1900s are now subsumed under "White." Their designation as distinct racial groups has been lost from public discourse. The Civil Rights movement and ensuing integration of schools, neighborhoods, and workplaces made great strides in severing the explicit association of "race" with imputed behavioral attributes and their related valuative gradations (although not entirely: it keeps resurfacing in relationship to intelligence; see, e.g., Herrnstein and Murray 1994). But the notion that "race" reflects both genealogical (bodily-biological, genetic) and geographic (environmental) differences has largely and commonly been retained, as can be seen in the dictionary definitions that begin chapter 3. For the most part, the valuative hierarchical rankings that degraded so many have been routed; but echoes of that remain embedded in the logic of category making and use, as we shall see in subsequent chapters.

Studying Categories

The analytic approach presented in this book is a mode of interpretive policy analysis, reflecting ideas from phenomenology and hermeneutics. Phenomenology focuses on the individual's lived experience as the source of meaning making, including in self-understanding. Hermeneutic views of social acts see artifacts—language, acts, physical objects—not only as human creations but, importantly, also as the embodiment of human meaning projected into or onto them by their creators (and interpreters; see, e.g., Polkinghorne 1983; Ricoeur 1971; Taylor 1971). This creative, meaning-endowing process does not work in one direction alone: every time an artifact is engaged or used, its underlying meaning(s) is (or are) sustained—or, potentially, changed.[23]

Interpretive approaches treat acts of meaning making and interpreting as central to human endeavor, including in the capacities of scientists, policy makers, and administrators implementing public policies. The language, physical artifacts, and acts operative in the situation being studied can be analyzed to see what meanings they embody, tacking back and forth among the specific artifacts (whether language, objects, or acts), their creators/users, and the contexts of their use. Analysis typically begins with the artifacts themselves, seeking to tease out their context-specific meanings in an inductive fashion, rather than beginning with a set of generalized meanings and seeking to find them, deductively, in the artifacts. Seeking to understand the lived experience of—the meanings made by—actors in a specific situation, yet recognizing the difficulties people often have in reflecting on and articulating their own meaning making, interpretive analysts often look to such a "textual" or narrative reading of artifacts to help reveal meanings.[24] Categories are one such artifact that can be studied in this fashion.

A number of related fields engage category analysis along these lines. Cultural anthropologists explore acts, language, and physical artifacts as reflective of meaning. They analyze "the symbolic forms—words, images, institutions, behaviors—in terms of which, in each place, people actually represented themselves to themselves and to one another" (Geertz 1983b, p.

58). Anthropologists have also long been involved with classification practices, categorizing kinship systems, languages, potsherds, and so on (see, especially, Durkheim and Mauss 1903/1963). Mary Douglas, in particular, has combined the analysis of symbols with category construction, exploring the relationships between category names or concepts, the acts entailed in using category members, and the meanings these have for the community, society, or polity in and out of which the categories have grown (1966, 1982/ 1973, 1975).[25] "Systems of symbols," she writes, "get their meaning from social experience. They are coded by a community with a shared history" (1982, p. xix). Given their origins in a collective past, they may appear to us in the present moment as naturally occurring. But, as she shows throughout her work, they are "culturally learned and culturally transmitted. . . . [T]here are no natural symbols; they are all social" (1982, pp. xix–xx).

While cultural anthropologists attend to language as one among many forms of human action, cognitive linguists focus on language as the conceptual system with which humans make sense of their experiences. In this view, language both reflects prior understanding and shapes subsequent action. It is both a model "of" and a model "for."[26] The linguist George Lakoff has explored categorizing in application to political action (1996, see also 1987, and Lakoff and Johnson 1980). Meaningful concepts, in his and other cognitive linguists' view, are rooted in what is meaningful to human beings, rather than being generalized and abstracted from human experience (see also Freire 1973 on this view, in the context of education). Categories are the central way in which humans make sense of experience; they are basic to human thought. Lakoff challenges the traditional view that category membership is inherent in the features of the elements being categorized. Rather, as he extensively argues and shows, categorization is a human act, and categories reflect the point(s) of view and/or experience of their human creators. In this approach, as with Douglas's, there is nothing natural about categories: they reflect the human mind more than they reflect the natural, "objective" world.[27]

In linking meaning making and language to political acts, the study of symbolic politics brings these two approaches together. It focuses on language as a central, though not exclusive, means of communicating a polity's ideas, at the same time that it looks at public policies and administrative practices as the enactment of those ideas. Language itself is seen as a form of action (and not only "as a means to promote rationality" [Edelman 1995, p. 24]).

Murray Edelman extensively explored how political language and action communicate meaning, shaping and shaped by practice. As he so often noted, classification is central to political concerns and acts (1977, 1995). Political category making is typically not driven by scientific analysis, but rather reflects and shapes political meanings at that moment in time. "Categories are especially powerful as shapers of political beliefs . . .when they appear to be natural, self-evident, or simple description rather than devised . . ." (Edelman 1995, p. 129). They appear to be natural, in part, because members of a society acquire them as children, through parents, schools, and other authorities, and through the language and images of conversations, schoolbooks, films and television, art, and so on. These activities lend the world and its categories a sense of stability and continuity. It is not easy, then, to recognize that categories are human creations, rather than fixed entities, and that as such they are subject to change (Edelman 1995).[28]

Category names, in these views, are not conceptual isolates. They represent and encapsulate broader sets of ideas, some known explicitly, some tacitly. They serve thereby as a sort of verbal shorthand or linguistic proxy, facilitating public conversation about a wider set of ideas than what is explicitly stated. The task for the analyst is to learn to read these ideas in category labels and language. Stein (2001) provides an interesting example of this in the context of educational policy. Exploring the implementation of Title I of the Elementary and Secondary Education Act (ESEA), she found teachers invoking "Title I" as a category of schoolchildren. In classroom use, it became a verbal shorthand for a nest of interrelated socioeconomic indicators, from poverty levels to parental marital status to domicile. When teachers told children to "line up for integration," they used the policy program name as a proxy for this wider set of ideas. Used in the teachers' room, it enabled a conversation about pedagogical practices far broader than the term itself. Her analysis makes these tacitly known (to teachers) elements explicit.

What policy analysis brings to the anthropological and linguistic discussion is an appreciation for the role of the state in the construction and maintenance of those categories implicated in public policy and administrative practices. In this view, such categories are not just manifestations of individual identity. Rather, they comprise ways in which states exert their influence over their citizens and residents, by naming and counting them for administrative purposes. Such purposes are not just military or paramilitary in character; states categorize people for purposes of schooling, healthcare delivery and monitoring, housing—the full panoply of state-provided services. In this process of naming and counting, choosing the salient features according to which populations will be categorized, states narrate stories or tales about collective identity. In so doing, they establish the parameters deemed necessary for membership in the polity at that moment in time.

There is a growing movement in public policy, administrative, and planning analysis to explore the narrative dimensions of individual and organizational acts, as ways in which identities are shaped, expressed, and communicated (see, e.g., Abma 1999, Fischer and Forester 1993, Roe 1994, Schram and Neisser 1997). Given that categories entail naming in a way that extends identity to the thing(s) or person(s) being named, they lend themselves well to an exploration of their narrative aspects. Such an approach brings out another dimension of meaning-focused interpretive analysis.

With Respect to What? Analyzing Race-Ethnic Categories

In this book I analyze race-ethnic categories as linguistic artifacts and explore their creation and use in public administration and public policy as practices, in order to elicit how race and ethnicity are being understood in the United States today. This entails, among other things, seeking to discover the point of view embedded and reflected in the logic of the architecture of category creation, much as notions of the "Middle" or "Far" or "Near" East, or the "Orient," reflect specific, situated points of view. The analysis also entails considering questionnaires as physical artifacts and the act of asking someone to answer a questionnaire as an artifactual enactment of meaning.

Such an approach rests on the understanding that category names and their associated objects and acts have meaning beyond their literal denotation. In common usage, category sets—the set of terms that label collections of entities presumed to be internally similar while distinct from one another—do not spell out their criteria for differentiation and collectivization. "The same/Different *with respect to what?*" is neither asked nor answered—or at least, rarely, and even more rarely by a member of the interpretive community using the terms, and yet more rarely still in print hard by the category terms themselves. This is the task of the analyst. Interpretive category analysts identify ("collect") the set of terms and then seek to explicate the logic according to which these terms order the world. If studying an interpretation or community foreign in some way to her own, the analyst would likely engage community members in conversations, interviews, discussions out of which she gains (she hopes) an understanding of how they make sense of these differentiating and unifying schemas. In studying interpretive communities of which he himself is a practicing member, such as I am doing here in exploring American ethnogenesis, the analyst perhaps relies more heavily on his own lived experience, at the same time seeking to "estrange" himself from what is so familiar. Perhaps, since it is often puzzles about their familiar world that launch researchers into such research, he is already "estranged" from it in some way. So, in any event, it has been with me.

I began this research by contemplating the five initial OMB category names and their definitions, the list of census category names printed on the 1990 form at questions 4, 7, and 13, and the other names the census provided enumerators and reported in its analyses, as I sought to discern the embedded logic and meaning making that made the categorical elements used for "race" alike and different, and that made the ones used for "ethnicity" alike and different. With respect to what did they make sense—or not make sense? Such an approach is similar to metaphor analysis. Using a definition of metaphor as the perception of similarities among dissimilars, the researcher asks: In what way(s) is the object (or focus) of the metaphor like the literal or source meaning of its vehicle? In what way(s), for example, are new immigrants like an animal's immature horns (greenhorns, that is)?[29] So it is with category analysis. But here, too, as with metaphor analysis, the researcher needs to engage the question, how are these categorical elements *un*like what they are purported to resemble? In this fashion, working back and forth between similarity and difference, analysis proceeds. It is a constant tacking back and forth between the specific—category members, such as, here, Armenian, Georgian, and so on—and the general—"with respect to what?"[30]

These methodological issues are present in instances of public discourse about race and ethnicity. A cursory look at several survey questionnaires shows that category sets and names vary from one to another. One survey lists "Caucasian, African-American, Asian, Hispanic, Native-American, Other" while another lists "White, African American, Hispanic/Latino/Chicano, Asian, Pacific Islander/Filipino, Native American, Middle Eastern" without an option of "Other" and without hyphenations, and yet a third lists "African American/Black, Arab American, Asian American, European American/White, Latina/Latino American, Native American/Indian, Other"— no hyphens, but in alphabetical order. (Several such questionnaires are included by way of illustration of this variety as Appendix 1.1.) To judge from the varieties of category set names found in contemporary questionnaires, Americans seem to be very confused at the moment not only about what "race" and "ethnicity" are, but also about what specific race-ethnicities are among us.

Notes

1. Their intention in the book was to provide data on groups about which information was not abundant and readily available. They say that this is not the situation for these three groups.

2. This is a characteristic of human action as seen from hermeneutic and phenomenological points of view: that meaning is projected into texts and "text analogues" (the phrase is Taylor's, 1971). Methodologically, interpretive analysis, which seeks to understand these embedded meanings, focuses on the more concrete, symbolic (i.e., representational) manifestations (in language, physical artifacts, acts) of these more abstracted meanings. I discuss this more fully in Yanow (1996, chap. 1, and 2000a).

3. See, e.g., Goldberg (1992) for an overview on race, and Yinger (1985) for a review of ethnicity that in current reading reveals the changes in understanding over the last decade, as well as Haney López (1994), Omi and Winant (1994), and other referenced sources.

4. On a theoretical note, we might distinguish between narratives and stories: narrative is the broader term, encompassing story as well as other forms of telling, such as chronicles of events, genealogies (e.g., biblical "begats"). Stories have plots; narratives do not, necessarily. An "emplotted" narrative (i.e., a story) arranges its narrated facts toward some purpose: each element of the narration relates to the arc of the initial problem-development-denouement plot structure. Characters and/or situations introduced in the beginning are developed through interactive tensions and conflict, until the initial problem finds resolution. (This is, of course, a "modernist" definition of story; a postmodernist story might have no resolution at all, and perhaps no development, either.) Among the list of story themes—search, exile, theft, injury— are identity and origin stories.

5. This is a different treatment of the concept of story from that used to analyze personal, individual narratives. It is less psychological, more collective, and it draws on different research methods. See, for example, Chock (1995a) on congressional "talk" and methods of researching it. By contrast, researchers such as Riessman (1993) access individuals' personal narratives.

6. Stone (1988, 1997, chap. 7) has an excellent discussion of the political aspects of numbers and counting. The power of counting is also illustrated in the Bible: in 2 Samuel 24, God tells David to count his people, but after he does so, David is punished. The reason is not clear, but it has made Jews very cautious about counting, and a folk process has evolved of counting the quorum for a prayer service by enumerating "*not* one, *not* two, *not* three," and so forth, or tallying the requisite ten by reciting a biblical verse that has ten words. I am not aware of other cultural groups that have prohibitions against counting people, but I would not be surprised to discover that they exist.

7. Steven Maynard-Moody (personal communication, 2001) suggests that fuzzy set theory would lead to very different understandings of the properties of categories. While it might be useful to see what this would bring to a theoretical or prescriptive study of race-ethnic categories, in moving inductively from usage to general principle I have not found it operative: public policies and their administrative applications insist on categorical clarity—you either are Black or you're not—rather than allowing for the kind of ambiguity of membership that fuzzy set theory would imply.

8. I have been aided in thinking through this point by the discussion in Potter (1989, pp. 142–143).

9. Or not different at all; see Edelman (1995, p. 139) for an example.

10. Berger and Luckmann (1966, Part II) discuss this process at length, with the hypothetical example of an aboriginal couple, A and B, whose choices become naturalized until person C comes along.

11. Other societies do not have a binary sex-categorization scheme, and children with both male and female genitalia are often considered specially blessed and as adults are assigned special roles and status within the community.

12. This is the question Thomas Kuhn maintains does not need to be answered for the practice of normal science (T.S. Kuhn, *The Structure of Scientific Revolutions*, 2d ed. Chicago: University of Chicago Press, 1970; quoted in Schön and Rein 1994, p. 46).

13. This scheme provided Lakoff (1987) with his book's title. He uses the Borges tale in his discussion of categories and cognition (p. 92). It was also invoked by Michel Foucault in *The Order of Things* (New York: Pantheon Books, 1971).

14. See Lakoff (1987, pp. 59–60) on marking.

Interestingly, the notion of "norm" is operative with respect to the teaching of American Sign Language. According to Douglas C. Baynton, schools for the deaf, first created in 1817 by Thomas H. Gallaudet, fell out of favor after Darwin: "'. . . to be human was to speak. To sign was to step downward in the scale of being'" (quoted in Kenner 1997, p. 30). Normality, says Baynton, was used descriptively as well as prescriptively, growing out of "'the need for standardized measurements, interchangeable parts (and workers), a common technical language and compatible products and technologies'" (ibid.)—hence, marking deafness and deaf people as "abnormal," eliminating them from public involvement, and curtailing the need for ASL or even for teaching them at all.

15. Davydd Greenwood (personal communication, 1992) has noted that the "dynamic and ambiguous characteristic of so-called natural categories" reflects a Darwinian view of the world. He expands on this argument in Greenwood (1984).

16. Latour (1987, pp. 199, 200–201) presents a lovely discussion on this point, using the example of anthropologist Ralph Bulmer learning the Karam's set of categories for birds, into which the "cassowary" (Bulmer's term for "kobtiy," the Karam's word) would not fit, despite his efforts to get them to see it as a bird. In Douglas's view, classificatory possibilities are shaped by, embody, and reflect a society's "core" statements, "a set of abstract organizing principles which affects the very shape of experience" (Douglas 1979, p. 186).

17. See Minow (1990) on the implications of category use in legal decision making in such issues as bilingual education, handicapped access, and medical care.

18. The idea that varieties of bodily measurements could yield scientific taxonomies has not been limited to racial knowledge. In 1917 Albert Abrams, M.D., published his findings that ovaries and testicles emitted radioactivity, and he produced a machine to measure the emissions and a scale according to which homosexuality could be measured. In his sample of six known "homosexualists," four had ovarian reactions and two, ovarian-testicular reactions with ovarian predominating. He proposed that this test would be of value to the military in preinductive screening in eliminating homosexuals, thereby saving the time and money that would be required to discover and eliminate them later. The original article appears in *International Clinics* Vol. 1, 27th ser. (1917) and is reprinted in *Medical Review of Reviews* 24:9 (September 1918), pp. 528–529. I thank Gary Lehring for bringing this to my attention.

19. In fact, it is apparently not uncommon in forensics for "racial" misdiagnoses and misidentifications to be made. Bronner (1998) mentions an example given by anthropologist Alan H. Goodman (in an article in *The Sciences,* March/April 1997) of a severed leg found after the explosion of the Oklahoma City Federal Building in 1995. It was identified by a "top forensic anthropologist" as belonging to a White man, whereas it turned out to come from the body of a Black woman.

For the biological account, see, for example, Cavalli-Sforza, Menozzi, and Piazza (1994) on the genetic argument that humans of all "races" arrange themselves along a continuum, rather than as distinct subspecies. As one biologist observed, "Humans are one of the most genetically homogeneous species we know of" (Alan R. Templeton, Professor of Biology, Washington University, St. Louis; quoted in McDonald 1998,

p. A19). On the anthropological account, it is interesting to note that Montagu made the social constructionist argument for "race" as long ago as 1942 (see the 1997 reissue).

20. Others writing about race and ethnicity as socially constructed concepts, such as Haney López (1994) and Segal (1998), similarly note their existence as social (arti)facts rather than as objective "facts" grounded in genetic or anthropological science.

21. *Metapherein* in contemporary Greek means "moving van," carrying something from one place to another. Hence, metaphors "move" meaning from a source to a new focus. I have elaborated elsewhere on this metaphoric process in the context of policy and organizational metaphors (Yanow 1996, 2000a). See also Miller (1985).

22. I am indebted to Davydd Greenwood for helping me put my own rudimentary and early "knowledge" of these matters into historical context. This paragraph draws heavily on his treatment of this history (Greenwood 1984). He argues there that post-Darwinian, supposedly "scientific" concepts of race are, in fact, echoes of ancient Greek and Roman ideas about the four environmental elements and their associated humors. Steinberg (1989, pp. 77–81) discusses the Darwinist roots of the argument that it is the cultural traits of groups that allow them to rise in status. See also Goldberg (1992, pp. 545–546) on a Darwinian view of race.

23. These two schools of thought developed in continental Europe, especially in Germany, in the early to mid-1900s, largely drawing on the eighteenth-century writings of Immanuel Kant in a critique of positivist philosophy. See, for example, the discussion in Polkinghorne (1983) and the references in note 24.

24. This tacking back and forth between a specific artifact and its context is one aspect of the hermeneutic circle described by Dilthey and Gadamer. Developing "narrative" modes of analysis draw on literary theorists' methods of understanding the meanings of texts, including acts and objects as "text analogues" (the phrase is Taylor's [1971]; see also Ricoeur 1971). For discussions of these ideas and their applicability to public policy and organizational analysis, see Abma (1999), Burrell and Morgan (1979), Dallmayr and McCarthy (1977), Fischer and Forester (1993), Hawkesworth (1988), Rabinow and Sullivan (1979), Roe (1994), Schram and Neisser (1997), and Yanow (1995, 1996, 2000a).

25. See Wuthnow et al. (1984, chap. 3) for a fruitful attempt to make explicit the methodological and philosophical underpinnings and implications of Douglas's work.

26. The phrase is Geertz's (1973, p. 93), although not in this application.

27. Lakoff (1987) notes a certain tension between the rules of category construction as popularly understood—what he terms "folk wisdom"—and the understanding of categories emerging in cognitive linguistics. While I find his argument persuasive, my own interest here, not being a linguist, is not in developing a more precise set of rules, but, as an interpretive social scientist, in understanding the consequences for political and organizational action of this "folk wisdom." So far, neither cognitive-linguistic nor social-constructionist arguments have succeeded in uprooting the commonsense understanding of race, ethnicity, and their categories, as the analysis in subsequent chapters shows.

28. This is the process also described by Berger and Luckmann (1966, Part II).

29. The literature on metaphor is vast. See, for example, for general discussion, Lakoff and Johnson (1980) and Ortony (1979), and Schön (1979), Miller (1985), and Yanow (2000a, 2000b) for applications to practice.

30. See also Geertz (1983a, pp. 68–70) on this form of sense making.

Appendix 1.1

Examples of questionnaires designed to collect race-ethnic data. Category sets vary from one to the next.

VOLUNTARY AFFIRMATIVE ACTION INFORMATION SURVEY

Dear Candidate:

I am pleased to know that you are a candidate for a position at Virginia Tech. The information we ask you to provide below will not affect your employment or be available to, or used in, any selection process. It will be used by the Office of Affirmative Action to compile statistics necessary to monitor the University's compliance with equal employment opportunity requirements. I hope you will assist us by providing this information.

_____
Assistant to the President

Position applied for _____ Date _____

Department _____

Ethnicity: American Indian/Alaskan Native _____   Hispanic _____   Asian _____

African-American (non-Hispanic) _____   White (non-Hispanic) _____   Other _____

Disabled: Yes _____ No _____   U.S. Citizen: Yes _____ No _____   Sex: M _____ F _____

Veteran - 30% Service Connected Disability: Yes _____ No _____   Vietnam Era Veteran: Yes _____ No _____

Month and year of birth _____

From what source did you learn of this position _____

If by advertisement, please name publication _____

Name (Optional) _____
Job ID # _____

ACADEMY OF MANAGEMENT
MEMBER'S ETHNIC BACKGROUND INFORMATION FORM

Please complete and mail with your membership renewal card. This information is voluntary and confidential. It is solicited as a means of tracing the ethnic composition trends in the Academy.

Since this is the first time this information is being collected, we would appreciate your comments. Please use the back of this sheet and feel free to include additional comments on a separate sheet if necessary. Thank you.

Ethnic Origin
(if U.S. Citizen)
Please Circle One

1. Caucasian

2. African-American

3. Asian

4. Hispanic

5. Native-American

6.)Other

Nationality
(if not U.S. Citizen)
Please Print

_____

Gender: Male _____ Female _____

UNIVERSITY OF MINNESOTA

Office of Equal Opportunity and Affirmative Action

Applicant Tracking Record For Academic Employment

Part I   This section is to be completed by the University Hiring Department(see reverse side)

Form 16/17 Number_____   (insert number assigned to this serach by the college)
(check all that apply)

Faculty (94XX):   Academic Administrative/Professional (P/A)

☐ Tenured   (P)   ☐ Administrative   (93XX)   ☐ Post-Doctoral   (95XX)
☐ Tenure-Trk (N)   ☐ Minnesota Extension Service   (96XX)
☐ Temporary   (T)   ☐ Professional Academic Staff   (97XX)

Part II   This section is to be completed by the applicant(see reverse side)

The University of Minnesota is required to collect this information to comply with Federal and State record keeping and re-
porting requirements pursuant to Executive Order 11246, Revised Order No. 4, Section 503 of The Rehabilitation Act
Amendments of 1974, Section 402 of the Vietnam Era Veterans Readjustment Assistance Act of 1974, Title VII of the Civil
Rights Act of 1964 and Minnesota Statutes, Section 363.073. Summary data, without names will be reported on the Higher
Education Staff Information (EEO-6) report and in the University of Minnesota's Affirmative Action Program.

Racial/Ethnic Categories (as defined by the Equal Employment Opportunity Commission):

_____
Applicant's Name (optional)

White: Persons having origins in any of the original peoples of Europe, North Africa, or the Middle East (not of Hispanic origin).

Sex (check one)
☐ M Male
☐ F Female

Black: Persons having origins in any of the Black racial groups of Africa (not of Hispanic origin).

Asian or Pacific Islander: Persons having origins in any of the original peoples of the Far East, Southeast Asia, the Indian Sub-continent, or the Pacific Islands. This area includes, for example, China, Japan, Korea, the Philippine Islands and Samoa.

Racial/Ethnic Group (check one)
☐ 0 White
☐ 1 Black
☐ 2 Asian or Pacific Islander
☐ 3 American Indian or Alaskan Native
☐ 4 Hispanic

The Indian Subcontinent takes in the countries of India, Pakistan,Bangladesh, Sri Lanka, Nepal, Sikkim and Bhutan.

American Indian or Alaskan Native: Persons having origins in any of the original peoples of North America and who maintain cultural identification through tribal affiliation or community recognition.

Hispanic: Persons of Mexican, Puerto Rican, Cuban, Central or South America, or other Spanish culture or origin, regardless of race.

Vietnam Era Veteran; A person who served on active duty for a period of more than 180 days, any part of which occurred between August 5, 1964 and May 7, 1975.

Veteran Status (check one)
☐ 1 Vietnam Era
☐ 2 Disabled - Vietnam Era
☐ 3 Disabled - Other Veteran
☐ 4 None of the above

Disabled Veteran: A person entitled to disability compensation under laws administered by the Veterans Administration for disability rated at 30 per centum or more, or a person whose discharge or release from active duty was for a disability incurred or aggravated in the line of duty.

Handicapped Individual: The Rehabilitation Act of 1973, as amended, defines a "handicapped individual" for the purpose of the program as any person who (1) has a physical or mental impairment which substantially limits one or more of such person's major life activities; (2) has a record of such impairments; or (3) is regarded as having such impairment.

Disability/Handicap (check one)
☐ Y Yes
☐ N No

The completion of this part does not constitute notification for purposes of accommodation.

Pres Form 24 - Rev 5/92
S 91381   ♲ Recycle This Paper

ETHNIC SURVEY FOR STATISTICAL PURPOSES ONLY

We need your voluntary cooperation in providing information to enable the School of Public Policy to complete reports on the ethnic composition of its applicants. Please note that the information will be used strictly for statistical purposes and *will not* be used to determine your eligibility for admission.

We ask that you indicate your ethnic identity below and return this form with your application. However, you are free to decline to complete this form. Whether you choose to indicate your ethnic identity or decline to state it, please return this form with your application.

Please check one of the following:

_____American Indian

_____Black/African-American

_____Chinese/Chinese-American

_____Chicano/Mexican-American/Latino: Specify_____

_____Caucasian

_____Filipino/Pilipino/Filipino-American

_____Japanese/Japanese-American

_____Korean/Korean-American

_____Vietnamese/Vietnamese-American

_____Other Asian-Pacific: Specify_____

_____East Indian/Pakistani

_____Other: Specify

_____Decline to State

APPLICATION FOR ADMISSION

CAÑADA COLLEGE

READ CAREFULLY, PRINT CLEARLY   COMPLETE BOTH SIDES OF THIS FORM
USE BLUE OR BLACK INK

TERM FOR WHICH YOU ARE APPLYING:
☐ SUMMER
☐ FALL/WINTER
☐ SPRING

1 SOCIAL SECURITY NUMBER

2 DATE OF LAST ATTENDANCE AT CAÑADA, CSM, OR SKYLINE.
MONTH   YEAR

3 LAST NAME (Print)

FIRST NAME (Print)

Middle Initial

PREVIOUS NAME USED AT CAÑADA, CSM OR SKYLINE IF DIFFERENT FROM CURRENT NAME
Last Name (Print)

First Name (Print)

Middle Initial

LEGAL ADDRESS (NOT A P.O. BOX)

☐ CHECK BOX IF YOUR MAILING ADDRESS AND/OR LEGAL ADDRESS HAS CHANGED SINCE LAST ATTENDANCE

NUMBER AND STREET   APT. NUMBER   HOME PHONE ( )

CITY   STATE   ZIP CODE   WORK PHONE ( )

MAILING ADDRESS (IF DIFFERENT)

NUMBER AND STREET   APT. NUMBER

CITY   STATE   ZIP CODE

4 ☐ MALE   ☐ FEMALE

5 ETHNIC BACKGROUND

AC = Chinese
AI = Indian Subcontinent
AJ = Japanese
AK = Korean
AL = Laotian
AM = Cambodian
AV = Vietnamese
AX = Other Asian
B. = Black Non-Hispanic
F. = Filipino

HM = Mexican, Mexican-American, or Chicano
HR = Central American
HS = South American
HX = Other Hispanic
N. = Native American/American Indian/Alaskan Native
O. = Other Non-White
P. = Pacific Islander
W. = White Non-Hispanic

6 I HAVE LIVED IN CALIFORNIA CONTINUOUSLY SINCE

MONTH   DAY   YEAR

7 BIRTHDATE
MONTH   DAY   YEAR

8 ARE YOU A U.S. CITIZEN?
☐ YES
☐ NO

9 IF YOU ARE NOT A U.S. CITIZEN, COMPLETE THE FOLLOWING:

2 = Permanent Resident Visa (Alien Number:)
3 = Temporary Resident – copy of work authorization required
4 = Refugee/Asylee
5 = Student Visa (F-1 or M-1)
6 = Other (Specify:) (copy of visa required)
6A = Undocumented

DATE OF ISSUE OF VISA
MONTH   DAY   YEAR
PORT OF ENTRY

EXPIRATION DATE
MONTH   DAY   YEAR
COUNTRY OF CITIZENSHIP

10 ENROLLMENT STATUS (student type)

1 = Attending college for the first time since high school
2 = Never attended Cañada, CSM or Skyline, but have attended or am currently attending another college
3 = Returning to Cañada, CSM or Skyline after attending another college
4 = Returning to Cañada, CSM or Skyline and have not attended another college since last term here
Y = Attending high school during the term for which I am applying

11 SELECT A MAJOR CODE FROM THE OPPOSITE PAGE

12 HIGHEST EDUCATIONAL LEVEL AND YEAR

0 = Not a high school graduate
1 = Attending high school during the semester for which I am applying
2 = Attending adult school
3 = High school diploma
4 = GED or Cert. of H.S. proficiency
5 = Cert. of Calif. H.S. proficiency
6 = Foreign secondary diploma/cert.
7 = Associate degree
8 = Bachelor's degree or higher

19___
Year Awarded

13 WHAT IS YOUR PRINCIPAL EDUCATIONAL GOAL?

A = Obtain a bachelor's degree after earning an A.A./A.S. degree
B = Obtain a bachelor's degree without earning an A.A./A.S. degree
C = Obtain an A.A./A.S. degree
D = Obtain a certificate
G = Acquire new job skills
H = Enhance current employment opportunities/job skills
J = Educational development
L = Complete credits for high school diploma
M = Undecided on goal

14 NUMBER OF HOURS YOU EXPECT TO WORK THIS TERM:

A = 1 - 9 hours per week
B = 10 - 19 hrs. per week
C = 20 - 29 hrs. per week
D = 30 - 39 hrs. per week
E = 40+ hours per week
N = Don't expect to work
X = Don't know

15 IS ENGLISH YOUR PRIMARY LANGUAGE?   ☐ YES ☐ NO

IF NOT, WHAT IS YOUR PRIMARY LANGUAGE?   N
1 = Chinese
2 = Spanish
3 = Tagalog
4 = Other

16 I INTEND TO TAKE:

1 = More than 6 units/day classes
2 = More than 6 units/evening or weekend classes
3 = More than 6 units/both day and evening classes
4 = 6 units or less/day classes
5 = 6 units or less/evening or weekend classes
6 = 6 units or less/both day and evening classes
7 = Distance Learning only

17 ARE YOU PRIMARILY A STUDENT AT ANOTHER EDUCATIONAL INSTITUTION AND TAKING COURSES AT THIS COLLEGE TO MEET REQUIREMENTS OF THAT INSTITUTION?   ☐ YES ☐ NO

ARE YOU CURRENTLY EMPLOYED AND TAKING ONLY CLASSES RELATED TO YOUR JOB?   ☐ YES ☐ NO

OFFICE USE ONLY

LEVEL	RESIDENCE	COUNTRY	VISA	MATRICULATION				CODED BY	DATE
01	5 6 8			N NM	DO DY OY				

RECEIVED BY   DATE   FEE RATE   ADMITTED BY   DATE

19

VENDOR CERTIFICATION FORM

Name: _____   Vendor #: _____

Please Complete the Following Information and Return in the Enclosed Envelope

Did we put your correct name and address?__ yes __ no
If no, please correct below:

Please answer questions 1-8 and return. See reverse for business classification definitions.

Legal Address

Company Name

Street Address

City   State   Zip

( )
Telephone Number

Remit Payment Address

Company Name

Street Address

City   State   Zip

( )
Telephone Number

Indicate Type of Ownership Arrangement

Corporation ___   Individual/Sole Proprietor ___

Joint Venture ___   Partnership ___

Other (Specify) ___   Parent Company ___

Please Sign Here

Owner's Name (Please Print or Type)

Owner's Signature   Date

( )
Telephone Number

1. Business Size   ___ Small   ___ Large

2. Disadvantaged-Owned   ___ Yes   ___ No
a. If yes, indicate status:

Black American   B ___
Native American   A ___
Hispanic American   H ___
Asian Pacific American P ___
Asian Indian American   I ___
Hasidic Jewish American J ___

b. Number of Employees   ___

c. Gross earnings last Fiscal Year   ___
------------------------------or------------------------------

3. Women-Owned and Controlled **W** ___

------------------------------or------------------------------

4. Protected Workshop   Z ___

------------------------------or------------------------------

5. Other Business Classification

Government   2 ___
Utility   3 ___
Foreign Owned   5 ___
USA-Owned with Offshore Build 6 ___
Other (including Non-Profit) 7 ___
Specify_____

6. Tax I.D. (9 digit) required to ensure prompt payment (or Social Security Number):

7. Dun and Bradstreet Number:

8. Principal Product or Service:

rev 2.0 042694 < vendor certification form >

LOAN #: 3894192

THE HOUSING FINANCIAL DISCRIMINATION ACT OF 1977
FAIR LENDING NOTICE

RE: Application/Loan No.

It is illegal to discriminate in the provisions of or in the availability of financial assistance because of the consideration of:

1. Trends, characteristics or conditions in the neighborhood or geographic area surrounding a housing accommodation, unless the financial institution can demonstrate in the particular case that such consideration is required to avoid an unsafe and unsound business practice; or

2. Race, color, religion, sex, marital status, national origin or ancestry.

It is illegal to consider the racial, ethnic, religious or national origin composition of a neighborhood or geographic area surrounding a housing accommodation or whether or not such composition is undergoing change, or is expected to undergo change, in appraising a housing accommodation or in determining whether or not, or under what conditions, to provide financial assistance.

These provisions govern financial assistance for the purpose of the purchase, construction, rehabilitation or refinance of one-to-four unit family residences occupied by the owner and for the purpose of the home improvement or any one-to-four unit family residence.

If you have questions about your rights, or if you wish to file a complaint, contact the management of this financial institution or:

DEPARTMENT OF CORPORATIONS
600 S. COMMONWEALTH AVENUE
LOS ANGELES, CALIFORNIA 90005

VOLUNTARY INFORMATION FOR GOVERNMENT MONITORING PURPOSES

If this loan is for housing purchase, construction, rehabilitation or refinance of a housing accommodation, the following information is requested by the State of California and the Federal Government to monitor this financial institution's compliance with the Housing Financial Discrimination Act, Equal Credit Opportunity Law, and Fair Housing Law. The law provides that a financial institution may neither discriminate on the basis of this information nor on whether or not it is furnished. Furnishing this information is optional. If you do not wish to furnish this information, please initial below.

This association is required to note race and sex, on the basis of sight and/or surname if the applicant(s) choose not to do so.

I choose not to supply this information. _____ (Applicant's Initials) _____ (Co-Applicant's Initials)

	Applicant	Co-Applicant		Applicant	Co-Applicant
Race/National Origin			**Sex**		
American Indian or	☐	☐	Male	☐	☐
Alaskan Native	☐	☐	Female	☐	☐
Asian or Pacific Islander	☐	☐	Age (in years)	___	___
Black	☐	☐	Marital Status		
Hispanic	☐	☐	Married	☐	☐
White	☐	☐	Unmarried	☐	☐
Other - Specify	☐	☐	Separated	☐	☐

2

Toward an American Categorical "Science" of Race and Ethnicity: OMB Directive No. 15

[Americans are a providentially guided]
band of brethren ... descended from the same ancestors,
speaking the same language, professing the same religion,
attached to the same principles of government,
very similar in their manners and customs.
—*John Jay, in the second* Federalist *paper
(quoted in Rogers 1997, p. 15)*

There is a certain irony in jumping from John Jay's late-eighteenth–century assertion of American uniformity—of heritage, language, religion, manners, customs—to contemporary variety along those same lines (although one element remains: a devotion to democratic principles of government; we may argue among ourselves as to how to enact those principles, but few argue in favor of a monarchy or oligarchy or communist form of government). The extent of this variety—perhaps even the strength of its contrast with the heritage of Jay's view—led to efforts to systematize these differences in a set of category names and definitions. The task of doing this eventually devolved upon one federal agency, the Office of Management and Budget (OMB).

Being "American"

The perception of such homogeneity in Jay's time rested on a population that was 80 percent of British derivation and virtually all Protestant (Philip

Gleason, quoted in Rogers 1997, p. 16). Segal (1991) argues that at an earlier point in American history, the category "European" was constructed as a mixture of racial, national, and class elements. In the first part of the seventeenth century, the unfree labor pool was not demarcated by race: slaves were of British and other "White" origins, as well as African. This perceptual definition changed after a series of working-class rebellions in the 1670s. European settlers, who had marked one another according to a status hierarchy, then began to consider "Africans" as a single "race-class"—creating a one-to-one correspondence between "African" and "slave." By opposition, this rendered "European" a singular race, internal national and class divisions notwithstanding. R. Williams (1990, p. 87) also dates the "creation of skin pigmentation as the dominant mark of vertical classification" to the late seventeenth century. One hundred years later, to be "American" meant to be "White" *and* "Protestant" *and* free *and* no-longer-British: "American national identity was now firmly rooted, not simply in whiteness, but in an Anglo-Saxon, Protestant species of whiteness" (Rogers 1997, p. 18)—although Maryland, in a major exception, was established as a Catholic colony, and, hence, state.[1]

Between the early 1800s and 1880, immigrants mainly came from northern Europe, although predominantly from outside the British domain: Ireland, Germany, and the Scandinavian countries (Rogers 1997, p. 16). The Catholicism of the Irish—one-third to one-half of the immigrants were Catholic (Rogers 1997, p. 17)—challenged this accepted, prevailing, commonsense self-understanding of what it meant to be American. The latter part of that century through the 1930s brought large numbers of immigrants from southern and eastern Europe—predominantly from Italy, Poland, and Russia, but also from Hungary, Spain, Romania, and Portugal (Steinberg 1989, p. 35)—with an even wider variety of heritage, language, religion, manners, and customs. "American" still meant "White," but Irish, Poles, and others were seen as—and called—"Black." Among dockworkers, for example, it was apparently common at that time to exclude Poles and Italians from "all-white" gangs, as in the question put by a member of the 1915 Industrial Relations Committee to a shipping company superintendent: "You employ seven gangs of white men and one gang of Italians on a ship?" (Kusmer 1996, p. 32). As Fuchs noted: American identity was identified

> with northern European, if not English ancestry; with Christianity, especially dissenting Protestantism, and its message for the world; with the white race; with patriarchal familial leadership and female domesticity; and with all the economic and social arrangements that came to be seen as the true traditional *American way of life*. (1990, p. 234)

The McCarran-Walter Immigration and Nationality Act of 1952 further expanded the cultural-national background of Americans by removing the ban on Asian and African immigrants. Gradually, toward the last decades of the twentieth century, Catholics and Jews came to be included more and more as "Whites."

By the 1970s, many more federal agencies than the Census Bureau and the Immigration and Naturalization Service in the Department of Justice were collecting racial and ethnic data. Data collection categories were apparently not standardized across these agencies. A 1973 report by the Subcommittee on Minority Education of the Federal Interagency Committee on Education (FICE) recommended that definitions of racial and ethnic groups be developed for data collection. The report was forwarded to the secretary of the U.S. Department of Health, Education, and Welfare, Caspar Weinberger, who apparently endorsed the recommendation. The FICE Ad Hoc Committee on Racial and Ethnic Definitions was created in June 1974; its initial set of recommended categories, submitted in April 1975, became "Revised Exhibit F" of the Office of Management and Budget's (OMB) Circular No. A-46 one year later (Robbin 1998a, pp. 9–10). Robbin notes in her analysis that there were debates and dissenting opinions regarding each of the proposed category names and definitions.

This OMB circular became OMB Statistical Policy Directive No. 15,[2] "Race and Ethnic Standards for Federal Statistics and Administrative Reporting." As of January 1, 1980, all federal agencies collecting racial and ethnic data had to use the categories established there. Although the federal government had been collecting such data for some 200 years, this marked the first time that the complete set of categories in use had been defined, explicitly and consciously, by the state in a policy document and codified in uniform and universal application to all federal agencies—as distinct, for example, from instructions given only about the application of the labels "quadroon," "octoroon," and so forth, and given only to census takers (and only in certain censuses; see note to Table 3.2). It might be reasonably argued that the state has been defining citizenship since its early days—the list of census classifications (Appendix 3.1) would be an example—but this reflects more of an analytic inference based on such lists of terms, rather than documentary evidence in which the state with conscious and explicit intent sets out in writing the criteria for membership of an American race-ethnic group.

The 1977/1980 form of Directive No. 15 named and defined these data categories as follows:

a. *American Indian or Alaskan Native.* A person having origins in any of the original peoples of North America, and who maintains cultural identification through tribal affiliation or community recognition.

   b. *Asian or Pacific Islander.* A person having origins in any of the original peoples of the Far East, Southeast Asia, the Indian subcontinent, or the Pacific Islands. This area includes, for example, China, India, Japan, Korea, the Philippine Islands, and Samoa.

   c. *Black.* A person having origins in any of the black racial groups of Africa.

   d. *Hispanic.* A person of Mexican, Puerto Rican, Cuban, Central or South American or other Spanish culture or origin, regardless of race.

   e. *White.* A person having origins in any of the original peoples of Europe, North Africa, or the Middle East.

Because the Bureau of the Census is a federal agency, it is also bound by OMB Directive 15. Debates and discussions about race-ethnic categories used by both agencies have been intertwined. In the aftermath of the 1990 census, in particular, many questions were raised about the names and definitions used, as well as about the adequacy of the category set to capture the experiences of people with multiple race-ethnic heritages and identities. As the questions emerged primarily in response to that census, I will defer their detailed analysis and discussion to the next chapter. However, they also prompted four years of congressional and OMB hearings, resulting in the publication of a revised OMB directive.

Directive No. 15, Revised

In the U.S. House of Representatives, it is the Subcommittee on Census, Statistics and Postal Personnel of the Committee on Post Office and Civil Service that is tasked—as its name indicates—with census policies. The subcommittee began holding hearings in 1993 on statistical concerns: various population groups in various states had been seriously undercounted in the 1990 census, despite efforts to the contrary, and the bureau had proposed the use of sampling (rather than a head count) in the next census. At the same time, matters of race-ethnic category nomenclature and definition were also the subjects of hearings. In addition to agency representatives, members of Congress, university-based researchers, and "multiracial" children and their parents, testimony was heard from several interest groups, among them the National Coalition for an Accurate Count of Asian Pacific Americans, Project RACE, the Association of MultiEthnic Americans, the National Council of La Raza, the Mexican-American Legal Defense and Educational Fund, the Arab-American Institute, and the National Congress of American Indians.[3]

   The OMB headed an Interagency Committee for the Review of the Racial and Ethnic Standards, comprised of thirty federal agencies including the

National Center for Health Statistics, the Bureau of Labor Statistics, the Justice Department, and the Census Bureau. Established in March 1994, this task force held hearings for three years, issuing its recommendations in 1997. Following the usual review period, OMB published a revised statistical directive in October of that year, entailing several definitional changes to the race-ethnic category set and two procedural changes.

Changes in category names and definitions. The revised Directive No. 15 restates the caution that the race-ethnic standards "should not be interpreted as being primarily biological or genetic in reference. Race and ethnicity may be thought of in terms of social and cultural characteristics as well as ancestry" (U.S. Office of Management and Budget 1997). It notes that the revised standards would consist of five minimum categories for data on race (as itemized below), and that there would be two categories for data on ethnicity: "Hispanic or Latino" and "Not Hispanic or Latino."

The following changes were made either to the 1980 category names or definitions, or both. The affected texts are underlined (marking additions or revisions to the 1980 text) or lined out (marking deletions), and the differences are annotated in brackets.

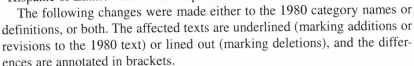

    a. *American Indian or Alaska̶n̶ Native.* A person having origins in any of the original peoples of North <u>and South America (including Central America),</u> and who maintains c̶u̶l̶t̶u̶r̶a̶l̶ ̶i̶d̶e̶n̶t̶i̶f̶i̶c̶a̶t̶i̶o̶n̶ ̶t̶h̶r̶o̶u̶g̶h̶ tribal affiliation or community r̶e̶c̶o̶g̶n̶i̶t̶i̶o̶n̶ <u>attachment.</u>

[The *"n"* is dropped from "Alaskan" in the category name. The geographic parameters of the definition are broadened to include "South America (including Central America)," and the language of the last phrase is reworded.]

    b. *Asian or ~~Pacific Islander.~~* A person having origins in any of the original peoples of the Far East, Southeast Asia, <u>or</u> the Indian subcontinent o̶r̶ ̶t̶h̶e̶ ̶P̶a̶c̶i̶f̶i̶c̶ ̶i̶s̶l̶a̶n̶d̶s̶ including, for example, <u>Cambodia,</u> China, India, Japan, Korea, <u>Malaysia, Pakistan,</u> the Philippine Islands, S̶a̶m̶o̶a̶, <u>Thailand,</u> and <u>Vietnam.</u>

[The category name has been divided in two. In the definition of Asian, "or the Pacific Islands" and Samoa are dropped, and five examples are added: Cambodia, Malaysia, Pakistan, Thailand, Vietnam.]

    c. *Black or <u>African American</u>.* A person having origins in any of the black racial groups of Africa. <u>Terms such as "Haitian" or "Negro" can be used in addition to "Black or African American."</u>

[African American is a new addition to the category name, and a second sentence has been added to the definition.]

    d. *Hispanic or Latino*. A person of <u>Cuban</u>, Mexican, Puerto Rican, <u>South or Central</u> American, or other Spanish culture or origin, regardless of race. <u>The term, "Spanish origin," can be used in addition to "Hispanic or Latino."</u>

["Latino" has been added to the category name. The revised document notes that Hispanic is more commonly found in the eastern United States, Latino in the West. The order of geographic origins is changed—"Cuban" moves from third to first place; "South" and "Central" exchange places—and a sentence has been added to the definition.]

    e. *Native Hawaiian or Other Pacific Islander.* A person having origins in any of the original peoples of <u>Hawaii, Guam</u>, Samoa, or other Pacific Islands.

[This is a new category, expanding on "Pacific Islander" from the 1980 category to which Native Hawaiian has been added. Hawaii and Guam are added to the definition as examples, and Samoa is moved here from the 1980 API category list.]

    f.. *White*. A person having origins in any of the original peoples of Europe, <u>the Middle East, or North Africa</u>.

[The 1980 order of "Middle East" and "North Africa" in the definition is inverted.]

It is also interesting to note what arguments did not prevail. Requests for separate categories for Middle Easterners, Cape Verdeans, Creoles, European-Americans, and German-Americans were all turned down, although the Middle Eastern question is still under study (having foundered on the question of whether such classification would include Jewish Israeli-Americans along with Arab-Americans). Hawaiians had requested to be moved from "Asian or Pacific Islander" to "American Indian or Alaska Native," but are now grouped in "Native Hawaiian or Other Pacific Islander." The revised directive notes that "Native Hawaiian" as a term "does not include individuals who are native to the State of Hawaii by virtue of being born there" (U.S. Office of Management and Budget 1997).

Changes in procedure. The two procedural changes that were instituted emanated from widespread public discussions about problems raised by the 1990 census for many people who found that the categories for race and ethnicity did not reflect their sense of their own identities. The first of these, adopted in 1997 for Census 2000 (and for other data-collection practices that allow in 1997 for Census 2000 (and for other data-collection practices that allow self-identification), addressed a major aspect of the sense of "dislocation": it enabled multiracial people to identify all the sources of their heritages. The second procedural change placed the Hispanic origin question ahead of the race question. Both of these changes, each in its own way, were adopted in the hope that the number of people answering "Other" to the race question would diminish, rather than grow even more, as it had between 1980 and 1990. However, this was not to be: in results published in the spring of 2001, the number marking off "some other race" had grown by 5.6 million—a rate of nearly 57 percent—in ten years, from 9.8 to 15.4 million, 97 percent of them Hispanics.

Federal agencies and their state and local affiliates were given until 2003 to conform to the new standards. The Census Bureau indicated that it would publish population totals for each category and for every possible combination of categories—a prospect of sixty-three categories in all, including White only; White and Black; White, Black, and Asian; and so on. Opposition to revising the category names came from members of those groups that rely on federal funds for various programs. They feared that their agencies and/or programs would lose federal dollars as a result of anticipated analytic difficulties in comparing statistics from one census to the next across changed categories. Opposition to making a "choose all that apply" procedural change came from a much broader range of associations, who feared a similar diminution of their numbers as people self-identified as something other than "pure" Black or other minority group.

As of this writing, the problem of statistical comparability is still being worked out. But the numerical results themselves surprised Census Bureau statisticians. Nearly 7 million people nationwide identified themselves as multiracial, constituting 2.4 percent of the population (Schmitt 2001c). The number of people self-identifying as American Indian grew: 2.6 million marked that box alone, with an additional 1.5 million marking American Indian plus another category. Among those identifying themselves solely as American Indian, growth ranged from 8 percent (in Oklahoma) to 80 percent (in Texas), with a 26 percent average growth nationally; adding those who identified themselves as American Indian and some other "race," the growth ranges from 55 percent (Oklahoma) to 228 percent (New Jersey), with a 110 percent national growth (Morello 2001). Among African-Americans, the number identifying themselves as being of more than one race varied from one geographic location to another. In general, it seems that where there were more opportunities for African-Americans to intermingle with other race-ethnic groups, as on or near military bases, more of them reported multiple race identities (8 percent of the population in Comanche County, Oklahoma); whereas in other locations, African-Americans reported lingering fears and doubts concerning the federal government's intent in allowing mixed race reporting, and fewer marked multiple boxes (less than 1 percent in Warren County, Mississippi; Schmitt 2001b).

Investigating American Race-Ethnic Definitions

Despite these changes, the 1990 census categories are perhaps still the best place to start an exploration of how public policies and administrative practices are shaping contemporary notions of race and ethnicity. The 1990 census served as a turning point in public discussion of race, ethnicity, and the categories, sparking extensive debate in Congress and in the Census Bureau itself, as well as in various print and oral media. It is in the census that race-ethnic matters are treated most fully, most explicitly, and most widely. It exemplifies the creation not only of racial and ethnic categories—an American ethnogenesis—but also the construction of the concepts "race" and "ethnicity" themselves. Looking at the 1990 census in its historical context highlights these creative acts and debates and frames the context for changes to category names and definitions.

In both its versions, OMB Directive No. 15 points to several of the questions that surface in analyzing the 1990 census questionnaire and practices of other agencies collecting race-ethnic data. The categories are not treated identically, in the following ways.

1. What does it mean to "*have origins*"? With respect to Hispanics, the Census Bureau notes that origin "can be viewed as the ancestry, nationality group, lineage, or country of birth of the person or the person's parents or ancestors before their arrival in the U.S." (U.S. Bureau of the Census 1989). Here is where ancient notions of race and ethnicity emerge: ancestry and lineage reflect genealogy; nationality group and country of birth reflect environment (i.e., the particular combination of earth, air, fire, and water that characterize a geographic site). But this definition of origins raises its own questions: how far back before arrival are genealogy and geography to be traced—to just prior to arrival? many generations earlier? to the immediately previous country of residence? to birthplace or country of citizenship? to ancestral homelands?

The definition seems to presume some fixed, stable state of affairs at some point in the past, as if migration were a recent phenomenon. This relates to a second question:

2. Who were the "*original peoples*" of Europe, North Africa, the Middle East, the Far East, Southeast Asia, the Indian subcontinent, the Pacific Islands, and North America? Neither Canadians nor Mexicans are considered

Native Americans; but neither are Caucasian Canadian-Americans European-Americans except by some appeal back to earlier generations. How far back in time do origins originate?

3. Why do Whites, Asians, Pacific Islanders, and American Indians and Alaska Natives have origins in *original peoples,* while Blacks have origins in black *racial groups*? This suggests that Blacks are not original to their lands, and that racial groups are not peoples (or vice versa). The language assigns "race" to Blacks alone, while granting the others the heritage of a unified, even sovereign identity (as in "the people Israel" or "Let my people go"). At the very least, it marks Blacks off as different from all other peoples.

4. Why are Whites, Asians, Pacific Islanders, and American Indians or Alaska Natives seen as having origins in original *peoples* and Blacks, in black *racial groups*, whereas Hispanics are seen as deriving from *cultures or geographic origins*? By definitional logic, this opposition appears to deny shared culture to members of the first five, divorcing genealogy and peoplehood from geography while positing an identity between culture and country of origin that is problematic.

5. Why are American Indians and Alaska Natives the only group required to maintain *tribal affiliation or community attachment*? Even though the 1997/2000 revision drops the requirement for "cultural identification" through self-initiated affiliation or externally imposed recognition, it still requires a standard not demanded of the others.

Additional questions emerge from other parts of the directive. OMB 15 also stipulates that "the designation 'nonwhite' is not acceptable for use." But at the same time, in tabulating data, "when the most summary distinction between the majority and minority races is appropriate," the collective descriptions of minority races should be labeled "Black and Other Races" or "All Other Races." For all intents and purposes, as the majority "race" is (in most places still) White, that creates a "nonwhite" category without using that name for it.

Second, when the distinction is among the majority race, the principal minority race, and other races, the appropriate categories, as stipulated by the directive, are "White," "Black," and "All Other Races." "Whites" may be included with "All Other Races" when making a distinction with a particular minority race or races. This policy problematizes even further the definitions of the various "racial" subgroups and our understanding of race. In both instances, if presumptively different races can be mixed together for statistical purposes, "race" would seem to lose all descriptive meaning and acquire (or reflect) political meaning alone.

These are the kinds of questions that category analysis brings out in a close reading of policy and administrative texts concerning race and ethnicity creating and managing are not racial or ethnic groupings that exist in the natural world, but categories. An analysis of census practices underscores this.

Notes

1. I thank Mary Hawkesworth for reminding me of this.

2. Apparently, its designation as a "statistical" policy directive is a holdover from the early 1970s when statistical policy was still a function of the Office of Federal Statistical Policy and Standards, in the Department of Commerce. That function was transferred to the Office of Information and Regulatory Affairs within OMB (Robbin 1998b, p. 31, n.1, citing personal communication from Suzann Evinger, title not given, OMB). The title of the document is still in widespread use and has been retained.

3. See, for example, "Review of Federal Measurements of Race and Ethnicity," Hearing before the Subcommittee on Census, Statistics, and Postal Personnel, Committee on Post Office and Civil Service, House of Representatives (Committee Serial No. 103–7, April 14, June 30, July 2, November 3, 1993). Earlier hearings on the same subject include "Content of 1990 Census Questionnaire: Race, Ethnicity, and Ancestry," Hearing before the Subcommittee on Census and Population, Committee on Post Office and Civil Service, House of Representatives (Committee Serial No. 100–13, May 19, 1987); "Review of 1990 Decennial Census Questionnaire," Hearing before the Subcommittee on Census, Statistics, and Postal Personnel, Committee on Post Office and Civil Service, House of Representatives (Committee Serial No. 100–48, April 14, 1988); "Revisions to the Standards for the Classification of Federal Data on Race and Ethnicity," Office of Management and Budget (http://www.whitehouse.gov/OMB/fedreg/ombdir15.html; October 1997).

Part II
Making Race-Ethnicity
Through Public Policies

[While a writer] may disagree with the majority of people
in his native land, still, the language, the people themselves,
the customs, the landscape, the sense of belonging
remain the same. He—or she—will not suffer
the anguished dislocation, the discontinuity,
of those of us in the Diaspora who once felt—and lost—
a deep sense of belonging and the identity that stemmed from it.
—Henry Roth
(quoted in Nicholls 1995, p. 19)

In legislating and implementing various public policies, the state creates categories for classifying population groups.* There is nothing natural about them—these groups do not exist in nature, nor do the criteria for the categorizing and classifying practices which enact them. But various "common sense," everyday practices (re)present and treat them as if they were natural—and make them appear that way to others (citizens and other residents, primarily).

The census is the policy instrument most often used for categorizing and classifying populations. In the United States, it is the one policy practice that engages race-ethnicity at its fullest and in its most extensive complexity. Chapter 3 shows how the Bureau of the Census creates race-ethnicity by naming, counting, and establishing the parameters of the concepts of "race" and "ethnicity" through its questions, forms, and counting practices. And it has done so throughout its 200-year history.

---

*I will use the phrase "the state" to refer to the conceptual entity of a national government, American or otherwise. Where I mean to indicate the government of one of the fifty U.S. states, I will use "the state government."

Census 2000 represents a significant shift in the state's organization of race-ethnic identifiers. To treat this reconceptualization in context, I begin chapter 3 with an extensive analysis of the 1990 census questions and categories, locating them in the 200-year history of census categories. This history provides the backdrop against which the more recent changes are significant.

Categorizing and classifying entail naming, and naming is a process of establishing identity. Comparing Census Bureau policy with Equal Employment Opportunity Commission and other agencies' policies in chapter 4 reveals a central issue in ethnogenic practices: Who defines race-ethnic identity? Can I name myself? Will I "count"?

Although what follows in chapter 3 is a critical analysis of the categories as they are used, I do not intend it as a criticism of the Census Bureau and its staff. As noted in chapter 1, the present categories are a *constructed text,* reflecting contemporary American discourse, rather than an *authored text.* They reflect the particular history of and contemporary discourse about race-ethnic matters in the United States, at the same time that they shape it. All members of the polity in which these categories have been constructed are as much implicated in their creation and use as are Census Bureau staff members.

It is, then, our collective, public discourse about race-ethnicity that is reflected in the categories-in-use. If we are to assign responsibility for the present state of affairs, it should be to the conserving, incremental processes of societal change and the extent to which past practices—and an outdated, eastern seaboard point of view—are still embedded in census language, shaping not only the perceptions of bureau personnel but also the dominant public discourse.

3

Color, Culture, Country:
Race and Ethnicity in the U.S. Census

ethnic 1. Of or pertaining to a social group ... on the basis of complex, often variable traits including religious,
linguistic, ancestral, or *physical* characteristics.
> (*American Heritage Dictionary* 1975, p. 450)

1a. Of or pertaining to sizable groups of people sharing
a common and distinctive *racial,* national,
religious, linguistic, or cultural heritage.
> (*American Heritage Dictionary* 1992, p. 630)

2. Pertaining to *race;* peculiar to a *race* or nation; ethnological.
> (*Oxford English Dictionary* 1971, p. 313)

2a. Pertaining to *race;* peculiar to a *race* or nation; ethnological.
Also, pertaining to or having common *racial,* cultural, religious, or
linguistic characteristics. ..; hence (U.S. colloq), foreign, exotic.
> (*Oxford English Dictionary* 1991, p. 423)

1. Of or relating to a religious, *racial,* national or cultural group.
> (*Webster's II New Riverside University* 1984, p. 445)

race 1. A local geographic or global human population
distinguished as a more or less distinct group by
genetically transmitted physical characteristics.
> (*American Heritage Dictionary* 1975, pp. 1074–1075; 1992, p. 1488)

I. A group of persons ... connected by *common* descent or *origin*.
II. A group or class of persons ... having some common *feature* or features.
> (*Oxford English Dictionary* 1971, p. 87; 1991, p. 69)

3. A group of people united or classified together
on the basis of common *history, nationality*
or geographic distribution.
> (*Webster's II New Riverside University* 1984, p. 968)

(All emphases added.)

The long form of the 1990 census asked four questions that are relevant to a race-ethnic analysis: one each on race, Spanish/Hispanic origins, ancestry or ethnic origin, and home language use. Answers to these questions deemed appropriate by the Census Bureau may be found in three places: in the phrasing of questions on the census form itself; in instructions to enumerators; and in statistical analyses published in Census Bureau reports. In introducing a multiracial possibility into Census 2000, the bureau sought to address one of the fundamental questions that the 1990 census aroused, and so the earlier census serves as the starting point for this analysis. As Anderson and Fienberg (1999, p. 191) note, ideas and policies for one census are already being developed while the previous census is being analyzed. The question of racial mixture relates to a logical principle of category making that continues to plague American race-ethnic discourse: the boundedness of the categories.

Census Questions and Categories: 1990

Question 4 asked: "What is . . .'s race?"* The census taker was instructed: "Fill ONE circle for the race that the person considers himself/herself to be." The answer block printed on the census form provided the following possibilities:

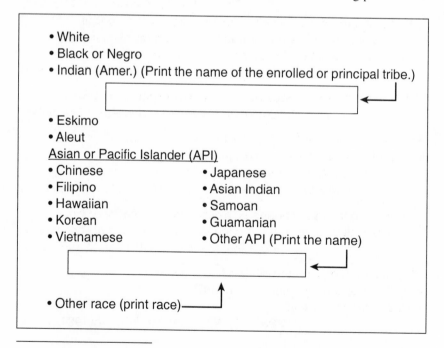

---

*Note: The ellipses in these questions are printed on the form.

Instructions given to the census taker offer the following possibilities for "Other API": "Cambodian, Tongan, Laotian, Hmong, Thai, Pakistani, and so on." The Census Bureau's analysis of the data included the following additional groups:

Asian	*Pacific Islander*
Bangladeshi	Tahitian
Burmese	North Mariana Islander
Indonesian	Palavan
Malayan	Fijian
Okinawan	Other
Sri Lankan	
Other	

The enumerator was further instructed, "If response is 'Other race,' ask— Which group does . . . consider (himself/herself) to be?"

Question 7 asked: "Is . . . of Spanish/Hispanic origin?" The census form offered the following as possible answers to the respondent answering in the affirmative:

Mexican, Mexican-American, Chicano
Puerto Rican
Cuban
Other

Instructions given to the census taker on "Other" identified "Argentinian, Colombian, Dominican, Nicaraguan, Salvadoran, Spaniard, and so on" as possibilities.

Question 13 asked: "What is this person's ancestry or ethnic origin?" The census form offers as examples: "German, Italian, Afro-American, Croatian, Cape Verdean, Dominican, Ecuadoran, Haitian, Cajun, French Canadian, Jamaican, Korean, Lebanese, Mexican, Nigerian, Irish, Polish, Slovak, Taiwanese, Thai, Ukrainian, etc."

And *Question 15* asked, "Does this person speak a language other than English at home?" The examples printed on the form are "Chinese, Italian, Spanish, Vietnamese."

These are the only questions that have direct bearing on racial and ethnic population features. Questions about religion are not included in the census following the principle of separation of church and state: the Census Bureau included a religion question in a 1957 survey as a pretest for the 1960 census, but it was so roundly protested (by Christian Scientists and by Jewish organizations) that it was abandoned; a renewed effort for the 1970 census was also aborted (Starr 1987, p. 42; Petersen 1987, pp. 221–222).[1] Language becomes significant as a race-ethnic demarcator when it comes to the criteria for "Hispanic." It is clearly related to language policies. That language mixes with more customarily noted race-ethnic criteria (e.g., skin tone, physiognomy, hair) is evident in the Canadian case. Three language terms are used in Quebec to denote the Quebecois equivalent of race-ethnic groups: Anglophone, Francophone, and Allophone. The latter term is used, apparently, with two possible meanings: someone whose mother tongue is neither English nor French; or someone whose ethnicity cannot be traced to either Great Britain or France. Sometimes it is used to mean both. However, "Allophone" is not used in reference to the eleven different First Nations peoples, some of whom speak English, some French.[2] In the U.S. case, the question of language use as a race-ethnic identifier is treated extensively in studies of the "English-only" movement (see, e.g., Schmidt 2000), and I will touch on it further here only as it is subsumed under the discussion of ethnicity through the other three questions.

The Census Bureau accepts the "standards on ethnic and racial categories for statistical reporting to be used by all Federal agencies" established in the OMB Statistical Policy Directive No. 15. As mentioned in chapter 2, the Census Bureau notes that Hispanic origin "can be viewed as the ancestry, nationality group, lineage, or country of birth of the person or the person's parents or ancestors before their arrival in the U.S." and may be of any race. According to bureau publications, "The concept [of race] is not intended to reflect any biological or anthropological definition." Furthermore, "we recognize that there are persons who do not identify with a specific racial group." And so "the 1990 census race question included an 'Other race' category with provisions for a write-in entry" (U.S. Bureau of the Census 1989).

Category Logic: 1990

The census and OMB labels suggest discrete categories with clear boundaries, in keeping with categorical logic more generally. This principle does not correspond, however, with individuals' reported experiences of their lives and identities, nor does it hold up to analytic exploration of the definitions-in-use of race and ethnicity embedded in the structure of the census questions.

For example, 9.8 million Americans (4 million of them from California) checked "other race" in 1990 in answer to Question 4, up from 6.8 million in 1980 (*Washington Post* 4/29/91, p. A9). People gave various reasons for choosing this category, making it something of a catchall. Some people chose it because they objected to the category name that the census gave their group. One woman, for instance, was angry that the form didn't have "African-American" as the category name and told census enumerators that she was neither "black" nor "Negro" (*Newsweek* 4/30/90, p. 23). Others objected to identifying people as other than generic "American." Still others found that the categories forced them to make a choice that reflected only a part of their complex race-ethnic background. The *Los Angeles Times* (1/13/91, p. E1) interviewed a woman born in Tokyo to a Japanese mother and an American father whose own parents were Blackfoot Indian and African-American, who said that the racial categories of Black and Asian-American did not capture her identity and experience. She argued for an additional category: "multiracial." Columnist Roberto Rodriguez wrote that as a mestizo—"mostly Indian, part European"—he couldn't find an appropriate box that fit his racial self-perception. "I tried to check American Indian—but was told Mexicans were not considered *American* Indians." Ruling out Asian left Black or White. ". . . [T]he great majority of the people of Latin America are indigenous/ mestizo, yet because of colonial legacies of race, are considered white," he wrote (Rodriguez 1990a). The choice forced by the census was apparently so irritating to some people that a reporter for the *San Francisco Chronicle* (R.G. McLeod, 3/23/90) wrote, an answer of "earthling" to Question 4 will bring the enumerator to your door.[3]

Such objections and resistance to categorization reflect a growing tension between individual, lived experience and state-defined categories. Underlying this tension is a perception that "race" and "ethnicity" as terms should correspond to some clear-cut, naturally occurring reality. That they do not— that their meanings-in-use are unclear—can be seen from category analysis exploring the underlying logic of the questions and their proffered and tabulated responses. Despite common perception (or "common sense") that "race" refers to physical traits and "ethnicity," to cultural ones, both are used, in practice, to refer to the same things. Even dictionary definitions, which might be expected to mark clear distinctions between the two, mostly define the one in terms of the other (as can be seen in the quotes at the beginning of the chapter). Analysis of the answers given by the Census Bureau to each race-ethnic question shows the overlap in meanings-in-use.

A. Question 4: "Race"

In a literal sense, census Question 4 is about race. But the categories and suggestions of possible answers indicate that it is asking about something other than the common definition of race as a human group "distinguished . . . by genetically transmitted physical characteristics" (*American Heritage*

Dictionary 1975, p. 1074). Analysis shows a different "common sense" understanding of "race" in the answers to Question 4. It is asking about racial groups not only in the sense of physiognomy or skin color. It uses "race" also to mean "ethnicity" or cultural heritage, as well as country of origin.

The three categories listed in Question 4 after White and Black/Negro are "Indian (Amer.), Eskimo, and Aleut." Eskimos and Aleuts made the argument that they are not American Indian "tribes": They do not share the same history, customs, language, and traditions as American Indians; and the Census Bureau therefore listed them separately in 1980 and 1990.[4] Shared history, language, religion, cuisine, customs, traditions, and so forth are commonly referred to as cultural traits. These are taken to be the hallmarks of "ethnicity," commonly making a distinction between "race" and "ethnicity" on this basis (reflected to some extent in the dictionary definitions). The census institutionalizes this distinction with a separate question, number 13, which asks about "ancestry or ethnic origin." But in accepting a culturally based distinction among Eskimos, Aleuts, and American Indians in Question 4, the census seems to be using "race" to mean "ethnicity."[5]

In addition to "color" and "culture," Question 4 suggests another possible meaning of "race." The subcategories listed for "Asian and Pacific Islander"— Chinese, Japanese, Filipino, and so on—are all nation-states, as are all the other possibilities suggested to enumerators and tabulated by analysts (with the exception of the Hmong, a mountain-dwelling group from Laos who, while living separately, do not have a separate government). Here, "race" appears to mean people who have a common geographic or national origin. This ties in with the ancient Greek notion that the elemental-humoral environment—the earth, air, water, and solar (fire) qualities that characterized a particular geographic place, and their associated humors—influences the behavioral characteristics of people born there (as noted in chap. 1; see Greenwood 1984). Peoples were characterized by whether they came from the East or West, North or South. "In the Western world, at least," Greenwood notes, "the question 'Where are you from?' really means 'What kind of person are you?'" (p. 75).[6] And so, Question 4, which asks about the respondent's "race," offers and tabulates ethnic and geographic answers as well—indicating that in Census Bureau practice, "race" means something other than physical features alone: not just "color," but "culture" and "country of origin" as well.

Moreover, by forcing a choice of a single category, the 1990 census (along with the initial version of OMB Directive 15) undermined the notion of "race" as a set of traits inherited through blood or genetic material. If race is indeed inherited, then there can be no choosing (or force-fitting into a single category): race is determined by one's ancestors. If this were the exclusive understanding of "race," there could have been no debate over adding a multiracial possibility or "Other" category: the logic of doing so would have been self-evident to all. That it has not been suggests that we are using "race" with additional layers of meaning.

B. Question 13: "Ancestry or Ethnic Origin"

The confusion of color (race), culture (ethnicity), and country (geography) also characterizes the suggested answers to Question 13, which asks about "ancestry or ethnic origin." Despite the fact that it appears to institutionalize the distinction between race and ethnicity, Question 13's proposed answers suggest the same mix of category logic as Question 4. German, Italian, Croatian (the census was prescient: Yugoslavian was not on the 1990 list), Cape Verdean, and others refer to specific geographic places. Afro-American, Cajun, and French Canadian refer to peoples who share such cultural elements as a common history, language, cuisine, and other customs (to a point). That means that Questions 4 and 13 are both asking about the same phenomena—country and culture—and using "race" and "ethnicity" to mean both.

But even Question 13's cultural sense of "ethnic origin" is not based on clear distinctions. For example, Lebanese and Nigerians come from countries with internal divisions along linguistic, religious, and other lines; hence, it is not clear that either constitutes a singular "ethnicity," as that term is commonly understood. Similarly, "Irish" includes two religious groups with different practices, Protestants and Catholics, whose differences might be reason to have two rather than one subcategory. And not all "Afro-Americans" share the same ancestry or "original" history, cuisine, religion, and so forth.

Further real and hypothetical combinations of race and ethnicity emerge from this analysis. A race (e.g., White), in this usage, may include many ethnicities (German, Italian, Croatian, Cajun, etc.). The various possible answers to Questions 4 and 13 suggest a distinction between Negro or Black as a "race" and Afro-American as an "ethnicity." By the categorical logic of this distinction, one could be racially "Black" and ethnically something other than "Afro-American." This, in fact, is the claim of immigrants from the Caribbean, who identify their heritage as Trinidadian, Jamaican, or, more generally, Afro-Caribbean.[7] One could also be ethnically "Afro-American" and racially non-Black, according to this category logic, which might be the situation, hypothetically, of someone raised in an African-American family who has "passed" (see chap. 4) or, by definitional happenstance, of a White African immigrant (or, perhaps, a non-Black with a heritage of enslavement). This was, in fact, the argument given by a White, American applicant to law school who identified himself as a "White African American," the son of three generations of Tanzanians through whose

Table 3.1

**Answers Deemed Suitable by the Census Bureau for Three 1990
Questions**

	Question 4 Race	Question 13 Ethnicity	Question 7 Hispanic
Native American	✓	x	n/r
Hispanic	x	x	[✓]*
Mexican	x	✓	✓
Dominican	x	✓	✓
Korean	✓	✓	n/r

*By definition, but not by usage: "Hispanic" itself is not given as an answer to Question 7.

stories and paintings "the African tradition became a part of my daily life" (Shea 1994).

C. Question 7: "Spanish/Hispanic"

The presumed distinction between race and ethnicity is further muddied by census Question 7, which asks about Spanish/Hispanic origin. Here, too, the possible answers suggested are geographic: Mexican, Puerto Rican, and Cuban are the subcategories on the census form; Argentinian, Colombian, and so forth, the additional possibilities offered.

At the same time, by noting that Hispanic peoples may be of any race, the census appears to suggest that "Hispanic" is an ethnic grouping. Using "Hispanic" to refer to both geographic and ethnic origins challenges the equivalence posited through usage, of nationality and culture. Yet, "Hispanic" is not included as a possible answer to Question 13, suggesting that it is not an ethnicity or ancestral heritage, any more than it is a race. "Native American" is also not an "ancestry or ethnic origin" (it is not included as a possible answer to Question 13, although it is included as a racial category in Question 4, unlike "Hispanic"). But Mexican and Dominican are proposed answers to both Question 7 ("Hispanic") and Question 13 ("ethnic origin"); and Korean is proposed as an answer both to Question 4 ("race") and Question 13 ("ethnic origin"). (See Table 3.1.) By this categorical logic, Mexican and Dominican are both Hispanic and ethnic markings, although "Hispanic" itself is not; and Korean is both racial and ethnic—although it is not clear, then, what this says about members of those groups or about the logic of the conceptual categories of race and ethnicity.

These usages illustrate the persistent confusion of meaning in these terms.

At least in their usage here, contra Goldberg (1992, p. 549), the conception of race as culture has not eclipsed other meanings. My point is not that we should be more exacting in our use of these two terms. If we recognize that both "race" and "ethnicity" are socially constructed, rather than naturally occurring, scientifically grounded terms, then we can begin to ask what sorts of features are highlighted in their use and what silences in public discourse are thereby enabled.[8] Those who argued for adding a "multiracial" category to the census or who do not find themselves reflected in existing categories are evidence not only that race-ethnic categories are not natural kinds, but also that the existing categories are increasingly less useful for capturing present American self-perceptions and demographic experiences. Further evidence of their nonnatural, socially constructed character lies in the fact that the categories and subcategories have changed in various ways over time, reflecting contemporaneous domestic and foreign policy concerns.

Constructing and Deconstructing Race-Ethnic Categories: Categorical Instability

The Census Bureau has not always asked about "race" and "ethnicity." First taken in 1790, the census was initially concerned with enumerating potential taxpayers, soldiers, and slaves, in part for calculating the size of state delegations to the House of Representatives (Anderson 1988).[9] Categorizing for purposes of military service, voting, and property ownership reflected individuals' civil status, thereby naming the criteria for being a "good" citizen (or, in the case of slavery, defining through oppositional contrast). In addition to changing purposes, category names themselves have changed over time, although the race-ethnic composition of the people they refer to has largely remained the same. (A summary of the early categories and subsequent changes is presented in Appendix 3.1.)

The word "color" first appears in the 1820 census, in reference to freed non-White slaves.[10] In 1850 "color" is first extended to Whites. For the previous six censuses, the dominant interest had been in documenting labor status: the "racial" categories (that word is not yet in usage) had been free whites, all other free persons (including "free colored persons") except Indians not taxed (i.e., living on reservation lands), and slaves. As slaves (of whatever "color" status) counted for three-fifths of a person in elections, this was tantamount to keeping tabs on potential votes and ties into the use of census data to determine congressional representation. Had slaves counted as full persons, the southern states would have wielded far more power. As only free persons could own land, only free persons (of whatever "color") counted as whole persons, and reservation Indians were excluded from the count, representation was tied through census categories to the interests of landowners, themselves predominantly "White." Interestingly, in 1850 color is subdivided into "white, black, or mulatto" for free inhabitants only; "slaves" has no color subdivisions.

The word "race" first appears in 1870, with the subcategories white, colored, Chinese (added now about two decades after the beginning of Chinese immigration), Indian. This census also tabulates "native or foreign born"—focusing attention on *place* of birth (and following an increase in immigration from Germany). A related question had been asked once before, in 1820, as "foreigners not naturalized"—but this focuses on citizenship (following the first great wave of immigrants from northern and western Europe) rather than on geographic origins per se. In neither case was sex, race, or other such demographic information cross-tabulated.

The 1880 census adds Japanese to the race list. In 1890 "race" becomes "color" as the category label, and "colored" is replaced by "Negro." In 1900 "Negro" is followed by the tag "(colored)" (as if "colored" had been dropped too soon, resulting in confusion over the denotation of "Negro"). In 1910 "(colored)" is dropped a second time, and "Negro" is subdivided into "Black" and "Mulatto" (the latter term reappearing for the first time since 1850). In 1920 the subdivisions of "Negro" are dropped, and the category name is changed to "color or race."

After fifty years of no changes in "nationality" categories, the 1930 census adds new subcategories: Mexican (following the end of Mexico's Civil War) and Philipino. These are supplemented in 1940 by Hindu, Korean, and "all other." "Indian" becomes "American Indian" in 1950, and Hindu and Korean are dropped. "Negro" becomes "Negro or Black" in 1960, Hawaiian joins the list (following statehood), and Korean returns (following the Korean War). In 1980 Negro and Black reverse order; Eskimo, Aleut, Asian Indian, Vietnamese (following the end of the Vietnam War), Samoan, and Guamanian are added. No new names were added in 1990. Census 2000 made several procedural and name changes, discussed below and itemized in Table 3.2 in the Appendix.[11]

Some of these changes—both additions of new categories and eliminations of others—reflect changing foreign and colonial relationships and policies, sometimes associated with states of war and ensuing obligations and immigrations, including the desire to track members of excluded groups: Chinese, Japanese, Mexican, Pilipino,* Korean, Vietnamese. The reason for the interplay between race and color terminology is less easy to pinpoint, although I surmise that the 1870 introduction of "race" reflects the influence of its increasing importance as a focus of statistical analysis, given the growth of that science, as well as its development as an organizing category among

---

*This spelling is preferred by members of this group. I use it unless a cited source uses a different spelling.

social philosophers involved with the growth of the eugenics movement.[12]

In general speech as well as in the census, changing usages of race-ethnic names also reflect historical moments. In the 1950 and 1960 censuses, Hispanics were tabulated in a separate question, identified as "Persons of Spanish Mother Tongue." In 1970 they were listed as "Persons of Both Spanish Surname and Spanish Mother Tongue"; in 1980 the "Hispanic" category was created; and in 2000 Latino has been added. In general parlance, "Chicano" was also in use for a while and is now frequently replaced by "Mexican-American" or "Latino/Latina," although usage varies across the United States, reflecting different population groups and political stances. "Black" and "Afro-American" have been giving way to "African-American," although many still prefer the term "Black." "Asian-American" has come into widespread use, although "Oriental" may still be heard on the East Coast and in the Midwest. "Native American" has replaced "Indian," although many Indians prefer that name (McCulloch, personal communication, 1996). "Alaska[n] Natives" have established that grouping as a separate category. The Small Business Administration accords "Native Hawaiians" separate standing.[13] Another recent development in daily usage is that "White" is being contested by "Caucasian" and by "European-American." The term "Anglo" suggests an opposition to "Hispanic," a less charged alternative to "gringo." As shorthand for Anglo-Saxon, it includes Celts, Protestant Irish, English, and Scots, as well as Germans and Scandinavians by reason of history and, by exile and immigration, New Zealanders, Australians, and Canadians. Its usage is broadening, although it is not yet as inclusive as "White": "Anglo" excludes Italians, Greeks, and others of Southern and Eastern European origin; and both "Anglo" and "European-American" exclude Arab and other peoples who are included in the OMB definition of "White."

The categories, in other words, are not fixed or stable—although census (and other administrative) usages imply that they are. They reflect choices to highlight certain features deemed important at particular moments in time. This has been the case throughout U.S. history, as the state has sought to classify its citizens and residents for various purposes. What is different now is the explicit attention to developing a uniform, universally applicable set of categories and to defining membership in those categories. It is this definitional process and its widespread application and implementation that lend the categories the aura of stability and permanence.

We can see this instability in further detail operating within each of the five original OMB groups.

a. *White.* The White category includes people who at other times it has excluded. Melungeons, whose ethnic history has recently been rediscovered publicly, are, according to one theory, descended from Moors—North African Arabs who had settled in Spain and Portugal and were expelled from those countries in the early 1500s. One story has it that a group of Moors landed off the South Carolina coast around 1580 and were eventually pushed to Newman's Ridge above the Powell River Valley along the Virginia-Tennessee border, where they have lived for the last 200 years. (Another possibility is that they were Turks, which would explain the eighty-year gap between their expulsion and landing: Many Moors took refuge from the Spanish-Portuguese expulsions in Turkey; language similarities between Turkish and Arabic phrases and "melungeon" support such an argument; and they described themselves in the mid-eighteenth century as "Portyghee"; Anthony 1998.) Along the way they married Cherokee and other Indians and English immigrants (*The Herndon* [VA] *Observer* 1/29/93: pp. 1, 4).[14] This suggests a third possibility, that Melungeons are one of several groups of so-called "tri-racial isolates"—including "Jackson whites";[15] New Jersey Moors; residents of the Indian Mound settlement in the Tennessee hills; the Wins of Coon Mountain, Virginia; and the so-called "mixed-bloods" of Drake County, Ohio, and Gouldtown, New Jersey (Frazier 1966, pp. 173–180).[16] What they have in common is a mixture of Black, White, and Indian heritage, and a longstanding geographic and social separation until the early 1900s, if not later, from both Black and White neighboring communities, sometimes self-imposed, sometimes imposed by neighboring Whites. They were originally included in the census as "free persons of color." Around World War II, their classification was changed to "white."

As mentioned in chapter 2, from the mid-1800s through the early 1900s, "all white" in reference to dockworkers meant Irish and German Americans, excluding Poles and Italians. And in Louisiana, Italians were excluded from "white Farmers'" associations, along with Blacks and Asians (Kusmer 1996, pp. 32–33).

Nor does White have universally stable meaning. In the West Indies, for example, a "Trinidad white" (or some other colony name modifying "white") is not a White Trinidadian, but a "modified" European—someone of "intermarried" European and island parents (Segal 1991). And "Caucasians" in Russia—Chechnyans, Azeris, Georgians, and other residents of the Caucasus region—are derogatorily referred to as "Blacks" in Russian ("*chorniye*"; McNeil 1998).[17]

b. *Black*. The nature of "Black"-ness is unique in American usage in one respect. Children born of one African-American parent are commonly registered as Black, even when that Black parent him- or herself is of mixed parentage (Davis 1991). This is a heritage of the so-called "one-drop rule" that has long operated in this country, that stipulated that any person with one drop of African blood was to be identified as "Black." The *Los Angeles Times* (1/13/91, p. E1) relates the story of children of a Swedish mother and Black father who are considered to be Black in all official records, to the mother's disbelief and dismay at finding her part of their heritage denied. The one-drop rule, established and long enforced through laws in many of the fifty states, continues to determine a set of administrative and social practices, as Davis (1991) shows extensively and as we shall see in chapter 5. Even with the option of checking off more than one box in Census 2000, many Blacks of mixed heritage chose to mark "Black" alone.[18]

The unstable, nonuniversal meaning of "Black" may be further seen by examining its meaning in other societies. In Great Britain, where an ethnicity question was first asked in the 1991 census, the categories included: Black-Caribbean; Black-African; and Black-Other (with a space to identify which other).[19] (Mexico, by comparison, has not asked a race-ethnic question for seventy years.) In the West Indies, there has long been a very elaborate set of categories for differentiating among persons of both European and African parentage.[20] Zena Moore (1995, p. 51) found herself "Black" in the United States, whereas at home in Trinidad, one is "either Trinidadian of East Indian descent, Trinidadian of African descent, or Trinidadian of mixed parentage." In Cuba, a person considered "Black" in the United States would be named according to various gradations of skin color and hair texture: "moro," "indiano," or "jabao" (Navarro 1997). In South Africa, "Black" sometimes includes people from India and those of mixed racial heritage (McNeil 1998). In Israel "Black" has been used by some older European-origin Jews to refer to Jews from the Middle East (e.g., Iraq, Iran, Syria, Lebanon, Egypt, the Yemen) and North Africa (Morocco, Tunisia, Libya, Algeria). Rita Arditti (in Bulkin 1984, p. 201, n. 7) elaborates on this point:

> ... the expression "Jews of color" ... seems to me a broad term that derives from the North-American division between white people in this country and blacks. . . . First of all, it seems to lump together all the Jews who are not "white." And who are "white Jews"? Are Ashkenazi Jews white?[21] How about Sephardic Jews from Italy, are they white and Sephardic Jews from Turkey or Morocco Jews of color? I can tell you that my family (Sephardim from Turkey, Ladino-speaking) would be very surprised to be called "Jews of color" and certainly they would not understand what you mean. So, who has the power of naming here? Are Jews from Ethiopia "Jews of color"? And Chinese and Indian Jews? . . . And finally, just to confuse you further, what would you call the Jews from Latin America, "color," "white," or what? In Argentina, for instance, about 25% of the community is Sephardic . . . from Syria, Turkey, Spain, Italy, etc., and the

rest are Ashkenazis, mainly from Russia, Poland and Germany. . . . Plus, there has been quite a lot of mixing.

Even within the United States, particularly in the southern states (and there, especially in Louisiana), an entire set of names denoting different mixtures of Black and White (and at times, Indian) heritage developed, including mulatto, quadroon, octoroon, and so on. Mexico and other Central American countries have added other names to the list, including mestizo and *pardo*. An old document in Spanish dating from 1780 lists two different sets of terms for different combinations, one with fourteen categories, one with sixteen. Among them are *gente blanca (de español y requinterona de mulato), cholo (de mestizo e india), chino (de mulato e india), sambo de indio (de negro e india), zambo (de negro y mulata)* in the one list; and *castizo (de mestizo y española), español (de castiza y español), morisco (de español y mulata), albino (de morisca y español), torna atras, lobo, zambaigo, cambujo, albarazado, barcino, coyote, chamiso* in the other (source unknown).

c. *Hispanic.* "Hispanic" or Latino identity is a similarly "unstable" category. OMB Directive No. 15 defines "Hispanic" as including those of "South [or Central, in the later version] American or other Spanish culture or origin." This could include Brazilians, who speak Portuguese, but not Portuguese-speakers from Portugal unless they consider themselves to come from a "Spanish" culture. The Small Business Administration, for example, in its Business Classification Definitions for Disadvantaged-Owned and Controlled, includes people whose origins are from "the Iberian Peninsula, including Portugal" as Hispanic Americans. The OMB category definition would also include Peru's former president Alberto K. Fujimori's children and others of Japanese and other Asian backgrounds born in South America who might immigrate to the United States, but who could also be considered "Asian or Pacific Islander" by the OMB definition. Former German citizens and their descendants immigrating to the United States from Brazil, Bolivia, Argentina would similarly be Hispanic Americans—and White. In 1940 the Census Bureau mandated that non-Indian Mexicans be listed as White (Haney López 1994, p. 51). The OMB definition would include S'faradi Jews—who come from a Spanish origin, often have Spanish surnames, speak a Spanish-Hebrew dialect, and live in many parts of the world; they could also be both Hispanic and White or Asian.[22]

d. *Native American.* In 1841 President William Henry Harrison invited "Native Americans" to his inaugural ball ("Topics of the Times," *New York Times* 1/10/93). But, as an astute letter writer pointed out, Harrison meant to include not American Indians, but White Anglo-Saxon Protestants such as those who belonged to the Native American Association, formed in 1837 to oppose the Irish and German immigrants of the era (Letters to the Editor, *New York Times* 1/20/93). In Tombstone, Arizona, of the early 1900s, White men established an association for their own gatherings called the "Improved Order of Red Men" (Wypijewski 1999, p. B15). On the other hand, "Mardi Gras Indians" (or the "Black Indians of New Orleans") refers to the descendants of unions between Africans and American Indians (Martinez 1995). In Mexico, indigenous people are now called "Indios" (McNeil 1998).

e. *Asian and Pacific Islander.* The 1990 postcensus update planned to include Asians (and Native Americans) in the "White" category, because their numbers were not statistically significant when considered on their own. And in Mexico, people from the Indian subcontinent are called "hindus," even if they are Christians or Moslems (McNeil 1998). As Moore (1995, p. 51) wrote, concerning American questionnaires, "If I were to select Asian, because my father is Chinese, does that deny my South American Indian ancestry . . . ?"

Reading Race-Ethnic Categories

This shifting of names and of membership over time and space suggests that race-ethnic categories *as they are used* have fungible boundaries, depending on their intended use, rather than the fixed boundaries implied by categorical logic. If, indeed, race-ethnic categories are not natural kinds but social constructions that have changed over time, and "race"-in-use means not only physical characteristics, but also ethnicity (genealogy, heritage) and geographic origins, then it is reasonable to ask about the attributes of the public discourse on race-ethnicity reflected in these categories. Which characteristics are being highlighted, and which are being obscured or occluded? The census case illustrates two central features of this discourse.

The categories-in-use reflect a high level of aggregate lumping. This "categorical lumpiness" masks distinctions within each category, thereby implying, enacting, or imposing a unity that by some measures is not there. Categorical logic implies clear membership criteria and sharp boundaries that, in practice, are neither. Classifying practices follow an "accurate enough" categorization that treats "almost the same" as if it were "entirely the same." Such a practice suppresses elements that differentiate among category members. It allows administrative and everyday practices to proceed according to certain assumptions and perceptions about the people melded into these categories, to create and tell identity stories about individuals and groups in terms of "cultural" histories that are much broader than any category's shared cultural attributes. Second, treating these categories as if they were universal, uniform, and mirroring nature, without attending to that "as if" quality, allows a masking of the point or points of view from which the categories have been created. This has been done both with "non-Whites" and with "Whites."

1. Categorical Lumpiness and the Modern American Adam

Aside from the issue of multiracial or interethnic identity, the categories in use in the census mix people together who by some criteria—language, for example, or religion, or cuisine and other customs—are quite distinct. Let us examine some of the oddities of this lumping, looking first at "people of color."

a. *"American Indian"* or *"Native American."* The category "American Indian" or "Native American" diverts attention from the sorts of differences that one might anticipate among the over 540 distinctive groups (McCulloch and Wilkins 1995)—119 of them recognized as "tribes" by government treaty—suggesting a homogeneity that from another point of view may not be there.[23] The underlying principle of classification seems to be "race," but it is race in the sense of "blood" composition, as well as a "cultural" sense, that demarcates Indian from non-Indian. To claim Indian heritage for U.S. legal and administrative purposes, a person must document a minimal percentage of blood composition, as well as self- or other-identification with a federally recognized tribe. Note that this is the only group for which the OMB definition stipulates such affiliation, and that there is a legal (and social) history of the role of blood in defining "African-American" as well. The focus on blood has led to its own nomenclature, counting "half-breeds," "full-bloodedness," and other proportions of ancestry, to 1/256.[24] At the same time, although the initial OMB Directive 15 defines Native Americans as "original peoples of North America," Rodriguez found himself excluded as a *Mexican* Indian, as noted earlier (and even the later additions of South and Central America would not help with this).[25]

b. *"Hispanic"* or *"Latino."* In their research Rodolfo O. de la Garza and his colleagues found that the cluster terms "Hispanic" and "Latino" suggest a "cultural homogeneity" and a "political unity" that do not exist—that Cuban-Americans, Mexican-Americans, and Puerto Ricans, the three largest "Latino" groups in the United States, often differ as much from each other as they do from non-Hispanic Whites (de la Garza 1993; see also Coughlin 1991). The appropriateness and meaning of the "Hispanic" label has been the subject of extensive newspaper and news magazine attention as well. Here, too, aggregated categorical lumpiness implies and enacts a homogeneity that, from the point of view of category members, does not exist. Including immigrants from Central and South America together with those from the Iberian peninsula features language as the classificatory principle, at the same time that it includes some who speak other languages.

Figure 3.1   **Map Showing Territories of Origin of Asian and Pacific Islanders**

Source: "Three Self-Guided Tours: The Asian Galleries." Reprinted by permission of the Department of Public Education, Museum of Fine Arts, Boston.

Note: The category excludes the (former) Soviet Union, Afghanistan, and the area to its west. Not identified on the map, but included in the census category list, are: the Philippines, Laos, the Hmong people, Myanmar (Burma in the census list), Bangladesh, Malaysia, and the Pacific islands of Hawaii, Samoa, Tonga, Okinawa, Tahiti, Fiji, North Mariana, Guam, Palau.

c. *"Asian-American" or "Asian and/or Pacific Islander."* The API category masks generational and economic characteristics, as well as geographic and cultural ones. It includes fourth-generation Japanese-Americans, like 1992 Olympic gold medal skater Kristi Yamaguchi, and a newly arrived immigrant from Pakistan.

The 1990 census list of possibilities for API has twenty-five different countries, covering 6,000 miles and many languages, religions, cuisines, customs, traditions, and physical features. A visual display of the territory covered by this category, as in the map in Figure 3.1, highlights the arbitrariness of where the category line is drawn, as well as the contiguity of the peoples involved. For example, some Iranians and Soviet Asians, although not included in the API category, share a language, religion, cuisine, and other customs, as well as physical features, with adjacent peoples who are included in the API list. The classificatory principle here appears to be continental land mass or geography. Even dividing the category in two, as Census 2000 has, preserves this principle, the broad inclusiveness, and the arbitrariness of boundaries.

Forcing this vast diversity into a single pan-Asian category conveys the implication that all API member groups achieve similar educational and economic standing, in keeping with the stereotype of the high-performing "Asian-American." But school dropout and poverty rates are higher among Hmong, Cambodians, and other Southeast Asians than they are among South Asians (Sengupta 1997). And as one letter writer who immigrated to the United States from Korea in the 1970s noted, "To be known primarily as an Asian-American rather than as 'Chinese' [the name by which he was often "identified generically"] . . . tempt[s] anonymity and invisibility. . ." (Kang 1996).

d. *"Black" or "African-American."* This category similarly masks generation of immigration and country of origin. For example, an African-American from Chicago whose ancestors were brought as slaves and who was raised in the South and a recent immigrant from Nigeria living in Boston are both "Black," according to the census, as is the Jamaican immigrant living in California. This brings one of the OMB definitional problems to bear on Question 13: how far back in time is an individual to go in tracing "ethnic origin"? To take this to its logical extremes, if current theories of the origins of Native Americans are true, then they are "Whites" whose ancestors crossed the polar cap from Europe. And, if Africans and African culture originated in Egypt, as some currently argue, then African-Americans, Afro-Caribbeans, and other Blacks are Whites (by definition, the classification of those originating in the peoples of North Africa). As with Native Americans, the principle of classification is blood, institutionalized in the one-drop rule, still a matter of practice and beliefs in many ways (see Davis 1991), although no longer supported by law.

These four categories seemingly share no common classificatory principle according to which they have been created. The requirements for membership suggest that while American Indians and African-Americans are categorized by blood, in a partial holdover from ancient humoral practices, Asian-Americans are classified by geography, and Hispanics, by accent.[26] The shared classificatory principle emanates from elsewhere, in the point of view from which these groups are being perceived, a point of view that is unspoken, though implicit in the categorizations. That perceiving eye belongs to a contemporary "Adam" who, looking out at the world, describing its inhabitants and naming them "according to their kinds," sees and defines an "Other."

Note the order in which the categories are typically given. When we want to suggest status equality among categories, we often list them in alphabetical order. This is not the case in the census (or in most such questionnaires): it (like most) begins with "White." Nor is it a chronological sequencing, which would establish categorical equality by a different criterion: the Pilgrims in Plymouth faced the local Indians before they faced Africans. The list is given in order of difference, of Otherness, beginning with the "normal," unmarked category. It follows a descending order of otherness, reflecting a single-point perspective.

This American Adam is the collective embodiment of a "White" communal perspective. From his perspective (and in many respects, this modern-day Adam has also been male), the salient unmarked characteristics against which he perceives "Otherness" are "white" skin, Northern European facial features and hair, and "unaccented" English. More finite distinctions—that there are noticeable physical or speech differences between a "Black" from Chicago or from Jamaica and one from Ghana or Nigeria, or between an "Asian" from New Delhi and one from Korea, or between a Navajo and a Mashpee—have typically not been visible to him (even though Whites, especially east of the Mississippi, have made minute judgments of recognition among themselves based on physical features and names with reasonable degrees of accuracy, differentiating among English, Irish, Italians, Jews, Greeks, and others[27]).

This collective Adam is from the North-Eastern stretch that extends from the Atlantic coast to Chicago and southward. Such an identity may be read from the portrayal of his "Other" in these categories: it is mostly "Black," as he sees his opposite in the black skin of his historical encounter with slavery, in the Civil War, and in the Civil Rights movement. This, despite the fact that there have been Asian-Americans in the West for over 100 years and "Hispanics" in the Southwest and American Indians across the continent for longer than there has been an "America." He is typically not (yet) conscious of being of a race himself: in his mind's eye, he sees himself as "normal," unmarked, regular. (Although, to judge from public and academic discourse, this is changing: his conscious self-awareness as "White" is emerging as it is reflected back to him by his Others and by growing public discourse on cultural diversity in schools, in the workplace, and in the media, including in "White Studies" programs in universities and attendant papers and publications.) Until very recently, our Adam has been Anglo-Saxon and Protestant (I will return to this shortly); he still is Christian, which makes "Others" of Moslems, Hindus, Bahais, Jews, Buddhists, Shintos, and so forth. These collective historic experiences and mind supply the perspective from which Others are labeled. Perhaps because this perspective is relatively undifferentiated, the categories created are highly aggregated and "lumpy." The categories homogenize identity; yet actual persons "belonging" in each category, marked by the identity established by the category, often do not share that identity—as illustrated by Roberto Rodriguez's story at the beginning of the chapter. The categories make less sense with respect to the attributed similarities of their members than they do relative to their aggregate differences from this defining Adam. It is this, perhaps, that makes the American race-ethnic world appear to many still to be a "Black-White" world, despite the fact that that vision is more accurately a reflection of the Northeast-to-Chicago stretch than of Miami, California, the Southwestern states, and elsewhere: the aggregate differences of the category structure suggest a bifurcated, "White/non-White" world.

2. White Is a Color, Too

"White" is also a lumpy category. It is no more fixed or stable than the others. It includes a few dozen different Eastern and Western European groups, plus Turks, Iranians, Iraqis and other Arab groups, and so on.[28] Current usage often conflates "White" with "European," and in doing so, reflects a changed sense of the historical experience of immigrants from European countries, at the same time that it ignores others—Arabs and other Middle Easterners, primarily—included in the category.

Until recently, the race-ethnic identity of the dominant American culture as perceived by themselves and others was not only White, but Northern European and Protestant as well. Other non–Northern-European and non-Protestant "White" groups became "hyphenated-Americans": Irish-Americans, Italian-Americans, Polish-Americans.[29] The hyphen denoted their Otherness. It is the marked category; "American," the unmarked norm. That they were also "white"-skinned Caucasians was not reflected in the categories of the time. Their contrasting features stood out more: physical (that they were redheads [Irish] or swarthy with dark, curly hair [Greeks, Italians, Jews], rather than fair-skinned blonds); religious (that they were Roman Catholic or Greek or Eastern Orthodox or Jews); cultural (that they spoke with accents, even though their children spoke accent-free English, and gesticulated when they spoke). Ironically, in Great Britain the English had identified the remaining Irish as a "distinct minority race with much lower social value" than the emigrating Irish (Williams 1990, p. 130) and than the English themselves, but both are joined here in a single category. Their otherness had economic as well as social implications: the phrase "Irish and Jews need not apply" was still known well into the 1960s in East Coast city and suburban newspapers and shop windows, as were streets where owners had pacts not to sell their homes to "Jews and Negroes."

Recent usage of the category "Whites" implies that this distinction between Protestant Anglo-Saxons and non-Protestant non–Anglo-Saxons has broken down. The European ethnics have made their way into the workplace, the boardroom, and the country club; there has been an Iacocca at the head of a major corporation, a Freedman at the head of an Ivy League college, and a Kennedy as president (but not a Ferraro as vice president—the gender problem intrudes). The use of the phrase "People of Color" has strengthened the oppositional categorization "Whites." And the turn to hyphenization among other Others—Asian-Americans, African-Americans, Latino/a-Americans, Native Americans (even without the hyphen)—has invoked a new oppositional category, "European-American."

What has been gained, and what lost, by this undifferentiated lumping? The aggregation of people with different cultural heritages and geographic origins under the label "Whites" masks recent and continuing discriminations against various "White" subgroups.

On the one hand, its promise is to even the playing field conceptually: Americans now come in five varieties (or six, if Pacific Islander is separated from Asian).[30] The nation is no longer a jumble of Negro, Oriental, Indian, Spanish-surnamed, and hyphenated marked, special cases in addition to unmarked, "normal," plain Americans. The once-demeaning hyphen has become almost a mark of status: all Americans are now hyphenated-Americans, and this conceptual categorization renders its members conceptually equal. As essayist Barbara Ehrenreich (1992) noted, "it [has] begun to seem almost un-American not to have some sort of hyphen at hand, linking one to more venerable times and locales."

This would suggest that European ethnics are no longer "Other." If this were the case, then in terms of equality, all have gained. However, late-twentieth-century presidential campaigns, from David Duke to intimations of Mario Cuomo's links to the Mafia to concerns about Paul Tsongas's 1992 candidacy—"Another Greek?" after Michael Dukakis—indicate that this animosity isn't entirely gone. The City University of New York, for example, includes Italian-Americans in its protected classes for affirmative action purposes.[31] And this conceptual equality doesn't extend to non-European, "White" Moslem and Christian Arab-Americans, whose "Otherness" was made visible in the last decade of the twentieth century during the 1991 Gulf War against Iraq, in character depictions and lyrics in the 1993 Disney film *Aladdin*, and in characterizations of the 1995 Oklahoma City bombing suspects as being of "Middle Eastern appearance,"[32] and again with the attacks on September 11, 2001.

At the same time, the blurring of distinctions between ethnicity and race has also fostered the designation "Caucasian" to mean a "White cultural group" (in the same way that the categories also imply the existence of aggregate African-, Asian-, Hispanic-, and Native American cultures). Creating this "White" category engages in the process that Omi and Winant (1994) call "racialization," "through which racial meaning is extended to a previously unclassified relationship, social practice, or group"—but in this case, without any of the cultural hallmarks of common language, religion, foods, customs, and so forth that give an ethnic group its identity. Perhaps the unspoken definer in this case is an Adam "of color," comparable to the WASP Adam who has racialized the other lumpy groups.[33]

This bleaches Caucasian women and men of the cultural characteristics that have defined them, much as has been done in lumping together members of the other, non-Caucasian categories, denying internal diversity. For those who find sources of identity in an ethnic culture, this is a loss. Ironically, it is not only the so-called European ethnics' culture that is lost in the lumpiness of "European-American" or "Caucasian." The WASP culture, portrayed, for example, by A.R. Gurney in his plays (e.g., *The Cocktail Hour*, *The Dining Room*), also disappears into this aggregation. "English" is absent as a possible answer on ancestry in Question 13.[34] This is the latest manifestation of a conceptual system that used "ethnic" to refer to Southern and Eastern European groups and the Irish, as if Swedes, Dutch, and others had no ethnic traits. Developing a category labeled "European-American" creates an identity that is conceptually equivalent to other hyphenated identities and yet at the same time so distanced from many Caucasians' self-perceptions that it, too, is devoid of substance. This is accomplished even more through the category "White": it is an oppositional form to "people of color," but it is colorless, without any cultural essence or referent, except when used as a synonym for "WASP."

Census 2000 and the Revised OMB Directive 15: Category Name Changes

The Census Bureau recognizes that "[r]acial and ethnic identity is a social process that is changing for some proportion of each of the racial and ethnic groups identified in Directive No. 15" (U.S. Bureau of the Census 1997, p. 2-10). The bureau initiated changes both in nomenclature and in procedures, in part in response to revisions in OMB Directive No. 15. In the Census 2000 race question (number 8 or 6 on the short form, 6 on the long form), "White" remains unchanged, but the category "Black or Negro" now adds "African American" to the formal name. This encompasses those who want recognition of their status as Americans, as well as those who feel that with a different background (e.g., the Caribbean) and/or without the heritage of American slavery, they are not *African* Americans.

By including South and Central America in "American Indian," the category emphasizes the indigenousness of many Latino/as. The addition would seemingly address the problem encountered by Roberto Rodriguez when he tried to identify himself as a Native American—until we remember that he was denied as an indigenous Mexican, and Mexico is considered part of North America. One hopes that explicitly naming Central and South Americans will raise awareness of the existence of Mexican and Canadian North American Indians, too. In emphasizing indigenousness, however, the new category explicitly introduces a third "racial" element (Indian) into a nonracial category: Hispanics/Latino/as are defined as having that identity "regardless of race," and now may be identified as non-Indian (along with non-Black and non-White).

Census 2000 scrambles the subcategories of the old "Asian or Pacific Islander" group, dividing them in list form between the two new OMB categories, "Asian" and "Pacific Islander":

Asian	*Pacific Islander*
Asian Indian	Native Hawaiian
Chinese	Guamanian or Chamorro[35]
Filipino	Samoan
Japanese	Other Pacific Islander
Korean	
Vietnamese	
Other Asian	

The revised OMB Directive No. 15 lists the following groups, from those reported in Census 1990 tabulations, as additional potential inclusions under Pacific Islander: Carolinian, Fijian, Kosraean, Melanesian, Micronesian, Northern Mariana Islander, Palauan, Papua New Guinean, Ponapean (Pohnpelan), Polynesian, Solomon Islander, Tahitian, Tarawa Islander, Tokelauan, Tongan, Trukese (Chuukese), and Yapese (U.S. Office of Management and Budget 1997). Splitting the larger category in two recognizes the vast range of physical, cultural, and geographic backgrounds that had been forced within a single categorical boundary (as shown in Figure 3.1), but it retains a high level of lumpiness within each of the two new categories (e.g., "Asian" encompassing Indians, Pilipinos, Thais, and Koreans). Although corresponding with a continental land mass, "Asia" still presents a degree of arbitrariness in drawing its western boundary. Naming "Native Hawaiians" with "Other Pacific Islanders" makes clearer their categorical locationing, although distancing them from "American Indian or Alaska Native" privileges geography (proximate location) over history. The revised directive also reports an inconsistency noted by some Native Hawaiians in the decision to exclude them from the American Indian or Alaska Native category that includes "descendants of Central and South American Indians—persons who are not original peoples of the United States," despite their own status as original peoples.

The "Spanish or Hispanic" origin question (number 7 or 5 in the short form, 5 in the long form) is also now more embracing in its addition of "Latino," which recognizes the colonial origins of the prior category name. The OMB definition moves "Cuban" to the first place in the list, rendering the sequence alphabetical and thereby suggesting a categorical equivalence among the suggested possible answers, rather than reflecting perhaps the chronological order of the United States' relationship with the three countries.

The ancestry or ethnic origin question is now the last in the sequence (it appears in the long form only, where it is Question 10). The section with suggestions to the enumerator makes the following changes to the 1990 form (italics designate newly added or moved terms): "Italian, *Jamaican, African-*American, *Cambodian,* Cape Verdean, *Norwegian,* Dominican, French Canadian, *Haitian,* Korean, Lebanese, *Polish,* Nigerian, *Mexican,* Taiwanese, Ukrainian, *and so on."* (German, *Afro-*American, Croatian, Ecuadoran, Cajun, Irish, Slovak, and Thai have been dropped.) The list has no self-evident order: geography and alphabet intermingle. It becomes clearer in this usage that African-American is taken to be both "race" and "ethnicity."

Procedural Changes and Category "Errors" or "Mistakes"

In addition to changes in category names, Census 2000 practices also entailed two procedural changes. Both were intended to address various problems—category "errors" or "mistakes," in terms of category-making principles—that had become more acutely felt during the 1990 census and entered public discourse much more widely, including into Congressional and agency hearings on the OMB definitions and census procedures.

One can be a category "error" conceptually in two ways. First, one may not fit the definition of any category—the English immigrant, "surely" a European-American, who was a Black-Pakistani at home in London. "Other" has only recently been added as a formal category option, and often on questionnaires this possibility is still not available. One must fit the available categories—by conceptual force if necessary. Otherwise, one does not "fit in," literally and colloquially: one is a by-product of the "prototype effect" discussed in chapter 1. For example, to nonmembers outside the category, the prototype of "White" is skin shade. From that perspective, light-skinned Arabs and Jews are "White." But many in both these groups do not see themselves as such. Many Arabs and some Jews do not include themselves with "original peoples of Europe" (the OMB phrase). Many Jews, as well as others, see the prototype of "White" as Anglo-Saxon Protestants and, given the history of exclusion and discrimination they have experienced at the hands of American WASPs and of Europeans before them, do not see themselves as sharing a cultural history or heritage with them.

Each of the five categories has its own prototype. In this sense, historically hyphenated Americans have been categorical marginals. "Real" Americans conform to the central, prototypical traits; following the category logic identified by Lakoff (1987), all others are American "by virtue of their relation to the ideal case . . ." (p. 76). The ideal case—Caucasian Protestant from northern Europe, native born, English-speaking with no "foreign" accent—stands for the category and defines societal and cultural expectations of it (see Lakoff 1987, p. 82). Kinds of Americans are deviations from this central case. The traits attributed to each of the five categories are, with rare exception, those of the prototypes.

The other way to be a "mistake" is in fitting more than one category, the case of "mixed race" peoples. As Scales-Trent (1995) so eloquently shows, being an "error" has often been accompanied by long-held personal silence, reinforced by the societal silencing instantiated by a nonexistent category; hence, an invisibility arises from the inability in a publicly available vocabulary to tell one's story as a member of a group. Given the longstanding strength of societal taboos on intermarriage and miscegenation, until recently with legal support, it is no wonder that there has been no category labeled "mixed race" before now, and wonderful that that silence began to be publicly broken finally in the mid-1990s.[36] Such silence, self-imposed and imposed from without, has often also been accompanied by a sense of shame. This shame arises from not fitting clearly into one of the five categories—not having a group identity—and the ensuing sense of not being a "real" American.[37]

One procedural change was designed to address the first type of category error, the geometric growth in the number of people who identified themselves as "Other" on Question 4 ("race") in the 1990 census. Statisticians felt that many of these were "Hispanics" who did not identify themselves with White, Black, Asian or Pacific Islander, or Native American.[38] Their analysis focused on the order of the questions: the opportunity to self-identify as Hispanic (Question 7, 1990) came after respondents had already encountered the "race" question (Question 4, 1990). In their analysis, a person having the opportunity to self-identify as Hispanic before engaging the racial identity question would be more likely to self-identify as a specific race, rather than the more generic "Other." This led to a change in the sequencing of these questions in Census 2000: the Spanish/Hispanic/Latino question now precedes the race question in both short and long forms. Given, however, that many Latino/as are of mixed "racial" heritage (e.g., White, Black, and Indian; or Latino/a and Asian), it is possible that the choice of "Other" was not a reflection of question sequencing.

The second procedural change—and it is a major departure after 200 years of census taking—addresses the second situation. For the first time, the Census Bureau designed a questionnaire allowing respondents to self-identify according to the full range of their "racial" backgrounds. Instructions to the enumerator say: "*Mark one or more races to indicate what this person considers himself/herself to be.*" This choice was made in lieu of creating a separate "Mixed race" or "Multiracial" category. That would have suggested that people of multiple heritages identify themselves as "mixed." Despite the growth of interest groups adopting a "mixed race" identity, the bureau's decision reflects a different stance: that people of multiple heritages are often aware of each of them and would appreciate the opportunity to identify accordingly. This practice addresses the problem of forced choice: one need no longer choose one parent over another or one ancestral heritage over others.

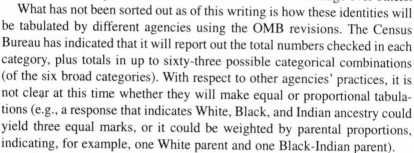

What has not been sorted out as of this writing is how these identities will be tabulated by different agencies using the OMB revisions. The Census Bureau has indicated that it will report out the total numbers checked in each category, plus totals in up to sixty-three possible categorical combinations (of the six broad categories). With respect to other agencies' practices, it is not clear at this time whether they will make equal or proportional tabulations (e.g., a response that indicates White, Black, and Indian ancestry could yield three equal marks, or it could be weighted by parental proportions, indicating, for example, one White parent and one Black-Indian parent).

As noted in the previous chapter, several agencies and interest groups are concerned that these counting issues will render the 2000 numbers incomparable to the 1990 figures, which would make redistributive and programmatic uses difficult. (Because of such arguments, the bureau did not change the 1990 Asian and Pacific Islander subcategories; see chapter 5.) If statistical analysis could show the totals for each category separately (relative to the total number of responses), it seems to me that such comparability might be achieved (but only if the bureau does an actual head count; there is insufficient knowledge of population mixtures to allow for projections based on sampling).

Comparative Race-Ethnicity:
Australia, Spain, Israel, New Zealand

This chapter has explored the variability of American race-ethnic categories as they have changed over time and encompassed different groups of people. It began by raising questions about the very notions of "race" and "ethnicity" themselves, and it is useful at this point to return to those concepts, however briefly. Americans with little experience outside of the United States or outside of their own particular race-ethnic group might think that the American categories—as imperfect as they might be—nonetheless accurately reflect race-ethnic categories throughout the world. After all, "everyone knows" that Asia, Africa, Europe, and North and South America are the major continental classifications, and every immigrant to every country has to come from one of them or from an island. Even a superficial look at ways in which other nations use the concepts of "race" and "ethnicity," however, and categorize their populations shows that none of these are natural. For instance, Malaysian public policies distinguish among *Bumiputra* ("son of the soil")— that is, indigenous Malays (60 percent of the population); ethnic Chinese (30 percent); and ethnic Indians (10 percent; Dorgan 1997). In the United States, all three would fall into a single category as Pacific Island– or Asian-Americans. As local uses of "race" and "ethnicity" also become the grounds for redistributive policies, the role of the state in creating race-ethnic identity also becomes more visible when comparing United States' to other practices.

The demographic organizing principle in Australia, for example, seems to be a combination of geography and language. The Australian government has created a category for people of non–English-speaking background (NESB), in an attempt to make various social and other programs (e.g., health care) accessible to all. Membership in NESB is determined by geography of birth; that is, birthplace becomes a proxy for linguistic ability, itself seen as the primary demarcator of socioeconomic disadvantage and "Otherness." An immigrant born in Papua, New Guinea belongs to the category; someone born in an Australian city does not. But the geographic principle seems to assume a sort of immobility: Children born to Anglo-Saxon Australians, who otherwise might be expected not to need state protections or assistance since they come from an English-speaking background, but who were living at the time of their birth in Papua, are considered NESB; children born to Serbo-Croatian–speaking parents living in Sydney, who use English only at school, are not.[39]

Geography is also the explicit principle currently for rendering ethnicity in Spain, although underlying it is the concept of the purity of blood (*limpieza de sangre*), documented in writing from the fourteenth century on (Greenwood 1984).[40] The new constitution developed in Spain after Franco's death establishes a regional basis for "ethnic" differences, whereby Catalunya, Galicia, Andalucía, and the Basque regions are enabled to develop their own languages and other cultural-administrative practices, rather than being forced to adhere to the practices established by the long-dominant Castilian state. "Rights," under the new constitution, adhere not to individuals, but to regional "ethnic" groups.[41] "Soil"-derived ethnicity moves with the individual: a Gallego (someone from Galicia) is still a

Gallego in Barcelona (in Catalunya). This would be the closest case to an American race-ethnic identity based on region (Southerner, New Yorker, Californian, and so forth); but American mobility often (though not always) diminishes that sense of geographic identity. All Californians, according to one popular saying, are from somewhere else. But to say that acknowledges an aspect of their "California-ness."[42]

Ethnicity among Jews in Israel appears to depend on intersections of geography and blood, expressed in the biblical language of peoplehood with internal land-based divisions. Ethnicity—the comparable modern Israeli Hebrew term is *edah*, roughly meaning "tribe," in reference to the biblical twelve tribes of Israel—is a matter of country or continent of origin prior to immigration to Israel; but since Jews have historically been forced to emigrate often, some *edah* categories refer back 500 years.[43] Many Jewish Israelis proclaim that through intermarriage (the mixing of home cultural practices and blood), these long-held lines of distinction will be blurred. This hope appears to be based on the assumption that in such unions, the dominant ("majority") ethnicity will prevail culturally.[44] Although skin color and other marks of physiognomy play a part in some distinctions, they are not present in all of them. For redistributive social policy purposes, however, the state in the 1970s created the category of family size based on the number of children (originally set at five, it was later lowered to four), which correlated roughly with *edah*.[45]

Ethnicity in New Zealand reflects settlement and colonial histories, specifically the encounters between English settlers and various Maori tribes. The distinction evolved into Maori and non-Maori; the Maori word *pakeha* (accent on the first syllable) is used to refer to the latter. But whereas pakeha originally meant "White" or "European," in reference to the English, Scots, and Dutch settlers, today it is being stretched to include immigrants from various Asian countries (Indians, Chinese, Japanese), Jews, Americans, and other Pacific Island immigrants—although for some state purposes, the latter are classed along with Maoris (Gershon n.d.b), with whom they share some historical and cultural background (at least, from a pakeha perspective) but from whom in other respects they are markedly distinct. As the government increasingly returns land and fishing rights to the Maoris, in keeping with the Waitangi Treaty of 1840 long honored in the breach, it seems that the Maori themselves will be responsible for redistributing wealth among themselves.[46]

I am intentionally not bringing into the discussion the racial laws developed and used by the Nazis to classify Roma,[47] Jews, and others. Although this is a clear case of the state's interest in race-ethnic categories—developing detailed genealogical criteria for "blood" content and charts of nose shapes, and so on as criteria for Jewishness and then classifying Jews as "subhuman" made it easier to eradicate them[48]—the circumstances are so extreme as to be dismissed as an outlier, rather than treated as just another—yes, extreme—example. However, the South African case is commonly perceived, rightly or wrongly, as less extreme, and yet the state laws for apartheid (see Bowker and Star 1999, chap. 6) echo, eerily, in their degree of excruciating detail the exactitude of the Nazis' Nuremberg laws,[49] as well as earlier American case law (Haney López 1995).

What becomes visible through such a comparative approach is not only the high degree of variability of race-ethnic categories, and, indeed, of the meanings of "race" and "ethnicity" themselves—where NESB is a language- and birthplace-based "race-ethnic" group, a category almost inconceivable in U.S. terms (as if "Bostonian" or "New Yorker" or "Southerner" were a protected class based on accent, and one could become a member of one of these groups by virtue of birthplace if one's parents were passing through). What comparative analysis also renders more visible is the role of the state in identity creation and construction.[50] Self-identity depends to a degree on categories created by the state—and individuals' self-identification becomes, then, "in some ways contingent on who the state claims they are or allows them to be, . . . as participants in the policy processes that [constitute and] legitimate the state" (Greenhouse and Greenwood 1994, p. 6). What becomes even more visible is the way in which the very acts of counting and reporting census data themselves create and maintain race-ethnicity and race-ethnic groups.

This process of state-defined race-ethnic identity can be read as an assimilationist story. We began historically in the United States by creating undifferentiated Blacks. We are now making undifferentiated Whites. "Asians," "Pacific Islanders," "Native Americans," and "Hispanics/Latino/as" are en route, if the conceptual logic of these categories is pursued. In this ethnogenesis, how is identity being negotiated?

Notes

1. It is not possible from the census to know what the Jewish population of the United States is, except by inference. The instructions to enumerators on Question 14 in 1980, for example, said: "A religious group should not be reported as a person's ancestry." One can infer that some percentage of those tracing their ethnic origins to Eastern European countries are Jews or derive a figure based on those who give Hebrew or Yiddish in answer to Question 15 about whether a non-English language is spoken at home. Neither of these identifies S'faradic Jews (see note 21); none yields exact numbers, nor do they indicate that Jews could be of many race-ethnic groups: Hispanic, Black, Asian (e.g., from India), Native American, as well as White.

2. For clarifying this, I thank Mike Regenstreif (personal communication, 10/30/95), a third-generation, English-speaking Jew whose grandparents immigrated to Canada from Eastern Europe.

3. American resistance to the census ranges from anger and annoyance to humor. Felicity Barringer in the *New York Times* (4/15/90, p. 12) reported that someone listed a family member's name as Puss E. Cat; his race in Question 4 was listed as Siamese.

4. "Indian" first appeared as a separate category in the census count in 1860. Prior to that, they would have been counted among "all other free persons," unless they lived on reservation land (in which case they were not taxed and therefore not of interest to the census, and, hence, not counted). "Indian" became "American Indian" in 1950.

5. This same confusion of meaning appears in noncensus questionnaires that list Hispanic together with White and Black. Since by OMB stipulation Hispanics may be of any race, by definition, the three used together in this way cannot denote racial groups: the categorical equivalence renders White and Black, ethnicities.

6. Similar in underlying framework of meaning, perhaps, is the rhetorical, derisive question, Don't you know your place? Many East Coast people who have relocated to California notice that Californians typically do not ask others, "Where are you from?" perhaps because everyone is from someplace else; and I know at least one California-born living in the East who is discomfited by the persistent Eastern habit of asking, "Where is your last name from?"—a version of geographic locationing that stands in for typing personal characteristics. See also the discussion on these latter two questions in Satris (1995, pp. 57–58).

7. I follow the usage here of Rogers (1997, see note 11, p. 5). He marks the term as a collective referent for first- and second-generation immigrants to the United States of African descent by way of Anglophone Caribbean countries: the stretch of islands from Jamaica to Trinidad plus Guyana, Surinam, and Belize on the continent. It excludes Spanish- and French-speaking islanders who, he notes, "typically claim a distinct ethnic or racial identity." Among Afro-Caribbeans themselves, he further notes, there is extensive cultural and linguistic heterogeneity, although by virtue of their common experience as immigrants to the United States, they have been forging a pan-Caribbean identity.

8. That "color," race, and ethnicity are socially constructed, rather than being natural kinds, is widely accepted in ethnic studies, anthropology, and other fields, although not (yet) in policy and administrative practices. See, for example, M.M.J. Fischer (1986), Sollors (1989), and R. Williams (1990). Williams also explores the societal value attaching to such "social designations" and why we treat them as natural phenomena.

9. This built on prior Revolutionary War experience, as the colonies had estimated their population sizes "to determine their war readiness, tax capacity, and so on" (Anderson 1988, p. 11). This sort of tabulation became important again during World War I, extended now to include data on explosives and "leather stocks" (p. 127), and in the 1940 census, to assess defense industry capacity and potential internal alien threat (p. 192).

10. It seems important to note that the labor category "slave" in American history is not coterminous with any race-ethnic category, let alone with the color category "Black." Slaves included Creoles and American Indians, as well as Whites. According to historian Jacqueline Jones, colonists did not make sharp distinctions between slaves and indentured servants (cited in O'Neill 1998). More important for the devel-

opment of American race-ethnic categories is the process by which African-Americans (and others, by opposition) came to be seen exclusively in terms of skin shade.

11. See also Goldberg's (1995, pp. 239–242) discussion of census categories.

12. Arguably, the introduction of "deaf" and "dumb" in the 1830 census and the addition of "blind" and "insane" in 1840 also represented the influence of the eugenics movement and the desire to control for the breeding of a physically unimpaired "pure" race.

13. The Small Business Administration (in its Business Classification Definitions for Disadvantaged-Owned and Controlled) also accords protected standing in its list of socially and economically disadvantaged business owners to Hasidic Jewish Americans.

14. An account of a seemingly different but possibly related group is given in Frazier (1966, pp. 175–177). The name "Melungeon" does not appear; the group is claimed to have originated in Delaware with the intermarriage of either Spanish Moors or "Negro slaves, probably of Moorish origin" with Irish and Nanticoke Indians. "A small community of their descendants has been established across the Delaware River near Beacon's Neck in Cumberland County, New Jersey" (p. 177).

15. According to one version of their origin, "Jackson whites" are descendants of a British officer named Jackson and of his soldiers. Jackson commanded a fort that included organized prostitution with enslaved African women. By some arrangement, his descendants were classed as "white" although their mothers were African—hence, their name (Orion White, personal communication, 1991).

Zack (1993, pp. 89–90) led me to an entirely different explanation of their origin in Frazier (1966, pp. 173–175), who identifies them as a mixed-race community in Ramapo Hills, thirty miles north of New York City. According to his informant, the community had been founded in the 1800s by four "Boers" (Dutch immigrants, it would seem) who were joined by Tuscarora and Delaware Indians and slaves owned by a family living nearby, one of whom was named Jackson, hence the name. Frazier's informant noted that there were two types of Jackson Whites, a white variety living on one side of the town, and a variety of "predominating Indian and colored types." See Fuchs (1990, p. 331) for yet another explanation that draws on bits and pieces of both stories.

16. Daniel (1992, p. 99) adds to this list the Van Guilders, Clappers, Shinnecock, Poospatuck, Montauk, and Mantinecock in New York; the Pools of Pennsylvania; Nanticokes of Delaware; Narragansetts of Rhode Island; Gay Heads and Mashpees of Massachusetts; Wesorts of Maryland; Guineas of West Virginia; Carmelites of Ohio; Ramps, Issues, and Chickahominy in Virginia; Lumbees, Haliwas, Waccamaws, and Smilings of North Carolina; Chavises, Creels, Brass Ankles, Redbones, Redlegs, Buckheads, and Yellowhammers of South Carolina; and a "host" of others in Louisiana. I note that some of these groups have been in court in the last twenty to thirty years seeking to establish identity as Native Americans, and that according to Frazier, not all of them have "refused" (as Daniel puts it) identification with Black or White communities.

17. Much as "black" has come to be used, metaphorically, for the "darker" side of human emotions and affairs—for example, "I'm in a black mood"—"white," too, has had a metaphoric usage with race-derived connotations. W.E.B. Du Bois described a woman of his acquaintance as "a 'white Black girl' from New Orleans; that is, a well educated young white woman who was classed as 'Colored' because she had a Negro great-grandfather" (*Worlds of Color*, Millwood, N.Y.: Kraus-Thomson, 1976, p. 9;

quoted in Lott 1992–93, p. 187, n. 68). Lott also notes that nineteenth-century "black Americans sometimes referred to themselves non-pejoratively as 'Anglo-Africans.'" Linda Gordon quotes James Young, "a black man at the Contention mine in nearby Tombstone," Arizona, as saying, toward the end of the 1800s, "Si White and I were the first white men in Tombstone . . ." (quoted in Wypijewski 1999, B15).

18. A number of recently published memoirs and essays document the flexible, unstable nature of Black and White categorical membership. G.H. Williams (1995), for example, writes of learning from his father at the age of ten that he was "colored" and subsequently, as he and his younger brother moved into their new neighborhood and school in Muncie, Indiana, of "learning how to be niggers" (the title of his chapter 5).

19. The non-Black categories were: White; Indian; Pakistani; Bangladeshi; Chinese; Any other, with a space to identify which other. See Ni Bhrolchain (1990) for a discussion of the background of this question.

20. See Segal (1991) on this, as well as Davis (1991). Historically, the southern U.S. states also demarcated among quadroons, octoroons, and so on, with such delineations most marked in Louisiana (Davis 1991, pp. 36–37).

21. "Ashkenazi" Jews are those whose ancestors came from Germany (*Ashkenaz*, in Hebrew) and other countries of Eastern and Western Europe to which German Jews migrated. "S'faradi" or "Sepharadi" Jews trace their ancestry to Spain (*S'farad*) or Portugal prior to their expulsion (1492 and 1497), when they migrated to the countries of North Africa, the Middle East, and some European states (typically Greece, Bulgaria, Italy, and Holland). Israel's Jewish population is roughly split between the two groups. The first Jews in the United States were S'faradim from Amsterdam who came to Nieuw Amsterdam (later New York) in Peter Stuyvesant's time from Recife, Brazil, where their ancestors had settled. See Bahloul (1994) for a discussion of the construction of S'faradi identity among Jews, and Yanow (1999a, 1999b) on Jewish Israeli race-ethnicity.

22. Anthropologist Ruth Behar encountered this set of problems about what it means to be "Hispanic" in a personnel decision at the University of Michigan (Behar 1992). A third-generation Cuban who had immigrated to the United States as a girl, she maintains that she was denied a tenure-track faculty position as a minority scholar at the university since "there was some question as to whether I was an authentic-enough Latina . . . because my grandparents had been European Jewish immigrants to Cuba."

Residents of New Mexico descended from Jews expelled from Spain who immigrated to Mexico and then moved north present another interesting departure from a "fixed" category. In some cases they married native peoples. Many continued to practice Jewish rites, although in secret, after their conversion to Catholicism (to escape the Inquisition), and without explanation to their children, because they still feared the consequences of discovery. Many of their descendants are now exploring why they follow a family tradition of secretly lighting candles on Friday nights and other Jewish customs. Some of them are converting "back" to Judaism. (They were "discovered" in the early 1990s and have been the subject of numerous newspaper and magazine articles.) Their lived experiences and identities would seem to cut across many of the census questions about racial, Hispanic, and ethnic origin.

23. See McCulloch and Wilkins (1995) for a discussion of the extent to which federal recognition has depended on a group's matching the socially constructed image of what a "tribe" is.

24. Wilson (1992, p. 121). See his discussion of Indians and blood. He tells of a friend who described himself as a "mixed-blood full blood": the grandson of four "full-blooded" Indians, each of whom came from a different tribe. See also Montagu (1997, chap. 14) and Wilson (1992) on race and blood.

25. Although the census allows individuals to register their self-perceptions, OMB No. 15 allows American Indians to be so identified by "community recognition." EEOC policy, however, as we shall see in chapter 4, requires identification according to the administrator's point of view (although this appears not to be uniform practice). This question of "in whose eyes?" has led to problematic court deliberations for Native Americans, usually around land claims. The Mashpee are a well-known earlier case (see, e.g., Clifford 1988 or Minow 1990, pp. 351–356); but the matter was even more recently before the Senate in the case of the Lumbee of North Carolina, which was decided against them (Healey 1992; *Wall Street Journal* editorial, 3/18/92; see also McCulloch and Wilkins 1995).

Haney López (1995, p. 45) notes that blood figured in naturalization law at the end of World War II for "white persons," "persons of races indigenous to the continents of North or South America or adjacent islands," Filipinos and their descendants, Chinese and their descendants, and "persons of races indigenous to India," in addition to "persons of African nativity or descent."

26. The blood criterion was still explicitly central to citizenship policies at the end of World War II. Naturalization criteria rested on a "preponderance" of blood in some cases or a mixture of "as much as one-half blood" of some "and some additional blood" of others (Haney López 1994, p. 45).

27. As social psychologist Judith White notes, "'We tend to see more differences within our own group than within other groups,'" and "While the majority seems to bifurcate the social world, minorities are keenly aware of a multiplicity of groups" (quoted in Hodder 1998, p. 24).

28. A 1978 source named seventeen European groups: Germans, Italians, Irish, Poles, Canadians, Jews, English, Swedes, Scots and Scots-Irish, Norwegians, Slavs, French, Hungarians, Greeks, Danes, Finns, Portuguese (cited in Steinberg 1989, p. 41, Table 2: Net Immigration of Various European Nationalities, 1820–1930). The table seemingly uses "nationality" in the sense of ethnic group, as Jews, Scots-Irish, and Slavs are not citizens of any single nation-state. Missing from the list, but present in the United States today, are Spaniards, Czechs, Slovaks, Russians (the latter three possibly the Slavs of the list), Romanians, Albanians, Yugoslavians, Lithuanians, Estonians, and so forth.

29. See Steinberg (1989), for example. Gusfield (1963) gives an interesting analysis of the impact of these Others on the then-dominant culture as expressed in the battles over Prohibition and Repeal. That we have never had "Catholic-Americans" or "Moslem-Americans" suggests that Jewish-Americans saw themselves, and were seen, as more than a religious group (having ethnic origins in various nation-states). Jews lobbied to keep religion and state separate in the census as well, in an effort not to draw attention.

30. Buker (1987, p. 26) made a parallel argument about the category "Black Americans" (or "Blacks"). In replacing "Negroes," it signaled a different status for its members: rather than signaling a nation with a few Negroes, she writes, the new category name implicitly argued that Americans were both Black and White.

31. Although this, too, is not uncontested: see Collison (1993). In addition, hearings were held in 1999 by the House Judiciary Committee (subcommittee on the

Constitution) regarding the proposed Wartime Violation of Italian-American Civil Liberties Act, which calls on Congress to recognize the discriminatory restrictions directed at Italian-Americans during World War II ("Italian-Americans Air W.W. II Loss of Liberties," 1999).

32. As Kusmer (1996) points out, "no one felt the need to explain" what that description signified. At the very least, the crime was assumed not to have been committed by a native-born White American. Samhan (1993, pp. 5–6) describes the vulnerability of Americans of Middle Eastern origins.

33. We find an example of the result of this noncultural racialization of "white" in one reporter's comment that "84% of Americans are white, . . . but 24% are members of a racial or ethnic minority" (Crispell 1991). This puzzling statement might mean that 8 percent of Americans (the surplus over the 100 percent total) are both white and members of a race-ethnic group (both white and Asian? white and Nigerian? white and Arab?). An example of racializing as Omi and Winant (1994) meant it can be seen in the present shift from writing "white" and "black" to "White" and "Black." Linguistically, the use of the capital letters moves the terms from adjectives to nouns. As categories, the capitalized words become conceptually equivalent to the other capitalized race-ethnic terms.

34. I thank Mary Timney for this observation.

35. "Chamorro" refers to the original people and language of Guam and the Mariana Islands. "Guamanian" is a referent derived from the name of the nationality. I thank Rica Llorente for helping clarify this.

36. Although there have been designations of admixtures before now—for example, mulatto, octoroon, "half-breed"—these were seen within each lumpy category. That is, mulattos and others were a subcategory of "Black"; half-breeds were a type of "Indian." There has never before been a category that explicitly names mixture, that administratively acknowledges more than one origin, or that gathers all "nonpure" mixtures into a single group.

37. The extent of shame among Native Americans has greatly surprised me. At the end of the 1992 conference session at which I first presented this research, two colleagues approached me, one after the other. The first told me that his father, who had recently died, had on his deathbed identified his own mother, my colleague's grandmother, as an Indian. Asked why he had not told her before, the father admitted that he had not wanted his son to be embarrassed. My second colleague asked if I knew whether there was indeed a tribe known as "Cree" and where they might be located. There was a family rumor, she said, that her grandmother might have been Cree. She remembered when she was a little girl brushing her grandmother's hair, which hung down long and straight and blue-black, as she sat in a chair.

More recently, a student in a graduate seminar on race-ethnicity and public administration identified herself on the first night as "White." She arrived at our second session quite agitated by the idea expounded in the readings, that race and ethnicity might not be scientific terms: "Why don't we know that?" she asked. At the last session she asked whether it was illegal for someone who was less than full-blooded to self-identify as a Native American. Only after we had discussed the question of tribal identity and enrollment issues did she say that one of her grandparents was a "full-blooded" Native American, and that her mother had always told her not to identify herself as a "quarter" Indian because it was illegal and because then she would not get where she wanted solely on merit. It is possible that it is the gradual overcoming of such silencing that accounts for the recent geometric increase in numbers of students and others self-identifying as Native Americans, far more than any romantic or opportunistic attempt by Whites to lay claim to a heritage not theirs (the explanation offered by the press and by some agency officials).

38. Much as many persons immigrating to the United States from sub-Saharan African countries have to learn how to be "Black," from North African and Islamic Middle Eastern countries to be "Arab," from Cuba to be "Black" and "Hispanic" (Navarro 1997), from much of Israel to be "Jewish," so "Hispanics" are put in the position by these classificatory policies of choosing to be "Black" or "White."

39. My thanks to Hal Colebatch for the case and the examples.

40. There is a long and ancient tradition of individual identity deriving from bodily fluids, whether blood, mother's milk (in Jewish tradition), or some other. It intersects in curious ways with the other tradition of the four humors and their geographic sources.

41. See Greenhouse and Greenwood (1994) and the essays in Greenhouse (1998).

42. That is, mobile, from somewhere else, by definition; as distinct from "native Californian," a sometimes intentionally ironic oxymoron.

43. "S'faradi" Jews, for example, as noted above (note 21), are those who trace their ancestry back to Spain prior to the expulsion of 1492 or to Portugal prior to the expulsion of 1497. An American Jew whose grandparents immigrated from Russia is an "Ashkenazi," from the word for Germany, even though his grandparents' last ancestors to live in Germany may have left in the 1700s. Both of these groups have internal ethnic divisions, many of whose members have intermarried.

44. Madison Grant (cited in Kusmer 1996, p. 20) sees intermarriage among White and non-White as diluting the stock, as distinct from Israeli attitudes toward Ashkenazi-S'faradi intermarriages, which have been seen as increasing the numbers of Ashkenazim.

45. One should also note the high correlation of large-sized families with religiously observant European-origin Jews. I explore these ideas further in Yanow (1999a, 1999b). See also Dang (n.d.) for a fascinating discussion of the meaning of "ethnicity" in Vietnam, reflecting distinctions among nationality, ethnicity, and local group; the role of language as a marker; and aboriginal and immigrant histories.

46. I thank Bob Williams (personal conversations, July 1996) for this latter observation. See King (1985, 1991) and Bell (1996) for more on these matters.

47. The people known commonly, at times pejoratively, as "gypsies."

48. For just such a discussion, see W.H. Tucker (1994, chap. 3).

49. Passed on September 15, 1935, and amended on November 14, these laws defined "Jewishness" and placed citizenship, marriage, and other restrictions on full-, half-, and quarter-Jews.

50. Nobles (2000) explores these ideas in a comparative analysis of Brazilian and U.S. census histories and policies.

Appendix 3.1
Early Census Categories

The first census, taken in 1790, had six categories for race-related divisions: five of them counted free people ("free white males" older than fifteen and older than twenty-one, "free white females" younger than fifteen and in general, and all others), the sixth, "Slaves" (Segal [1991] and Steinberg [1989]). Note that among the slaves were Indians and Whites as well as Blacks. The next census refined these into four categories: age gradations of free white males, age gradations of free white females, all other free persons except "Indians not taxed" (i.e., those on reservation lands), and slaves. In 1820 the list was revised by the addition of "foreigners not naturalized" and "free colored persons." The gender of slaves was first noted in 1820. "Free colored persons," first counted that year, are also tallied by gender.

In 1830 the categories are simplified into three: free white persons; slaves and free colored persons; and "deaf and dumb," divided between whites, and slaves and colored persons. Neither slaves nor free colored persons were counted by gender. Gender tabulation of slaves and free colored persons returns in 1840. This census adds "blind and insane" to deaf and dumb, separated between white and colored persons. The 1850 census simplified the count with two categories: free inhabitants and slaves. Each had four subcategories: "age; sex; color; deaf, dumb, blind, or insane, idiotic." The latter disappears altogether as a category after this census.

The 1860 census is the first to resemble contemporary "racial" categories. There are four: white, free colored, Indians, slaves.

These and subsequent changes are outlined in the following table.

Table 3.2

Changes in Category Labels and Names, U.S. Census 1790–2000

Note: After 1790, only additions (denoted by +), deletions (denoted by ✗), and new language (denoted by ✗ > or **bold**) have been noted. Where the categories remain the same, they have not been repeated.

1790   free white males over 15
free white males over 12
free white females younger than 15
free white females
all other free persons
    except Indians not taxed
slaves

1800   free white males [with 5 age subcategories]
free white females [with 5 age subcategories]

1810   [no change]

1820   + free **colored** persons
+ **foreigners not naturalized**

1830   free white persons [by age and sex]
+ **deaf and dumb**
   • white persons
   • slaves and colored persons
~~foreigners not naturalized~~

1840   + deaf, dumb, **blind, or insane**
   • white
   • ~~slaves and~~ colored persons

1850   free persons
    color: white
             black
             mulatto
slaves
    color: white
             black
             mulatto
deaf, dumb, blind, or insane, **idiotic**
place of birth, by U.S. state or territory or foreign country

1860   ~~free persons~~ > white
                > free colored
+ Indian
slaves [with no color divisions]
~~deaf, dumb, blind, or insane, idiotic~~

(continued)

Table 3.2 *(continued)*

1870 **race**
    white
    black
    mulatto
    Chinese
    Indian
    + **foreign birth of father, mother**
    + **mixtures of Indians across tribes or with white, black, mulatto, including non-Indian adoptees into tribe**

1880 [no change]

1890 ~~race~~ > **color**
    ~~colored~~   > **Negro**
    + **quadroon**
    + **octoroon**
    + **Japanese**

1900 Negro **(colored)**
    + **percentage of white blood in Indians (0–1/8)**
    ~~mulatto~~
    ~~quadroon~~
    ~~octoroon~~

1910 Negro ~~(colored)~~
    Black
    Mulatto
    + **percentage of Indian blood that is Indian, white, and black other**

1920 **color or race**
    Negro
        ~~Black~~
        ~~Mulatto~~

1930 + **Mexican**
    + **Filipino**

1940 + **Hindu**
    + **Korean**
    + **all other**

1950 ~~Indian~~ **American Indian**
    ~~Hindu~~
    ~~Korean~~

1960 + **Hawaiian**
    + **part-Hawaiian**
    + **Korean**

(continued)

Table 3.2 *(continued)*

1970   Negro **or Black**
        **+ origin or descent: Mexican, Puerto Rican, Cuban, Central
        or South American, Other Spanish, None of the Above**

1980   **Black or Negro**
        + Eskimo
        + Aleut
        + Asian Indian
        + Vietnamese
        + Samoan
        + Guamanian

1990   no change

2000   Black, **African American**, or Negro
        American Indian **or Alaskan Native**
        Native Hawaiian
        Guamanian **or Chamorro**
        Other Asian, Other Pacific Islander
        ~~Eskimo~~
        ~~Aleut~~
        Spanish/Hispanic/**Latino**

Sources: Anderson and Fienberg 1999, pp. 177–178; Short 1996, pp. 334–341; Nobles 2000, pp. 28, 44; U.S. Bureau of the Census 1989. Some of the information provided by these sources is contradictory, possibly due to variant primary sources, possibly due to differences of interpretation. I have followed the census documents in these cases.

I note that the 1870 birthplace question instructed enumerators to give specific German states, "as Prussia, Baden, Bavaria, Wurttemburg, Hesse Darmstadt, etc." instead of entering "Germany" (Short 1996, p. 338, n. 5). This had changed by 1890: "The names of *countries*, and not of cities, are wanted. . . . If born in Canada or Newfoundland, write the word 'English' or 'French.' . . . *This is a most important requirement and must be closely observed in each case and the distinction carefully made*" (Short 1996, p. 339, n. 12; original emphasis). (Keep in mind that this is from the time when census-takers made these identifications.) By 1900 enumerators are being told not to "write Prussia or Saxony, but Germany" (Short 1996, p. 339, n. 14).

4

Identity Choices?
Agency Policies and Individual
Resistance

Congressman,
... in certain parts of the country,
like Milwaukee where I come from,
the name Schimmelpfennig
for example,
would be accepted as a good American name,
and nobody would question probably whether [he] ... was illegal;
but if somebody named Sanchez came along....
—*Andrew Biemiller, Director, AFL-CIO, 1975*
U.S. HR subcommittee hearings on immigration reform,
addressing Congressman Hamilton Fish, Jr.
(quoted in Chock 1991, p. 283)

America must be kept American.
—*President Calvin Coolidge, 1924*

Everyone knew what he meant.
—*Peter Brimelow, Senior Editor,* Forbes, *1992*
(quoted in Fuchs 1993, p. 180)

There is a central tension at play in policy and administrative practices with
respect to race-ethnic identification, between those that allow individuals to
self-identify and those that restrict or eliminate such opportunities for self-
expression. This tension is manifested in two sorts of practices. For one,
some agencies allow or require individuals to self-identify, while others require an outside observer to identify people without asking them how they
identify themselves. Since 1970 the Census Bureau has instructed the enumerator to put down whatever racial or ethnic identity the respondent names.[1]

On the other hand, the Equal Employment Opportunity Commission (EEOC), for example, removes that self-expression or sense of choice by instructing employers to identify their employees without asking them; and other agencies follow analogous practices.

Second, even when individuals are asked to self-identify on various forms (What is your race? What is your ethnic heritage?), the forms typically make available only a set of categories predetermined by someone else, as we saw in the last chapter, occasionally with the option of choosing "Other." The front-line workers—police, nurses, school administrators, mortgage bankers, employers—who present Americans with these forms and ask them to fill them in constitute, in Michael Lipsky's term, "street-level bureaucrats." In Lipsky's (1979) analysis, these administrators are often seen by the people they interact with not only as agents of the bureaucracy, but, crucially, as the agency's very policy makers. The analysis in this chapter and in chapter 5 suggests an even stronger association: when it comes to race-ethnic practices, these workers are seen less as employees of their respective agencies than as agents of the state (whether federal or local). The perception is not so much that the school or the hospital wants to know the race-ethnic identity of oneself or one's child, but that the American government (or the California or other state government) does. Moreover, as individuals are often asked to fill out the forms directly, it is often the forms themselves, produced by agencies acting on behalf of the state, as much as the workers, that are seen as standing in for the state. In a kind of transitive process of synecdoche (see Miller 1985), the forms "become" the state. The proclamation of one's own identity, then, is illusory: one selects an identity from a menu prepared by the state acting through agency employees and/or agency forms. Self-expression is mediated through a physical object (the form with its list) that constitutes and reflects back notions of identity at the same time that it constrains them.[2]

In these and other ways, policy and administrative practices concerning race-ethnicity play a role in constructing individual identity. That statement might appear problematic in its formulation: common perceptions of identity formation consider it to be the realm of individual, not institutional, action. But individual race-ethnic identity construction works and reworks conceptual and affective material drawn not only from the self, but also from surrounding cultural-societal-political, communal, and familial contexts, in an interactive process. Group identity is constructed in interaction with the state and with other groups.

The opening footage of the classic film *Twelve Angry Men* (released by United Artists in 1957) provides an example of the way in which context affects and shapes identity construction. The camera pans slowly up the stairs of the courthouse, between the pillars, through the marbled lobby, up the staircase and down the long corridor into the courtroom, over the judge's shoulder to the jury, across their faces and back, finally coming to rest on the defendant seated behind the desk—a young teen with dark, curly hair and wide, dark, fear-rounded eyes. Clearly (the camera seems to be saying), the jury is going to find him guilty—because of the race-ethnic identity suggested by his looks (southern European, or perhaps Puerto Rican) in contrast with theirs (the majority of them Anglo-Saxon or northern European). Lacking an understanding of the visual identity codes of the 1950s and 1960s, a contemporary audience misses those clues and the meaning of much of the tensions among the twelve jurors.

This chapter begins with an exploration of identity construction from a collective, interpretive point of view and then turns to two specific aspects of it. One of these is the tension between self-identification and the ascription of identity by the state through its agencies, looking at EEOC and other agency policies and practices. The second is the case of "passing," the practice of individuals attempting to mask a subdominant race-ethnic identity in the physical and cultural trappings of the dominant identity, in order to escape the burdens attached societally and administratively to the collective identity being passed out of, in a subversion of other-identification. The chapter concludes with a discussion of the categorical logic and scientific presuppositions that make these practices conceivable and possible.

Context and Identity: Interpretive and Collective Approaches

While the extensive work in psychology on individual identity formation, ranging from Erik Erikson's historical narratives to psychoanalytic approaches, is perhaps more familiar, the analysis here focuses on interpretive approaches to collective actions, expressed through policy and administrative practices. Such practices are seen as social constructionist processes that provide a context within which individuals create and shape their identities, in interaction with that context. In this, I am following Mary Douglas's (1986) injunction to see the collective reflected in the individual: we would do well, she asserted, to see the individual as society writ small, rather than only seeing society as the individual writ large. As Kenneth Hoover (1993) notes, it is a misunderstanding of developmental theory, such as Erikson's, to consider identity development as entirely an individual undertaking, without also looking to the social, cultural, and political context(s) within which such development takes place and seeing it as a dynamic, emergent, interactive process encompassing both dimensions.[3] For Hoover, an individual-focused approach is promoted by "the identity myths of individual self-sufficiency," undergirded by conservative, individualist notions of the market (Hoover 1997, p. 68). An alternative would be to see identity creation as self-inscription in relationship to others, drawing on similar presuppositions to those Stone (1988) identifies as characteristic of a "polis" approach to policy community. In this view, identity formation takes place within public discourse.

An interpretive approach to the self suggests that individual acts and societal constructions of meaning are mutually dependent for constitution and change: *social*—that is, collective—constructions are realized (materialized), reinforced (re-created or maintained), and changed by individuals engaging those constructions. It is in this way that an interpretive, collective approach to identity construction brings into focus the societal, cultural, and/or political contexts within which these processes take place. It reflects a shift in perceptions of selfhood within political theory from the marketplace conceptualization of the individual as rational, economic, individualist, decision-making "man" to a reflective, expressive person bound up in and oriented toward community and other relationships (see, e.g., Hoover 1997; Stone 1988, 1997).

Context figures to some extent in traditional psychological theories of individual identity construction around notions of individuation from the mother or parents of infants and adolescents. Cultural psychologists Markus, Mullally, and Kitayama (1996) note that Western views of human development are more inclined to see identity construction as entailing separation from and in opposition to others, while theorists from other cultural backgrounds—Japanese, Korean, African—see the individual as developing in conjunction with family and community. One could also make a case for gender as a distinguishing factor in such theorizing: Gilligan (1982) also saw connection as central to American women's modes of adult development, in contradistinction to Kohlberg's focus on separation as the hallmark. In either case, identity-construction is an interactive, relational process, not a self-contained one.

Erik Erikson (1959) noted that "identity" is a concept with several meanings, ranging from a conscious sense of self, to unconscious personal character development, to inner solidarity with a group. Erikson himself (1963) used the concept to refer to the interactions among physical development, psychological stages, and social environments. Hoover (1997) makes clear the extent to which Erikson and other developmental theorists saw these processes as interactive. In this view, individuals develop and shape their identities out of challenges to the self that emerge from "the interface between life stages and social practices" (p. 17). He notes Erikson's emphasis on cultures, with their "mix of practices, customs and institutions," as shaping identities (p. 18). Competence and integrity, two of the elements that constitute identity, develop out of "transactions between the self and society," Hoover writes (p. 20). Social recognition validates individual competence. The crafting of identity "is driven not simply by ego, or some abstracted sense of self, but by the imperative of achieving a sense of competence and integrity amid the promptings of physical changes and the interplay of powerful social forces. . . . Identity grows and is nurtured or frustrated in a complex bonding of self and society. It is not simply asserted or assigned" (pp. 20, 21). As we shall see, assertions of race-ethnic identity take place within a field defined and constrained by the state and at times lead to acts of resistance.

Naming and Collective Identity Constructions

Because they entail naming, the creation and use of categories figure centrally in collective identity processes. As Edelman (1977, p. 29) notes: "When we name and classify [something] . . . , we unconsciously establish the status and the roles of those involved with it, including their self-conception." Geertz (1983b, pp. 64–68) describes a system of name-giving in Sefrou, Morocco, that illustrates some of these matters (see also Scott 1998, pp. 64–71 on other naming systems). He tells of the Arabic *nisba* that ascribes a classification— by occupation, by religious sect, by place (tribe, region, town, family)—to an individual, by attachment to his personal name. It is as if I would be called Dvora-the-professor, Dvora-the-Jew, East-Coast-Dvora or Dvora-the-Bostonian or -the-Needhamite, or Yanowa (as my grandfather's female cousins were, linking them to their father through the feminized version of his last name, following Slavic grammatical rules). The choice of the specific identifying attribute depends on context: the smaller the spatial area within which one is named, the narrower the range of the categorizing attribute. Individuals named in this fashion are, in Geertz's phrase, "contextualized persons": "their identity is an attribute they borrow from their setting" (p. 66).[4]

Categorizing Americans as European-, African-, Hispanic, Asian-, or Native attributes to them an identity borrowed from the contemporary setting. It places individuals in a context greater than themselves—greater than that designated by personal and familial names, greater than the psychically bounded self that Freudian or Western psychology and psychoanalysis theorize as the heart and essence of human identity. In a nation of high geographic mobility, such as the United States, where individuals tend to "float as bounded psychic entities, detached from their backgrounds and singularly named" (Geertz 1983b, p. 67), such categorizing locates residents in a context that marks them by membership in a larger group, creating borders that construct similarity within and difference from other groups. In a country whose communities are increasingly less bounded by the physical markers of neighborhood, place of worship, and civic association, the five or six race-ethnic categories are positioned to act as surrogates.[5]

Although individual identity comprises a wide range of elements, race-ethnicity has become a central facet in contemporary American identity formation and discourse.[6] As Hoover also notes (1997, p. 21), the state serves as an important actor in proffering elements that individuals draw on in identity construction and in certifying those identities. Through the list of race-ethnic category names and through the various administrative opportunities to name oneself and others, the state provides both the language for and the mode of identity expression in this one dimension. But when these elements, including category names, do not fit individuals' lived experiences and reflective sense making, tensions ensue. In privileging race-ethnic identity discourse and circumscribing choices for self-expression, the state provokes reactions against both (as in the individual mentioned in chapter 3 who included a cat of Siamese heritage in the 1990 census).[7] Contemporary American race-ethnic discourse, through its policy and administrative practices, embodies and reflects a struggle for public recognition and certification of self-proclaimed identity, at times including resistance to state-imposed modes of "self-identification."

Nisba attributes require or impute knowledge about only one aspect of the individual, but collectively the several dimensions encompass a wider range of identity sources than what the five American race-ethnic categories make available. The latter are reductionistic in two senses. They enable a limited discourse on identity, perhaps supplemented by sex (e.g., Asian-American female), but not explicitly with class, personal (rather than ancestral) birthplace, or any individual attribute (such as talent, occupation, hobby). They also limit the discourse on race-ethnic identity largely to continent-of-[ancestral]-origin. This stands in for "race" and thereby presumes and projects a one-to-one identity among color, country, and culture, with continent as the presumed source of cultural heritage. Such a discourse conceptually pushes Asian-Americans, for example, to look for a heritage in "Asia," rather than in Americanized adaptations of Chinese, Pilipino, and other customs. And so it is for other "lumpy" groupings, as noted in the previous chapter.

The original OMB Directive No. 15, after naming and defining the five groups, continues: "When [data on] race and ethnicity are collected separately, the number of White and Black persons who are Hispanic must be identifiable." This is, as we have seen, what is done in the census: separate counts for racial group and for ethnic origins, and for Hispanic/Spanish origins. But most other agency questionnaires implementing federal policy simply duplicate the OMB list. They do not tabulate race and ethnicity separately, and "Hispanic" takes on the weight of an equal but separate category, forcing a choice among heritages for those who are of mixed parentage. By the logic of such questionnaires, one may be either White or Black or Hispanic, but not both White and Hispanic or Black and Hispanic. By focusing explicitly only on White and Black combinations with Hispanic, these rules conceptually disallow the possibility of being Asian-Hispanic—such as Japanese Peruvians or Brazilians, should they or their children immigrate to the United States—or Native American–Hispanic—as many Mexican-Americans, for example, are. This is another way in which race-ethnic identity discourse is constrained. Through its documents, its implementation practices, and federal governmental definitions, an agent of the state creates a race-ethnic identity for those filling out the forms and imposes it on them.

It is not only around presumed distinctions between "ethnicity"—Hispanic—and "race"—the other four categories—that identity is being created. Another form of choice is being imposed here. Although the census uses questions that (at least in theory) allow respondents to distinguish among race, ethnicity, and language group and, since Census 2000, to mark multiple race-ethnic heritage boxes, most agency forms (used, e.g., for employment- or admissions-related affirmative action purposes) force a choice of one category only. Mixed-race heritage has no place here (unless an encompassing "Other" category is provided).

The commonsense, definition-in-use of "race" implies that it is inherited, determined by ancestors, reflected in physiognomy, skin color, and blood, and that the individual has no choice in the matter. By contrast, Waters (1990) shows that choices are made by some. She analyzed Catholics whose parents "intermarried," mixing European ancestries, who chose one of multiple possible ethnicities by which to identify themselves and/or their children.[8] Similar choices have been made by people who have intermarried across the five U.S. categories. Others "choose" to encompass both or all of their heritages, as seen in the demand for a mixed-race option in Census 2000.[9]

"Choice" is exercised in another sense when race-ethnic identification is made not by the individual but by someone else. This takes place, in American policy and administrative practices, in two ways: in the category names provided by the state through agency forms drawing on OMB No. 15, and through acts of identifying others in filling out those forms.

Although the census was originally used by the state to assess labor, military, and taxpayer strength, as noted in chapter 3, it has in recent years acquired other uses and layers of meaning. Its race-ethnic categories have taken on a role as part of the context for the constitution and expression of individual race-ethnic identity, supplying conceptual and affective material within and against which individuals make sense of themselves in race-ethnic ways. In recent and current census history, as individual self-perception has increasingly stepped outside of OMB and Census Bureau categories and questions, the sense-making effort has become more public a struggle. Highly visible at the time of the 1990 census, it remained salient throughout the decade: *Time* (Special issue, Fall 1993), *The New Republic* (October 1994), *Newsweek* (February 13, 1995), and other journals of general readership as well as newspaper reporting (e.g., the *New York Times,* July 6, 1966, pp. 1, 7) addressed category-related questions about "racial" definitions. Debates over adding a "mixed race" question to Census 2000 attracted headlines and stories through the rest of the 1990s, and the decision to allow multiple category checks on the race question was seen as addressing identity issues.

Within this seeming possibility for self-identification, however, the range of options is created and circumscribed by the state through its agencies. The struggle is, in large part, a battle to reconcile a race-ethnic identity created and imposed from without, by some administrative agencies of the state, with a self-named and internally developed sense of identity. That the population categories and their definitions mandated by OMB Directive No. 15 and enacted through the census explicitly create and shape (as well as reflect) common understanding of what "race" and "ethnicity" mean was discussed in the previous chapter. There are other, less explicit ways in which the directive defines U.S. race-ethnic identity. Naming categories and defining category membership explicitly create group boundaries and conceptualize individual identities; administrative practices accomplish this more indirectly.

Comparing Agency Policies: Self- Versus Other-Identification

> ... [T]he judge [ruled] that the plaintiff was indeed "white"
> because he had been well received in white society
> and had "commonly exercised the privileges of a white man."
> —*Brent Staples (1998, p. A14)*

Inscribing identities through category logic is not the only way in which state policies and practices are creating race-ethnic identities and enforcing categorical blood purity. When the Census Bureau or the university personnel office provides the option of answering "Other," the external imposition of identity is or can be mitigated. When there is no provision for self-identification, however—as when Roma or Jews, unlike their fellow citizens, are forced to identify themselves as such in identity cards under Soviet, post-Soviet, or Nazi regimes—the state's interest in individual identity becomes transparent. In the census and in employment and school enrollment questionnaires, the state, in an impersonal fashion, structures opportunities for self-identification, but the categories made available are predefined and preselected, and the state's role is much less transparent. Ironically and paradoxically, the state is seemingly rendered less faceless through the person of the employer acting under EEOC policy, who is required to identify employees him- or herself, using the same state-established categories. But the employer must do so without input from the individual.

The original OMB No. 15 stipulates: "The category which most closely reflects the individual's *recognition in his community* should be used for purposes of reporting on persons who are of mixed racial and/or ethnic origins" (emphasis added). Persons were to be defined by others, not by themselves; and only one of their ancestral heritages was to be selected.

This certainly has been the experience of many African-Americans, who have usually been considered Black if one parent is Black, following the "one-drop rule" (see Davis 1991).[10] Rules for assigning identity in such cases are spelled out in early instructions to census takers. By 1930, enumerators were being instructed to report mixed Negro-White as Negro; Negro-Indian as Negro, unless the "Indian blood predominated" *and* the person was perceived by the community as Indian; Indian-White as Indian, unless the proportion of Indian blood was "very small" and the person was perceived in the community as White. All those born in Mexico or to Mexican-born parents were to be reported as Mexican, unless they were clearly something else (White, Negro, Indian, Chinese, or Japanese). Any White–not White mixture was to be reported as the not-White identity; and except for Negro-Indian, all mixtures of not White–not White were to be reported according to the father's race (Short 1996, pp. 339–340, n. 17). In 1940 Mexicans were to be reported as White unless they were clearly mixed with a non-White race (n. 18). In 1960 Southern European and Near Eastern nationalities were to be reported as White (n. 19).[11]

By stipulating such practices—identification by a single heritage—in the case of people of mixed ancestry, the original OMB policy appeared to deny two possible social realities: the existence of individuals who (choose to) belong to more than one community, and the existence of a community that defines itself and its members as a "mixed race" community. In neither case would community recognition of such individuals produce a race-ethnic identity that fit into the five bounded categories. What is even more curious is that such practices take the determination of identity away from the individual and vest it in the hands of others. The EEOC takes the matter of self- or other-determination of identity further.

The Unemployment Relief Act of 1933, the first federal legislation to introduce principles of equal employment opportunity, listed "race, creed or color" as protected categories. The 1941 Fair Employment Practice Committee, established by President Franklin D. Roosevelt through Executive Order 8802, added national origin to the list. Title VII of the Civil Rights Act of 1964 (P.L. 88–352, Sections 704 and 705) dropped creed and added religion: it prohibits discrimination in employment practices on the basis of "race, color, religion, or national origin."

Other acts added other protections. The Equal Pay Act of 1963 prohibited wage discrimination on the basis of sex. The Age Discrimination in Employment Act of 1967 extended Title VII protections to persons over forty; the Pregnancy Discrimination Act extended Title VII protections to cover pregnancy, childbirth, and related medical conditions; Section 501 of the Rehabilitation Act of 1973, reinforced by the Americans with Disabilities Act of 1990, extended them to the handicapped. While these are important elements of U.S. antidiscrimination policies, I will confine this examination to protections of race-ethnic-related elements: race, color, religion, national origin, language, and so forth.

In 1961 President John F. Kennedy signed Executive Order 10925, creating the Committee on Equal Employment Opportunity and charging it with the responsibility of ensuring equality in employment in the federal government itself and in federal contracts with other agencies. In 1965 President Lyndon Baines Johnson signed Executive Order 11246, requiring government agencies and contractors to establish affirmative action plans for the inclusion of "minorities" in the workplace (Friedman 1991).[12] The 1964 Civil Rights Act created the EEOC and charged it with the implementation of Title VII and other guidelines. The U.S. Civil Service Commission administered EEO programs from 1965 through 1978, when they were transferred to the EEOC under the Civil Service Reform Act of that year. It is interesting to note that the Civil Rights Act did not define the meaning of race—it was apparently assumed to be commonsense knowledge—nor does it mention ethnicity. The Civil Service Commission defined "minority-group member" primarily to mean (in the terms most common at that time) blacks, Hispanics (Spanish-surnamed persons), American Indians, and Orientals, and sometimes also Eskimos and Aleuts (Rosenbloom 1980, p. 171).

EEOC Standard Form 100 (Rev. 3–97) provides additional instructions for the employer who must file Information Report EEO-1 documenting workplace racial composition. In the Appendix, prior to listing the definitions presented in OMB No. 15 (the 1980 version; the form had not yet been revised to comply with the 1997 definitions), it tells the employer: "You may acquire the race/ethnic information necessary for this report either *by visual surveys* of the work force, or from post-employment records as to the identity of employees. *Eliciting information* on the race/ethnic identity of an employee *by direct inquiry is not encouraged*" (emphases added).

And it carries the following proviso: "Race/ethnic designations as used by the EEOC do not denote scientific definitions of anthropological origins. For the purposes of this report, an employee may be included in the group to which he or she *appears to belong, identifies with*, or *is regarded in the community* as belonging. However, no person should be counted in more than *one* race/ethnic group" (emphases added). As with initial OMB policy, multiple memberships (as in mixed-race heritage) are precluded here, too. But more than that, the first and third criteria—"appears to belong" and "is regarded . . ."—require identification by others, either the employer (appears: to whom?) or community members (is regarded: by whom?). The second criterion—"identifies with"—would suggest asking the individual in question (e.g., With what race-ethnic group do you identify?). One university questionnaire asks students, "With which race/ethnic group are you most comfortable?" But the prior statement precludes this: "eliciting information . . . by direct inquiry is not encouraged." Again, persons are not to determine their own official, public race-ethnic identity, according to these policy statements.[13]

Until the 2000 revisions, OMB and EEOC policies stood in marked contrast to the Census Bureau's instructions to its enumerators since 1970 to write down whatever respondents tell them.[14] According to bureau publications, the concept of race the Bureau of the Census uses reflects self-identification by respondents; that is, the individual's perception of his/her racial identity (U.S. Bureau of the Census 1989). As the head of the bureau said, "The policy is people should be allowed to self-identify" (Chang 1999).[15]

The EEOC and OMB were not the only agencies to invoke such practices. The following text appeared on a mortgage approval form (used in 1994) under the heading, "The Housing Financial Discrimination Act of 1977: Fair Lending Notice" (emphases are added):

> . . . the following information is requested by the State of California and the Federal Government to monitor this financial institution's compliance with the Housing Financial Discrimination Act, Equal Credit Opportunity Law, and Fair Housing Law. The law provides that a financial institution may neither discriminate on the basis of this information nor on whether or not it is furnished. *Furnishing this information is optional.* If you do not wish to furnish this information, please initial below.

But choosing not to provide race-ethnic information does not mean it will not be provided. The form continues:

This association is required to note race . . ., *on the basis of sight and/or surname* if the applicant(s) choose not to do so.

I choose not to supply this information.
                                                                    _____
                                                                    (initials)

A box following this text asks for "race/national origin" of both applicant and coapplicant, listing the five standard categories and "Other-Specify."

Workplace practices may vary from EEOC policy. But what is of interest is the way in which the concept of assigning race-ethnic identity is institutionalized, possible variations in its implementation notwithstanding. To assume that race-ethnic identity can be made externally "by visual surveys" or "by sight" is predicated upon an understanding of "race" as the fixed, stable essence of a collective that each member instantiates and makes manifest. Contra Goldberg (1992, p. 564) and American notions of choice and self-determination, in these practices, "You are [*not*] what you take yourself to be."

The stipulation that visual criteria be used to define race-ethnic membership privileges physiognomy (skin color, hair texture, eye, nose, and skull shape) as the distinguishing feature of such membership. While surname may be intended to help in uncertain cases as a cultural-linguistic hallmark of heritage, given inter-race-ethnic marriage and name choice practices, it hardly seems promising as a tool for statistical accuracy. Visual race-ethnic identification of one person by another draws both on the common understanding of the meaning of "race" and on an understanding of the race-ethnic categories as groupings with distinct, uncrossable boundaries. Some cultural markings are or may be made more visible than "racial" ones, such as religious observances and dress, but these are typically not made public routinely in encounters with federal, state, or local agencies (with the exception of some forms of dress or diet[16]); and as their wearers have various national origins and racial affiliations, they are not incontrovertible indicators of race either. The policy problematizes the presumed distinction between "race" and "ethnicity," not least because it treats Hispanic identity as a race. It also reflects a tension between self-identification according to heritage and culture and other-identification according to physical characteristics, name, accent.

Haney López (1995, p. 5) notes that the courts based their determinations of racial membership on two rationales: common knowledge (what appears here as community perception or observer identification) and scientific evidence. As an example of the former, he notes an 1878 decision, *In re Ah Yup,* in which a California federal district court denied citizenship to a Chinese applicant because of the popular understanding that "[t]he words 'white person' . . . in this country, at least, have undoubtedly acquired a well settled meaning in common popular speech . . . ," as well as in its literature and "common parlance." The alleged scientific character of race-ethnic categorizing and counting is apparent in instructions to census enumerators. In 1880 they were told: "Be particularly careful in reporting the class *Mulatto* [orig. emphasis]. The word is here generic, and includes quadroons, octoroons, and all persons having any perceptible trace of African blood. *Important scientific results depend upon the correct determination of this class . . .*" (Short 1996, p. 338, n. 7). In 1890 the "scientific" determination changed: "Be particularly careful to distinguish between blacks, mulattoes, quadroons and octoroons. The word 'black' should be used to describe those persons who have three-fourths or more black blood; 'mulatto,' those persons who have from three-eighths to five-eighths black blood; 'quadroon,' those persons who have one-fourth black blood; and 'octoroon,' those persons who have one-eighth or any trace of black blood" (Short 1996, p. 338, n. 10). The extensive "scientific" detailing of categories and their characteristics extended beyond African-Americans. In the 1880 census, for example, enumerators were instructed: "Indians not in tribal relations, whether full-bloods or half-breeds, who are found mingled with the white population, residing in white families, engaged as servants or laborers, or living in huts or wigwams on the outskirts of towns or settlements are to be regarded as a part of the ordinary population of the country . . ."—that is, are to be counted, rather than exempted in the manner of Indians living on reservations (Short 1996, p. 338, n. 8).

Today, scientific evidence is by and large no longer advanced in justification of race-ethnic concepts and divisions, and these two rationales have merged into one, embedding the "scientific" character of race-ethnic judgments implicitly into "commonsense" categorical practices. That is, it is the institutionalized practice of external, visual, race-ethnic identification by administrative agencies that now embodies and sustains a common "knowledge" of the "scientific" character of such an act.

By presenting the individual, whether in the workplace, the housing market, or some other context, with a preselected range of options, state policies and practices impose a definition from outside. By forcing the individual to fit within a single category, the possibility of self-definition is further narrowed. Nevertheless, in both instances, an illusion of self-determination and choice may be preserved. Requiring observers to identify individuals without asking them, however, removes even that illusion.

Community recognition and other-identification arise in another context as well—the OMB definition of "American Indian or Alaska Native." No other set of individuals is required to maintain "(cultural identification through) tribal affiliation or community (recognition) attachment" (Directive 15, 1980 and 2000 versions). While this language is explainable in terms of the legal requirements established by the Bureau of Indian Affairs for federal recognition of Indian identity, it is senseless in light of the operative OMB assumptions that race and ethnicity are different—the directive's stipulation casts Indian or Alaska Native race in ethnic (cultural) terms—and that race is essential, inherited, and fixed: without cultural identification, "Native"-ness disappears, but White, Black, API, and Hispanic are not similarly escapable.

In the 2000 revisions, OMB Directive 15 not only made provisions for marking more than one "racial designation" (not ethnic: "There are two categories for data on ethnicity: 'Hispanic or Latino,' and 'not Hispanic or Latino'"). It also revised its methods of assigning race-ethnic identity: "self-reporting or self-identification using two separate questions is the preferred method for collecting data on race and ethnicity." Note, however, that the preference has to do with the form of the questions, not of reporting. The directive continues: "In situations where self-reporting is not practicable or feasible, the combined format [using one question for both race and ethnicity] may be used." The directive seems to be suggesting that when an agency administrator needs to make a race-ethnic assessment without asking the individual, it may be too difficult to assess Hispanic/Latino identity separate from African, American Indian, Asian, Caucasian, and Pacific Islander identity.

Passing as Resistance: Self- *and* Other-Identification

> My grandmother was as nearly white as a Negro can get
> without being white, which means that she was white.
> —*Richard Wright,* Black Boy
> *(quoted in Haney López 1994, p. 47)*

Another form of identity choice entirely subverts these practices of other-identification by taking them to an extreme: decisions to "pass." In this it is much broader than the range of choices considered by Waters (1990). In American usage, this concept derives from the phrase "to pass for," meaning "to be accepted as something one is not" (*American Heritage Dictionary* 1975, p. 957). Passing is an act of disguise: masking those features that mark one as a member of a subdominant group in order to be identified *by others* as a member of the dominant group. It is, in this sense, the ultimate in observer-identification. In the American context, the act has usually been given meaning in the context of race-ethnicity, and there, most commonly in reference to Blacks passing as White (although Daniel [1992, p. 92] notes that Blacks have also attempted to pass as Asians, Native Americans, or Hispanics, and Rogers [1997, p. 42] writes about middle-class African-Americans using "linguistic 'code switching' from Black English Vernacular to Standard English to distinguish themselves from poor or 'underclass' African-Americans"). Jews have also passed into "Whiteness," lower-class persons—across the "color" spectrum—have passed into higher classes, and gays and lesbians have made (and many still continue to make) efforts to pass as "straight." Here, I will focus on race-ethnic passing.

Intentions to pass range along a continuum, from an intention to disappear "forever" from one's birth community to an intention "to disappear" one's birth identity publicly while maintaining the masked identity in private, living a bicultural lifestyle in which the subdominant culture is maintained in a submerged, "underground" existence. Between these two poles are people who have passed but may make occasional forays back to family homesteads to maintain those ties. This, too, entails a dual identity, but the duality is not necessarily enacted daily. Daniel (1992, p. 93) also mentions another mode of "discontinuous" passing—the "brief trip across the color line," whether for reasons of amusement, revenge, or practicality. All of these involve conscious pretense, although those who pass "absolutely" may eventually lose that sense of constant hiding *de no ser notados*—so as not to be discovered and unmasked.[17] Passing, in other words, is a lived reality for only two of the three entities party to it: the person passing, and the family or community members left behind who are aware of the original race-ethnic identity. For the third party, the observer, the assumed and presented identity is taken as authentic, until revealed to be otherwise.

Passing would appear to be a matter of individual choice alone, but the terms on which it succeeds are determined societally—in a social constructionist process of fabricating race-ethnic categories and establishing the categorical ideal (or norm) according to which membership and deviance are judged. Fitting to this socially constructed ideal sometimes requires changes in physical appearance—"nose jobs," eyelid surgery, hair straightening (ironing) or bleaching, changing eye color (e.g., by wearing blue contact lenses), bleaching skin, carriage—and sometimes in mannerisms, clothes, food preferences, religion, and other customs. Sometimes it entails changing personal and/or family names and speech patterns (vocabulary, enunciation) or accent. At times it rests on physical resemblances to the dominant group that are already present, such as light skin shade and other physical features.[18] Marriage to a member of the dominant group is often a concomitant act, the features and manners of the spouse serving to cement the perception of the presented self or "face."

Passing, then, both relies on the facticity of the race-ethnic category structure and highlights the un-"reality" of it, at one and the same time. The ability to be perceived and accepted as a member of the unmarked group, based on "neutral" physical features and "unaccented" English, is the conceptual test case for working definitions of race-ethnicity and a variation on the concept of category mistakes. Matching the salient un-marked characteristics against which "otherness" is defined is what makes passing possible. The notion of "passing" depends on the existence of cat-egorical prototypes; hence, the requirements for category membership and for passing are similar. They entail both color and culture. Country of ori-gin does not figure here—one need not "go native" in England for a period of time in order to pass as a "European-American"—except as a proxy for color and culture. Both are externally determined: categorical membership is defined by the state, and the terms for affiliation are set by the dominant group (at times with state support, as in court cases; see Haney López 1995), in keeping with the prototype.

Passing depends, in other words, on possessing certain visible, observ-able traits that are perceived to be the central and sole elements of race-ethnic membership. It renders personal identity as an expression of communal identity in the form of group membership, as the passer takes on the appear-ance and acts of that group in accordance with the ideal or norm or proto-type, leaving behind the communal identity of the group being left. As all European-Americans do not share the same set of physical or other charac-teristics (any more than all members of any of the five American race-ethnic categories do), passers engage in stereotyping (or racial profiling in reverse) in adopting particular elements of dominant group identity as their own, while hiding (temporarily or permanently) aspects of their abandoned race-ethnic group membership. This is made conceptually, as well as actually, possible by the scientific character and the objectivity imputed to race-ethnic catego-ries through the logic embedded in category making, including the ascrip-tion of some demarcating "essence" to membership in each one and the sense of a categorical ideal.

Yet passing also requires intimate knowledge of the other group. Domi-nant passing into subdominant group membership is, therefore, much rarer (except, perhaps, as a sociological or literary experiment: Rosenhan [1973], in an extended experiment with seven colleagues, passed as mentally ill, with ensuing problems of return, thereby subverting then-entrenched diag-nostic categories; John Howard Griffin passed as Black to write about it in *Black Like Me*).

Because passing rests on visual identification, agencies and their employees acting for the state play a role in maintaining and enforcing the terms for
its success. Whether done by mortgage officers implementing federal policies through HUD forms or police officers choosing to stop a driver under
conditions of "racial profiling," "eyeballing" is the application to each case
of the unspoken, tacitly known "rules" for passing. This is what makes it
conceptually possible for the mortgage form to tell the prospective borrower,
"This association is required to note race . . . , *on the basis of sight and/or
surname* if the applicant(s) choose not to do so."

Passing is not, then, just the "ability of individuals to change race" (Haney
López 1994, p. 47). It rests on interactions between individual acts and the
identity-forming material provided by society. It is, in other words, as interactive as other identity-construction processes, and it entails a role for the
state, because the state, through its policies and administrative agencies' practices, provides socially known and accepted material for the construction of
race-ethnic identities.

Several passing stories have been published in recent years, of Jewish or
of Black children passed by their parents (G.H. Williams 1995) or whose
parents themselves or other adults in their lives had passed (Gates 1996;
Gordon 1996; and McBride 1996). The discovery usually comes as a shock.
Those writing about race-ethnic passing (e.g., Bradshaw 1992; Daniel 1992;
Haney López 1994, pp. 47–50) often note the psychological and emotional
burdens that accompany it, including a sense of betrayal, having to renounce
family and community ties, and a deep-rooted feeling of not belonging, aside
from feelings of dishonesty, deception, and fraud.[19] The author Philip Roth
quotes a friend's mother bemoaning all the relatives, from a family of "very
pale" Blacks, who had been "lost to all their people" (McGrath 2000). Because it is often motivated by economic factors, those who pass may be
perceived as opportunists. For them, failure can entail a double rejection: by
the dominant group and by the family that has been disowned. Although
Bradshaw (1992, p. 79) notes that it is "internalized negatively," this would
not necessarily be the case for those passing to save their lives (such as Jews
passing for Aryans under the Third Reich), although some of these may experience "survivor guilt" later on.

These autobiographical and family narratives suggest that the experiential meaning of passing varies from one race-ethnic context to another. Anecdotal evidence—stories told by my colleagues and students—suggests that
large numbers of Native Americans have chosen to pass (as urban Whites),
especially those who marry out and who leave the reservation, to escape the
stigma of being "Indian." People of mixed-race heritage have long chosen to
pass to escape the stigmas of "impurity" (of race or blood) and "miscegena-

tion," to "escape from marginality" (Bradshaw 1992, p. 79). American Jews, when they have passed, have not done so in religious terms alone: that would not require the physical changes (facial plastic surgery, hair straightening) that they have undergone. Theirs has also been a race-ethnic passing, requiring physical-"racial" along with religious and other cultural-"ethnic" changes (food, clothing, accent, gestures, mannerisms). Their passings and generational silences, historically, were motivated by survival challenges, from the fifteenth-century Spanish Inquisition to twentieth-century Nazi Germany (where the discovery of a single Jewish grandparent was sufficient to mark one for deportation and likely death).

These stories reveal that passing is not a process undertaken only by multiracial people (Bradshaw 1992, p. 80): McBride's (1996) mother, a Jew, passed as a light-skinned Black in her African-American neighborhood (illustrating the extent to which dominance and subdominance are contextually established relationships). Because passing takes place within a realm of masking and secrecy, it is difficult to imagine a systematic study of its processes and effects, and the few social scientific treatments of it tend to be speculative and not generalizable to groups other than those that are their subjects. Nevertheless, it is clear from these participants' accounts that passing raises some of the central issues about identity choice that are of concern in policy and administrative practices.

The choice imposed on bi- or multiracial people by the policy and/or administrative requirement, excluding Census 2000, of checking off only one box in a list of race-ethnic categories is one of the practices that underscores the stigma attached to race-ethnic mixing. But the state-directed choice to identify with one parent's heritage is not necessarily identical to the passing practices discussed here. Two anecdotes illustrate the difference. Margo Jefferson (1999) wrote:

> At a recent seminar I heard the singer Abbey Lincoln say that she was of African, Cherokee, Irish and English descent and then add . . . that the Africans were the only ones who claimed her. . . . [M]y great-uncle Lucius . . . could say that he was of African, Cherokee, Scottish-Irish and English descent, and . . . the Scottish-Irish and English were the only ancestors he claimed when he grew up and chose to pass for white.

Race-ethnic identity "choice," in other words, is sometimes volitional and sometimes imposed, sometimes self-directed and sometimes not. Even involuntary passing—on the telephone or the Internet, both of which can mask physical signs—has a second dimension, as others' "eyeballing" projects a dominant identity onto a person of a subdominant group without his or her necessarily intending to pass.

Defining Identity: "Scientific" and Literal Presumptions

You can't put half a check mark in "black"
and half a check mark in "white."
You have to check "Other"—
that means you're black and white.

—*Basketball star Michael Jordan*
(quoted in Swanigan 1993)

I have a child who is black to the school,
white to the Census Bureau
and multiracial at home.

—*Atlantan Susan Graham*
(quoted in "Population of Interracial Couples ..." 1993)

Ethnically, I am about as homogenous as it is possible to be:
...I was born in the same town as every one of my Sante
forebears at least as far back as the mid-16th century....
Having been transplanted from my native soil, though, and
having had to construct an identity in response to a double
set of demands, one from my background and one from my
environment, I have become permanently "other."

—*Luc Sante (1996)*

What conception of race-ethnicity allows the OMB, the EEOC, and other agencies to mandate race-ethnic identification of individuals by others, rather than by the individuals themselves? What makes it a "thinkable" policy—especially in a world that still remembers the Nazi regime in which population control and decimation depended on race-ethnic labeling and marking by the central government?[20]

One answer may lie in the way in which "race," "ethnicity," and their categories have come to be understood and used. Conceptually, these concepts and categories are treated as scientific entities that reflect a naturally occurring, objectively determined reality. Rather than "race" and "ethnicity" being seen as socially constructed terms reflecting particular times and places and the race-ethnic categories being seen as flexible and evolving continua, they have been accepted and used as if they were real and fixed. The EEOC's disclaimer that the definitions do not represent anthropological science does not engage this aspect of what establishes their scientific character. The disclaimer stipulates that the definitions do not correspond to anthropological definitions. It does not and cannot address the scientific character that their usage imputes to them, implicitly and tacitly, as they name a taxonomy and count and slot individuals accordingly: the concepts and categories are being used in and through these acts as if they constituted scientific practices themselves grounded in an externally observable reality. It is this ontological status—their reification as presumptively objective and scientific entities—that enables agencies to stipulate that race-ethnic identification be made by an external observer, the supervisor or street-level bureaucrat responsible for collecting and/or tabulating data.

Treating race-ethnic categories as scientific entities allows the EEOC to mandate "objective" supervisory identification of the individual employee, in keeping with the tenets of positivist science. Stipulating that an outsider *can* identify the individual builds on the presumably fixed, objectively factual nature of identity and group membership. Self-identification, on the other hand, is more in keeping with a phenomenological position that emphasizes the actor's lived experience. Moreover, the notion of multiple and overlapping sources of individual identity is postmodernism's hallmark. Complaints about census categories may be the first intrusion of postmodern claims into the public policy arena. Perhaps its allowance of self-identification is one reason why people have felt freer to criticize the census categories than the EEOC categories, where self-identification is, at least in policy, forbidden. At the same time, census categories are also external, state-administrative creations of race-ethnic identities. Perhaps that is why the census can allow self-identification: it is self-proclamation using pre-established terms.

Other-identification brings into play primarily only one of the three meanings of race-ethnicity: color, or phenotype. But it does so by creating a centrally weighted, broad, ideal type (or stereotype) for each of the five categories, each with its associated trait list. The one-drop rule still prevails in these administrative practices. There is little or no provision for mixture. Country and culture materialize only by association with color. To the extent that other-identification implicates identity, it is encased in its phenotype, without nuances, shadings, or varieties.

The proclamation of race-ethnic identity is contrary to what it means to be "American," in the liberal tradition of distinguishing between the public and private realms. Liberalism's construction of individual identity, at least in American forms of liberalism, rests on the independent, autonomous property owner. Sex (male) is assumed; religion (Protestant) is assumed; able-bodied-ness is assumed (to work the land, thereby to pay taxes, and to give military service); race-ethnicity (Northern European) is assumed—as is, indeed, the unmarked state of every attribute that names a protected class under civil rights legislations. None of these attributes requires marking, in classical liberalism. Paradoxically, these elements of private, individual identity are the requisite criteria for participation in the public realm: "a good citizen is one who actively participates in community affairs," in the view of Americans responding to a survey (Fuchs 1990, p. 5, summarizing Almond and Verba's 1965 comparative research on "civic culture"). Any variation from these elements—that is, the marked identity cases, such as race-ethnicity—is understood to belong in the private sphere, rendering it publicly undiscussable.[21] In an analogous fashion to the separation between church and state, American liberalism relegates race-ethnicity to the same private realm in which religious beliefs are to be held: one participates in society as an American, as an individual, not as a member of a group.

This is one way of understanding why John F. Kennedy, as a presidential candidate, was asked about his religious practices as a Catholic (in terms of his allegiance to the pope), as well as of understanding the character of his answer. As Fuchs notes (1990, p. 5), one of the founding principles of republicanism is that Americans who "comport themselves as good citizens of the civic culture are free to differ from each other in religion and in other aspects of their *private* lives" (emphasis added)—including, it seems to me, aspects of their race-ethnic identities.

This would explain, at least in part, why public discourse about race and ethnicity has been societally *verboten* (Yanow 1992a, 1996) until recently, and why such conversations are often still so difficult and partial. It would also explain prior generations' experiences of immigration and assimilation, which serve as a backdrop to current race-ethnic discourse. Eastern and Southern European immigrants of the late 1800s and early to mid-1900s kept their "ethnicity" a private matter, speaking English in public without any thought of demanding bilingual education in the schools; conforming to "American" foods, dress, religious habits, and observances;[22] and, in general, looking for and adopting other ways of "passing." Even being "Negro" was publicly undiscussable (that is, outside of the community) until the advent of the Black Power movement, and "being White" is only now being publicly spoken about. This pattern of keeping race-ethnic identity (and other elements of personal identity based on membership in a marked category) a "private" affair makes public discourse on identity issues very difficult, tantamount to breaking a taboo.[23] The roots of these practices in the liberal philosophical tradition explain, in part, the strength of that taboo, as well as the difficulty of overcoming it.

"America Must Be Kept American"

The years leading up to the 1960s and that decade were pivotal in many ways. Up until then, group names were largely assigned by the state. But the "Black" Power movement took back for "Negroes" a self-designated group name, which quickly became the name used for that group by others, institutionalized in the 1960 census. The last several censuses have been very sensitive, and at times responsive, to group requests for self-designation.

But also in the aftermath of the social legislation of the 1960s and 1970s, the census's categories and demographic data became freighted with a redistributive mission. Another aspect of the tension between self- and other-identification arises when supposedly scientific, and hence presumptively neutral, natural, demographically descriptive categories are used for political ends, to redistribute the nation's wealth and other resources (such as jobs, contracts, education, etc.). Census data have increasingly been put to such uses, compounding the problem of fixed categories that are not allowed to evolve with changing understandings of population characteristics. The Asian-American community, for example, protested (successfully) the Census Bureau's attempts to revise API classifications in 1990, arguing that all manner of social services dependent on federal funding required categories identical to those used in 1980, which formed the bases for redistributive formulas (Yanow 1992b). This raises the question of "the extent to which *individuals* have social reality and legitimacy beyond their *legal status* as 'representatives' [or members] of racial . . . groups" (Greenhouse and Greenwood 1994, p. 18; emphasis in original). In many ways, the policy and administrative standing of American race-ethnic categories has overtaken the ontological status of individuals who do not fit them. Ironically, public agencies' needs for "sameness" (through the creation of categories) were invoked by some of the very people whom the categories do not fit.

In other words, it is not just individuals qua individuals whose identities are being constructed by these policies and practices, but groups as well. Self-identification and other-identification interact: individual freedom to choose a category (or more than one) joins the group's lack of freedom, given state-defined categories. Race-ethnicity as a social reality helps us as individuals define our own identities—how we think about ourselves—at the same time that it shapes how we act toward each other. And the struggle over self- versus other-definition is a struggle of groups, as well as of individuals, resisting having their identities created for them.[24] This is a most salient issue for Native Americans, as individuals and as tribes, as seen in recent developments in university affirmative action admissions, in gambling laws and their proceeds, and in land claims: the success of Native Americans' legal claims often depends on Whites' constructions of tribal identity (McCulloch and Wilkins 1995).

The cost for the individual is that her story, her life, her Self become "unnarratable." Not finding one's personal identity in the categories makes one invisible in a particular way: left without a name or label, one is unable to tell one's own story because the vocabulary for that story is nonexistent. The individual is forced to speak through the vocabulary of other-determined categories, or into a posture of silence. The irony is that such a posture makes other-identification all the more possible. Alternatively, identity becomes determined in the negative, by what one is not. In this sense, individuals and groups define themselves in opposition to "Others."

Policies that mandate other-identification construct individual race-ethnic identities out of, in response to, or even against a repertoire of ideas present within the societal environment. The struggle over other-identification is one of self-definition within these ideas, of finding one's place in the definitions and thereby within the state: it is a struggle over what it means to be a "good" "American," as well as for a sense of individual and group agency in the face of state practices that are paternalistic and encourage dependence. Public silence about some aspects of American individual, group, and national identity is maintained, while those identities and discourse about them are shaped in other ways and directions. We are still struggling to keep America "American." The contest is over what "everyone" understands that to mean.

The discussion of the revisions to OMB Directive No. 15 published in the *Federal Register* notes that OMB's decisions "underscore that self-identification is the preferred means of obtaining information about an individual's race and ethnicity, except in instances where observer identification is more practical (e.g., completing a death certificate)" (U.S. Office of Management and Budget, 1997). Yet even in such "practical" situations, the state, through its agencies and their administrative practices, establishes decision-making rules that constrain such choice.

Notes

1. Within statistical "reason": until 2000, enumerators had to choose one box to check if the respondent gave more than one answer. See Short (1996, pp. 340–341, n. 23).

2. Anthropologist Jean-Loup Amselle (1995) has described this process as a "hall of mirrors." In his example, a collective typically appoints one member to represent the group to the media. This individual is identified in a news report as the "leader" of the community, and in the process of speaking on the members' behalf, he or she thereby constitutes both the "community" and his or her "leadership" of it. The broadcast reflects back to the group the media's rendering of the image that the group created. In this fashion, the broadcast constructs the group even as the group sees itself constructed through seeing its "reflection" in the broadcast.

3. For a somewhat different, yet still interactive, approach to identity, especially ethnic identity, see Stephan (1992).

4. Gershon (n.d.b, p. 22) notes that people in Papua New Guinea villages often had a variety of personal and clan names. This made census taking difficult, as the census takers assumed a one-to-one relationship between person and name.

5. Although the 1997/2000 OMB and Census categories define six groups, common parlance still names five (African-, Asian-, European-, Hispanic/Latino/a-, and Native Americans or their variations), and I will largely follow that custom.

6. I share Hoover's (1993) sense that much contemporary discussion of identity

is reductionistic and his sentiment that that is wrong. This is, in fact, one of the points that emerges from the analysis of contemporary workplace-oriented race-ethnic discourse (see chap. 6).

7. Hoover (1997, p. 40) takes this point even further, in noting that when the state has sought to provide an identity to its citizens, it retards individual growth, foreclosing identity formation, fostering stereotypes, and promoting negative identities.

8. At the same time, as Stephan (1992, p. 62) notes, "ethnic identities do not seem to involve conscious selection. One does not experience electing to be Hispanic, for instance, but instead experiences being Hispanic."

9. However, as Johnson (1992, p. 44) notes about biracial children, there is no biracial identity because there are "no cultural rituals, values, or artifacts with which to identify," and identification with biraciality is difficult because of the intangibility of the "group." It will be interesting to see if this changes in the aftermath of changes in Census 2000 practices.

10. Indeed, the assignation of race according to other-identification underlies a whole set of court decisions. See Haney López (1994) for an extensive discussion and case references.

11. See also Nobles (2000, pp. 187–190) for a set of instructions to enumerators from 1850–1960 and the discussion in chapter 2.

12. Executive Order 11375, signed by Johnson in 1967, extended antidiscrimination provisions to women.

13. I am aware of the fact that implementation of these policies on site may, and apparently does, vary. While this would be another interesting line of inquiry to pursue, I am concerned here with policies as statements of intended or desired practices, rather than with varying site-specific practices.

14. With the 1970 census, the bureau moved to the present-day practice of mailing questionnaires to homes, thereby calling on respondents to self-identify. In follow-up face-to-face surveys, printed instructions to enumerators indicate that they are to mark whatever identity the respondent names, with special provisions if the respondent names more than one.

On the other hand, the bureau does not always tabulate responses according to respondents' answers. For statistical purposes, subcategories have been combined. In 1990, for example, as noted in chapter 5, the Census Bureau proposed to combine Native Americans, Asian-Americans, and Whites in several California cities because there were insufficient numbers for separate statistically significant analyses.

15. Robbin (1998a) notes that the debate between allowing self-identification and mandating observer-identification dates back to the 1974 FICE Ad Hoc Committee Report (which recommended in favor of self-identification) and was also present in congressional hearings in 1993 and 1997, as well as in *Federal Register Notes* published between 1988 and 1997. She notes that the 1988 OMB proposal to require self-identification "was vigorously opposed by federal agencies," and that the Senate also opposed it for reasons of data-collection accuracy and "'uniform record keeping and reporting requirements'" (citing the *Review of Federal Measurements of Race and Ethnicity*, Subcommittee on Census, Statistics and Postal Personnel, Committee on Post Office and Civil Service, House of Representatives 103d Congress, 1st session, 1993, pp. 223–224).

16. For example, men's head coverings, facial hair, and dietary practices in prisons, and girls' and women's head coverings in schools and universities, especially in France and Turkey.

17. The phrase, meaning "not to be noticed," comes to me from Murray Baumgarten (personal conversation, 1991), who understands it to have been handed down from Inquisition times. Scholars of this period with whom I have corresponded have not identified it absolutely as language of that era. Gaspar Mairal Buil of the Universidad de Zaragoza suggests that its equivalent in contemporary Spanish would be *"pasar desapercibidos"* (to pass unperceived), which today would be expressed as *"de no degarse notar"* or *"de no hacerse notar"* (correspondence, 1/4/2000). Samuel G. Armistead offers "to keep a low profile" as the contemporary American equivalent, noting that Jews and Muslims, including *conversos*, would not have appeared any different from Christians, Moriscos (Spanish "Moors") arriving in Algeria in 1609 having been slaughtered because they were taken to be Europeans (correspondence, 11/19/2000). Several other phrases—to "go native," to go "slumming"—highlight some aspects of passing as masking, but none of them engages its race-ethnic elements per se. Going native comments on foreignness and self-estrangement; slumming draws on the entailments of class.

18. Skin shade has played a very strong role among African-Americans, as has "good" hair, in marking status hierarchies. See, for example, Russell, Wilson, and Hall (1992) for a collection of anecdotes on this subject. One of my students interviewed an African-American man who could have chosen to pass by virtue of his skin shade, who listed the following when asked if he'd ever been called "a racial name": "White Boy, Negro, piss color, lemon head, half-breed, yellow, yella, sheet, banana." Except for the first two, which were used by Caucasians, the other terms were used by African-Americans.

19. I have benefited from coursework on this subject by Aaron Scott. He called this "shedding the family skin." See Bowker and Star (1999, chap. 6) on passing under apartheid.

20. Memories of Nazi-imposed identity cards still have political impact today. The Netherlands passed a vote only in 1994 creating national identity cards. Several previous measures had been defeated, and that vote still raised the specter of identity being imposed externally by a central government.

21. I have been influenced in this thinking by Carole Pateman and other feminist theorists' critiques of the public/private dichotomy and the meaning of citizenship, in light of some comments of Jürgen Habermas in a lecture at Stanford University in January 1995. (See also Young [1990].)

22. I have in mind here the influence of Protestant ministerial styles and church architecture on Jewish models of professional rabbinic practice and synagogue design, as well as the extent to which many Jews and some Moslems and Hindus have adopted Christmas trees, lights, wreaths, and gift giving.

23. I am drawing a distinction between matters that are thought or talked about by individuals among themselves, in "private" family, social, or communal contexts, and those that would be and are "unthinkable" as topics of explicit conversation in the public sphere beyond the borders of family and community.

24. Paley (2000), in the context of Chilean survey research conducted by the state to assess population characteristics, also notes ways in which people resist, evade, or intentionally undermine the categories.

Part III
Making Race-Ethnicity
Through Administrative Practices

The previous two chapters show that American race-ethnic categories are not natural, but rather are created through public policy practices in the process of their enactment. Through these practices, the sense is sustained that the categories do correlate with objective features of the social world, sustaining also the widespread, common sense that they are natural and scientifically grounded. This sense is extended and supported by practices in two other realms: the administrative practices of state and local governments and their agencies, and the work of social scientists and management consultants applying social science research, both groups seeking to shape and advise those practices.

Administrative practices play a role in constructing understandings of race, ethnicity, and the race-ethnic categories. This process is mutually constituting: public policies and agency documents and practices enacting them are created based on the way(s) in which the concepts and categories are used and understood; and in these enactments, those understandings are recreated, sustained, and (potentially) changed. These administrative activities, explored in chapter 5, along with management-oriented research, treated in chapter 6, maintain and sustain the widespread belief in the naturalness of the concepts and categories. Indeed, these administrative practices are not isolated events, but part and parcel of a set of practices—including congressional hearings (Chock 1991), court cases (Haney López 1994), media stories, and so on—that show and teach their audiences and readers how to "do" race-ethnicity in America today.

Chapter 5 looks at some of the uses to which various public agencies put the race-ethnic categories, drawing largely on examples from California. Hospital practices for assigning newborns a race-ethnic identity and federal health statisticians' analytic uses of these data recapitulate the kind of identification practices discussed in chapter 3, inviting self-identification within the parameters of pre-established categories, but also generating statistics-driven rules for assigning race-ethnic identity. By contrast, police practices for determining the race-ethnic identity of alleged perpetrators of crimes rely on other-identification, enacting the visual, essentialist policies discussed in chapter 4. Implementation of job training programs also often entails administrative assignation of race-ethnic identity to others, a practice that makes some of those street-level bureaucrats uncomfortable. New adoption policies intended to eliminate race-ethnic-based discrimination against children and prospective parents in the best interests of the child bring questions of "blood" and "culture" to the fore, in a more forceful and visible way than any of these other policy issues. And elementary school practices illustrate how the best interests of the child can be subverted by redistributive social justice that allocates funding by race-ethnic categories. All of these cases are undergirded by the logic of category making discussed in chapter 1, as well as by the lumpy, reified character of American race-ethnic categories so much in evidence in the census, as presented in chapter 3.

Chapter 6 explores another dimension of the supposed naturalness of race-ethnic concepts and categories, in examining the role of social science in the process of generating and sustaining American race-ethnicity. Social scientific research under the heading of "managing cultural diversity" in the workplace and its extension to consulting practices undergirds and maintains the "common" sense that concepts and categories are objective, scientifically grounded reflections of social "realities."

5

Ethnogenesis by the Numbers, Ethnogenesis by "Eyeballing"

> The mistake is to assume that birth certificates
> and biographical sketches and all the other documents
> generated by the modern bureaucratic state
> reveal an anterior truth—that they are merely
> signs of an independent existing identity.
> But in fact they constitute it.
> The social meaning of race is established
> by these identity papers—by certificates ...
> and all the other verbal artifacts that proclaim race
> to be real and, by that proclamation, make it so.
>
> *—Henry Louis Gates, Jr.*
> *(quoted in Lustig 1997, p. 22)*

In 1992 an American city of about 200,000 was beset by a serious social problem: members of "the Oriental community" (in the language of the local resident telling this story), which constituted 2 percent of the city's population, were killing their infant daughters. Also, they were involved in other, seemingly drug-trade-related offenses. The city's police department wanted to place an officer undercover in the community. The department understood that its non–Asian-heritage officers would have difficulty and ultimately be unsuccessful in gaining entree. They also perceived that any Asian-American officer from the department or, for that matter, from any other department within the state would be known to members of the community, given its relatively small size statewide. The department applied for a federal grant to hire an out-of-state Asian-American police officer to go undercover and help solve the crimes.[1]

This might appear on the face of it to be a story with a simple resolution. It might continue, for example: The police department found a highly experienced Asian-American officer who successfully infiltrated the local Asian-American community, and the crimes were solved. But from another perspective, the story is more complex and raises several questions. What sort of Asian-American community was this? Which of the many disparate groups subsumed under the heading "Asian-American" did the police officer come from? The resolution of the story depends a great deal on the answers to these questions; and they, in turn, raise questions about the characteristics of the categories in use in contemporary U.S. discourse about racial and ethnic identity.

Federally established race-ethnic categories are used in employment practices and in identifying agency clients and others for program and service development purposes. These include schools and universities, hospitals and clinics, housing programs, services for the elderly, and welfare and police services, among others. A perusal of an index to American statistical reports yielded the following partial list of data collected in different policy arenas by "race and ethnic group" (U.S. Congressional Information Service 1988, pp. 858–863):

Policy area	Report topic
Agriculture and food	Dairy product consumption effects of prices and personal income
Communications and transportation	Traffic deaths and rates
Education	Degrees awarded; discrimination; test scores in literature and U.S. history
Government and defense	Military deaths; minority business contracts; TVA employment; voting age population
Health and vital statistics	AIDs cases; birth defects; cancer; cataract surgery; drownings; firearm accidents; hysterectomies; bubonic plague; smoking habits; suicides
Housing and construction	Mortgage availability; access to rental units
Industry and commerce	Business owner and management characteristics
Labor and employment	Employment and unemployment; labor force participation; financial services industry employment in NYC; union coverage
Law enforcement	Reported child abuse and neglect cases; drug law violation arrests; homicide rates; jail population
Population	Census; personal income; poverty

Public welfare and social security	Medicare enrollment; OASDI coverage
Science and technology	Number of Ph.D. degrees; employment and salaries of science and engineering graduates
Veterans affairs	Labor force status of Vietnam veterans

Banks are required "to compile such data . . . on the gender, race, ethnicity, national origin, or other pertinent information concerning individuals that utilize the services of the assisted institution to ensure that targeted population and low-income residents of investment areas are adequately served" (12 USC §4716). The Department of Agriculture is required to "collect . . . data on the racial and ethnic characteristics of persons eligible for, assisted, or otherwise benefitting under each community development, housing assistance, and mortgage and loan insurance and guarantee program" (42 USC §3608a). A percentage of Institute of Museum and Library Services funds is required to be made available for "targeted services" provided to "people of diverse backgrounds and abilities, that include, for example, Hawaiian Natives and Native Americans" (P.L. 105-128, Library Services and Technology Act of 1997; these three examples are from Robbin 1998b, p. 32, n. 5). The International Institute of the East Bay (California) Newcomer Information Clearinghouse uses census data to analyze domestic violence, mental health, substance abuse, public assistance recipients, occupational distribution, level of educational attainment, and other matters in Alameda County, all by race-ethnicity (Gasiorowicz et al. 1993).

Nor is such categorizing new. Immigration laws in the late 1800s and early 1900s categorized newcomers by nationality, "race or people," and complexion. The manifest of a ship that arrived at Ellis Island in 1921 identifies Irish-born immigrants as British by nationality, Irish by race or people, and "fresh" by complexion. Jewish immigrants born in Eastern Europe were identified as of the "Hebrew" race or people. Italians immigrating from the south were of a different race or people than Italians immigrating from the north, although both groups shared a "dark" complexion (Sachs 2001).

Some argue that the five race-ethnic categories currently in common use are necessary for administrative efficiency: they enable statistical comparability across geography and time. Others claim that the categories need to be retained for reasons of social justice, since they have been used in the past to distribute welfare moneys, social service programs, housing, and so on. A close look at how the categories are used in agency practices, however, challenges these claims to efficiency, at the same time that it raises other questions about social justice.

As the foregoing lists show, the agencies and practices touched by race-ethnic category usage cover a broad spectrum, from hospitals noting births to police departments helping victims and apprehending suspects, from job training programs to welfare agencies placing children for adoption, from schools tracking students to medical research, hate crimes, and university recruiting. It is not my intention here to single out any particular agency or practice for criticism, or for praise. There are many more agencies and practices that engage in race-ethnic identification than are dealt with here: we "do" race-ethnicity throughout our society. The ones treated in the next sections were chosen to illustrate different aspects of the issue. Many others could equally well have been featured or noted. What becomes clear in all the cases is the extent to which common, ongoing, everyday practices of agencies of the state naming race, ethnicity, and race-ethnic categories and sorting and counting people accordingly play a part in constructing these concepts and categories and sustaining them, and thereby contributing to them the aura of "scientific-ness" and, hence, natural reality.

Constructing American "Kinship" Patterns: Recording Births

In 1992 an anthropologist told of the birth, in a California hospital one year earlier, of his first daughter. When mother and daughter were to be released, a nurse brought them a form on which her race was to be noted. They looked at the choices—the five then-standard OMB categories—and stopped. Instead, they drew in a sixth box and line, marked it "Other," and wrote in: "human." The nurse returned in moments, handing them back the card. There was a black line drawn through their addition. They were told they had to fill out the standard, printed form or else their daughter would not be released. He explained their objections to the nurse, who reiterated the hospital's requirements. When he continued to persist in his explanations, she said the hospital could not change it, it was state policy; they would have to call Sacramento (the state capital). Fine, he said; call. The word came down from administrative headquarters some time later: Okay. And so their daughter was the first contemporary "human" to be born in the state of California (Segal 1998).[2]

At one time, most states recorded the race-ethnic identity of infants on their birth certificates. Artist and philosopher Adrian Piper, in an installation at the Museum of Contemporary Art in Chicago entitled *Cornered* (1988), displays two copies of her father's birth certificate, both issued by the state of West Virginia. Born June 5, 1911, he was designated "Black octoroon" (i.e., one-eighth black) on the birth certificate issued in 1953. The 1965 birth certificate identifies him as "white." Since then, the law in many states has changed, and race-ethnic identity is no longer named on birth certificates. But hospitals have not stopped collecting race-ethnic data on infants and their parents. They report these data to the National Center for Health Statistics (NCHS) in the U.S. Department of Health and Human Services (DHHS),[3] which publishes several series analyzing such things as infant mortality, birth weight, disease, and other information by the race-ethnic identity of the children or of one or both parents.

Although the race-ethnic category name does not appear on the certificate, it is encoded there and in hospital records. For this purpose, following the algorithm developed by the NCHS, the California Department of Health Services has a 24 cell × 24 cell "Matrix for Generating Race/Ethnicity of Child," with father and mother on different axes. The 1994 matrix provided eighteen specific possibilities for each parent's race-ethnic identity: White; Black; American Indian; Asian (Chinese, Japanese, Korean, Vietnamese, Cambodian, Thai, Laotian, and unidentified); Indian; Filipino; Hawaiian; Guamanian; Samoan; Eskimo; Aleut; Pacific Islander. There is also one code each for specified "Asian" and for specified "Other," as well as one for "refused to state" and one for "unknown." ("Spanish/Hispanic origin" is now tabulated separately from "race-ethnicity" in birth data.) The matrix, along with the explanatory codes, follows as Table 5.1.[4]

A child is "White" if and only if both mother and father are white. If either parent is Hawaiian, the child is Hawaiian, regardless of the race-ethnicity of the other parent. If the identity of either parent is unknown (simply so, or through refusal to state), the child's race-ethnic identity is that of the known parent. (If both refuse to state, or if both are unknown, the child is identified accordingly.) If the father's identity is unknown and the mother refuses to state hers, or if the father refuses to state his and the mother's is unknown, the child is encoded by the mother's response. If the father is White and the mother is not, the child is assigned the mother's race-ethnicity.[5]

In all other cases, save two, the child's race-ethnicity follows the father's, regardless of the mother's race-ethnic identity. When the father is Black, American Indian, any of the specific Asian designations, or any of the specific Other designations (Indian, Filipino, Guamanian, Samoan, Eskimo, Aleut, or Pacific Islander), so is the child, except in two sorts of cases. If the father is of unnamed Asian (code 40 or 41) or Other (code 51) race-ethnicity, the child follows the mother's designation if she is a member of a more specific Asian or Other group (such as Korean). In the case where the father is "Other-specified," the child receives the mother's race-ethnicity only when it is Indian, Filipino, Guamanian, Samoan, Eskimo, or Aleut (but not Pacific Islander: that child follows the father's designation).

Table 5.1

"Matrix for Generating Race/Ethnicity of Child" (1994), California Department of Health Services

MOTHER

FATHER	10	20	30	40	41	42	43	44	45	46	47	48	49	51	52	53	54	55	56	57	58	59	98	99
10	10	20	30	40	41	42	43	44	45	46	47	48	49	51	52	53	54	55	56	57	58	59	98	99
20	20	20	30	40	41	42	43	44	45	46	47	48	49	51	52	53	54	55	56	57	58	59	20	20
30	30	30	30	40	41	42	43	44	45	46	47	48	49	51	52	53	54	55	56	57	58	59	30	30
40	40	40	40	40	41	42	43	44	45	46	47	48	49	51	52	53	54	55	56	57	58	59	40	40
41	41	41	41	41	41	42	43	44	45	46	47	48	49	51	52	53	54	55	56	57	58	59	41	41
42	42	42	42	42	42	42	43	44	45	46	47	48	49	51	52	53	54	55	56	57	58	59	42	42
43	43	43	43	43	43	43	43	44	45	46	47	48	49	51	52	53	54	55	56	57	58	59	43	43
44	44	44	44	44	44	44	44	44	45	46	47	48	49	51	52	53	54	55	56	57	58	59	44	44
45	45	45	45	45	45	45	45	45	45	46	47	48	49	51	52	53	54	55	56	57	58	59	45	45
46	46	46	46	46	46	46	46	46	46	46	47	48	49	51	52	53	54	55	56	57	58	59	46	46
47	47	47	47	47	47	47	47	47	47	47	47	48	49	51	52	53	54	55	56	57	58	59	47	47
48	48	48	48	48	48	48	48	48	48	48	48	48	49	51	52	53	54	55	56	57	58	59	48	48
49	49	49	49	49	49	49	49	49	49	49	49	49	49	51	52	53	54	55	56	57	58	59	49	49
51	51	51	51	51	51	51	51	51	51	51	51	51	51	51	52	53	54	55	56	57	58	59	51	51
52	52	52	52	52	52	52	52	52	52	52	52	52	52	52	52	53	54	55	56	57	58	59	52	52
53	53	53	53	53	53	53	53	53	53	53	53	53	53	53	53	53	54	55	56	57	58	59	53	53
54	54	54	54	54	54	54	54	54	54	54	54	54	54	54	54	54	54	55	56	57	58	59	54	54
55	55	55	55	55	55	55	55	55	55	55	55	55	55	55	55	55	55	55	56	57	58	59	55	55
56	56	56	56	56	56	56	56	56	56	56	56	56	56	56	56	56	56	56	56	57	58	59	56	56
57	57	57	57	57	57	57	57	57	57	57	57	57	57	57	57	57	57	57	57	57	58	59	57	57
58	58	58	58	58	58	58	58	58	58	58	58	58	58	58	58	58	58	58	58	58	58	59	58	58
59	59	59	59	59	59	59	59	59	59	59	59	59	59	59	59	59	59	59	59	59	59	59	59	59
98	10	20	30	40	41	42	43	44	45	46	47	48	49	51	52	53	54	55	56	57	58	59	98	98
99	10	20	30	40	41	42	43	44	45	46	47	48	49	51	52	53	54	55	56	57	58	59	98	99

10-19	White (11–19 not currently used, reserved for future special studies)
20-29	Black (21–29 not currently used, reserved for future special studies)
30-39	American Indian (31–39 not currently used, reserved for future special studies)
40	Asian - Unspecified
41	Asian - Specified
42	Asian - Chinese
43	Asian - Japanese
44	Asian - Korean
45	Asian - Vietnamese
46	Asian - Cambodian
47	Asian - Thai
48	Asian - Laotian
51	Other - Specified
52	Indian (excludes American Indian, Aleut, and Eskimo)
53	Filipino
54	Hawaiian
55	Guamanian
56	Samoan
57	Eskimo
58	Aleut
59	Pacific Islander (excludes Hawaiian, Guamanian, Samoan)
98	Refused to state
99	Unknown

The general rule seems to be, fathers determine the child's race-ethnicity, except:

1. When the father's race-ethnic identity is unknown or unstated or is general Asian or Other, and the mother's identity is known and more specific;
2. When the mother is Hawaiian; or
3. When the father is White and the mother is not.

To put it in race-ethnic, rather than relational, terms: in a White/not-White "mixture," not-White prevails; in not-White/not-White "mixtures," the father's identity prevails, subject to the conditions and exceptions noted above.

These decision rules entail some curious practices. First, the determination is predicated on the assumption that either parent will have only a single race-ethnic identity. This means either that interracial or interethnic marriages are assumed not to have taken place very often in the prior generation (an assumption seemingly supported statistically by census data: the number of interracial couples tripled from 1970 to 1990, compared with a 23 percent increase in the number of married couples, although this could be an artifact of increased reporting rather than increased incidence: antimiscegenation laws still prevailed in some states into the 1970s—until 1987 in Mississippi [Fuchs 1990, p. 517, n. 11]—and the social stigma against "mixing" has been even stronger than the law). Or it means that children of the prior generation's intermarriages, who are now giving birth, are assumed to have chosen or developed (by their own volition or by assignment) a single race-ethnic identity, rather than an identity reflecting all of both parents' heritages.

Second, following this treatment, infants are assigned only one, categorically "pure," race-ethnic heritage.

Third, the table does not treat race-ethnic heritages, or gender, equally. To be "White" requires "full-bloodedness"—and it is the only case, where the father's race-ethnic identity is known and specific and not Hawaiian, in which the mother's counts equally. The one-drop rule—which assigned Black identity to anyone with "one drop" of Black ancestry, and which Davis (1991) shows holds sway in many social practices even though it has been declared illegal—obtains here across the race-ethnic spectrum: non-"White" trumps "White" across the board, except for Hawaiian. And maleness carries more weight, except for Hawaiian and where greater specificity of race-ethnicity in the mother outweighs the father's more general race-ethnic identification. The notion of race-ethnicity that underlies this approach appears to be based on the transmission of identity through semen, although expressed in terms of categorical blood purity.

The categories are not equal in another sense: only "Asians" are marked for subcategorical differences, and continental East Asians are treated separately from Indians and island "Asians" (from the Philippines, Guam, Samoa, and other Pacific Islands). Curiously, Eskimos and Aleuts—who argued to the Census Bureau that they are not American Indians—are categorized here with island Asians and Indians.

As a consequence of these practices, the number of "White" births is restricted, while the number of "non-White" births expands. Within the terms of this matrix, leaving aside the cases of unknown parentage, a newborn would have a mathematical chance of 1 in 484 of being White, but 22 in 484 of being either Black, American Indian, specific Asian, or specific Other.

This analysis leaves one puzzle: why does Hawaiian parentage, whether male or female, "trump" all other race-ethnic backgrounds? The answer appears to lie in federal support for Hawaiian state law establishing eligibility for "Native Hawaiian" status. Such a determination requires 50 percent Hawaiian "blood." This is important for Hawaiian inheritance rules: only "Native Hawaiians" are permitted certain types of land ownership.[6]

Public health professionals and departments argue that birth weight, disease, infant mortality, and other data are important to track by population group. It is undeniably important to know, for instance, for reasons of equal treatment, that infant mortality is higher for African-Americans than it is for European Americans, as Segal and Handler (n.d.) also note. But the enactment of this goal here shows that it is statistical data—at best—that constitute the initial "observations," not field data. With the exception of the "White" child, half (at least) of all genetic material contributed to the child is being lost as public health data, except in the case of parents from identical, single race-ethnic backgrounds. The only African-American babies, for example, being counted in California are those born to Black fathers, or Black mothers if the father is White or unidentified. Even in the case of the "White" child, the categories are blind to possible prior mixtures—the presence of an African or Indian ancestor, for example, in the case of someone in the line who has "passed."

The development and implementation of federally defined categories was intended to facilitate the use of statistical data in analyses of changes over time and place. But statistical practices themselves have changed. For example, up until 1989, all federal NCHS statistical analyses used parental information entered on the birth certificate to derive the child's race-ethnic designation (referred to as "race" in 1985 and "race or national origin" in 1988), and then used that designation in data analysis. Children were assigned the non-White parent's race-ethnicity in a White/non-White mixture, and the father's race-ethnicity in a non-White/non-White mixture, except when the mother (in 1985) or either parent (1988) was Hawaiian or part Hawaiian. In the case of missing data for one parent, the child was assigned the other parent's race-ethnic identity. If data were missing for both parents, the child was assigned the identity of the preceding entry (U.S. Department of Health and Human Services 1990, p. 39; 1992a, p. 4). (At least as late as 1978, NCHS reports were using both "race" and "color": color has two categories, "white" and "all other"; race tabulations "show data separately for the black population" [U.S. Department of Health, Education, and Welfare 1978, p. 49].)

Changes over the years in identity assignation practices for statistical purposes further illustrate the lack of stability or fixed character to the concepts of race and ethnicity (or national origin), the categories, and the categorizations. Prior to 1964, all missing data for race-ethnic identities were coded "White." Between 1964 and 1968, all missing data cases were encoded "white" if the preceding record was White; otherwise, they were designated "black." From 1969 on, all missing data cases were assigned the race-ethnic identity of the previous entry. In 1988, "White" included Hispanic births as well as "White" ones. In cases of uncertainty regarding an Asian parent's identity, birthplace was treated as race-ethnicity (i.e., an Asian parent born in China or the Philippines was categorized as Chinese or Filipino). When birthplace designation was inconclusive, the parent was assigned to "Other Asian or Pacific Islander" (U.S. Department of Health and Human Services 1992a, p. 4). The effect of these statistical assignments was to lower the number of children born to certain categories, relative to the number of mothers in those categories: in 1988, there were 1.8 percent more White mothers than there were White children born (the difference being attributable to non-White fathers), but 5 percent fewer Black mothers than Black births; 19.2 percent fewer American Indian mothers than births; 6.8 percent fewer Chinese mothers; 17.5 percent fewer Japanese mothers; 31.6 percent fewer Hawaiian mothers; 5.8 percent fewer Filipino mothers; 7.8 percent fewer Other Asian and Pacific Islander mothers; and 15.4 percent fewer "Other" mothers (U.S. Department of Health and Human Services 1992a, p. 5). These children presumably acquired their father's race-ethnic identity, the father (by the logic of the algorithm) being a non-White of some other group.

Beginning in 1989, the federal government no longer tabulated birth data by the child's race-ethnic identity, using, instead, the mother's. This would seem to make sense for epidemiological reasons: while it is perhaps arguable that the father's identity (assigned to the child in most cases) serves as a better socioeconomic indicator, the mother's state of health seems far more relevant in determining infant birth weights and other public health factors. Indeed, the technical notes to the 1989 and 1990 data analyses make that point: the 1989 revision of the U.S. Standard Certificate of Live Birth (used by all states in reporting data to the federal DHHS) "includes many more health questions that are directly associated with the mother, including alcohol and tobacco use, weight gain during pregnancy, medical risk factors, obstetric procedures, complications of labor and/or delivery, and method of delivery." Other data collected, including marital status, educational level, preterm birth, and receipt of prenatal care, also relate more closely to the mother than to the father. This makes it more appropriate to use the mother's race-ethnic identity than the child's (which is to say, the father's, in most cases; U.S. Department of Health and Human Services 1993, p. 5; 1994b, p. 5). Another report also notes that the analytic change to using the variable "mother's identity," instead of the child's, produces mortality rates "that are considered more realistic" (U.S. Department of Health and Human Services 1994a, p. 2), although it does not establish why that would be so.[7]

Additionally, in the statisticians' view, using the mother's identity makes for greater uniformity of data: births with no information on the father were already being assigned the mother's identity; these births were often to unmarried women, and the incidence of that had grown from 7 percent in 1968 to 15 percent in 1989. And using the child's (father's) identity in the case of inter-race-ethnic births (up to 3.4 percent in 1988, from 1 percent in 1968) suppressed the number of statistical births to White women and increased the number of births to non-White women (U.S. Department of Health and Human Services 1993, p. 5; 1994b, p. 5). That one report notes a 44 percent increase in Hawaiian infant mortality rates when using the mother's race-ethnic designation for birth identification than when using the child's (U.S. Department of Health and Human Services 1994a, p. 1) suggests that the rule for assigning Hawaiian identity to infants when either parent is Hawaiian was not being uniformly or consistently applied.

Mortality reports follow different rules of assigning race-ethnic identity: "On the birth certificate, race of parents is reported by the mother at the time of delivery. On the death certificate, race of the deceased infant *is reported by the funeral director based on observation or on information supplied by an informant,* such as a parent" (U.S. Department of Health and Human Services 1994a, p. 26; emphasis added). Mortality rates are also reported differently, using only "White" and "Black"; all non-Whites are subsumed into the Black category for statistical analysis.

What these practices illustrate is that consistency of statistical analysis across race-ethnic data sets—whether geographically, across the fifty states and the District of Columbia, or chronologically, across periods of data collection—has not been ensured by the development of federal definitions of race-ethnic categories. "Depending on the data source, the classification by race may be based *on self-classification or on observation* by an interviewer or other persons filling out the questionnaire" (U.S. Department of Health and Human Services 1992b, p. 322; emphasis added). Such procedural differences do not provide consistent data. Robbin (1998a, p. 37), citing other research, mentions one set of findings that the "ethnic" identity reported for an individual could change as many as four times over the course of a lifetime, depending on who was making the identification. There are several possible identifiers and moments for identification: the individual self-identifying; the mother at birth; state health statisticians analyzing hospital data; the employer later in life; the coroner at death. Other opportunities for race-ethnic identification are likely to arise between birth and death, given the current state of American race-ethnic administrative practices, such as at every school enrollment. As Tafoya (2000, p. 9) notes, both qualitative research and anecdotal evidence suggest the fluidity of race-ethnic identity. "The potential effect of such fluid identity on data integrity," she writes, "is unclear." She gives the example of inferences about workplace discrimination derived from the comparison of EEOC and census data, noting that "consistency across these two sources is vital for making valid inferences." Given that one relies on other-identification and the other, on self-identification, consistency would seem to be questionable.

Questions concerning categorizing practices also arise in epidemiological and other medical data collected by race-ethnicity. Researchers have apparently by and large not attended to the ways in which they have used race-ethnic categories in research design and analysis (Jones, LaVeist, and Lillie-Blanton 1991). If health policy analysts are intending to track patterns in low birth weight, infant survival, and so on, they need to make sure that they are not using "race-ethnicity" as a surrogate variable for socioeconomic class, family structure, or some other element that may be impacting the outcome; and if they are seeking to measure genetic factors in disease, they need an indicator that better reflects the full composition of individuals' race-ethnic backgrounds.

The sort of selective race-ethnic tracking in evidence in federal algorithms and the California matrix has important implications for other policy areas as well. The California Senate passed a bill in 1995 calling for research to generate good state data on the mortality rate of American Indian infants. Studies conducted in 1974 and 1984 appeared to reveal a high rate of error in recording the ethnicity of American Indian infants on death certificates: the numbers were half that of the national death rate for all races, and one quarter that of the rate for American Indians in all states. This apparent underreporting led to a loss of federal moneys for American Indian health care in thirty-seven rural counties in the state (California State Senate 1995).[8]

Identification practices mandated by the birth matrix would result in fairly high statistical underidentification, since a child is identified as American Indian only when the father is identified as American Indian (unless the mother is Hawaiian) or the mother self-identifies as American Indian and the father is White or not identified. The lost numbers in declarations of death are likely to have been elevated by the high degree of shame or embarrassment that still attaches to self-identification as Native American (see, e.g., the discussion in Wilson 1992), perhaps leading parents or kin to underidentify infants, or by the fact that administrative observers often identify Native Americans as "White" (Gillum, Gomez-Marin, and Prineas 1988, p. 488, who found that as many as 20 percent of Native American school children were misidentified in a health study).

Category-generation and identity-assignment practices for statistical purposes, in other words, build on and compound the data problems resulting from reified and lumpy categories. The logic of category making mandates discrete, self-contained entities, with no room for mixture. Assigning race-ethnic identity arbitrarily (or "electronically," as the NCHS reports' technical notes say) follows the logic of the rules of statistical analysis. But when those assignments eliminate increasing variation in and varieties of race-ethnic background, and their analyses become the bases for policy judgments, administrative actions, and related public discourse, some attention needs to be paid to the fact that mortality increases among "Asian" infants and rising birth weights of "Black" newborns are reporting only part of the nonstatistical story.

"Eyeballing" Physiognomy: Locating Victims and Suspects

One winter evening in 1996, the chief of the police department of a smallish city in California was preparing to file the monthly "Age, Sex, Race, and Ethnic Origin of Persons Arrested" report with the state's Department of Justice (DOJ), Division of Law Enforcement, Bureau of Criminal Statistics, which in turn would transmit the data to the Federal Bureau of Investigation (FBI) in the U.S. DOJ for its Uniform Crime Reports (UCR). The racial and ethnic origin categories used in the FBI's UCR program are the OMB names and definitions, and the program follows Directive No. 15 in collecting data separately for "racial designations"—White, Black, American Indian or Alaskan Native, Asian or Pacific Islander, by the names in effect that evening—and "ethnic designations"—Hispanic and Not Hispanic. As he looked through the numbers collected from his officers' reports, one case struck him as odd. A single individual—someone well known to members of the department (a "frequent flyer," in local parlance)—had been arrested eleven times that month.

On four of these occasions he had been identified in the reports as Hispanic. Six times he had been listed as White. And once he had been marked as Other. The police chief started thinking about race-ethnic identity and officer training.

It is not bodily fluids—whether blood or semen—that shape police departments' practices in identifying perpetrators of crimes or their victims by race-ethnicity. Rather, it is the practicalities of making a quick ID in the field, often with an uncooperative suspect or with a distressed victim or member of the latter's family. It is, in short, what the person "looks like" that drives these practices.

The California Law Enforcement Telecommunications System (CLETS), a database that primarily tracks wanted and missing persons, established nineteen categories for reporting race-ethnic identity (see Table 5.2).[9] These are used by officers in filling out various field report forms, such as for missing persons and child abuse (see Table 5.3).

Research into the practices of the police departments (PDs) of three neighboring California cities of varying sizes—I'll call them Able, Baker, and Charlie—found that all three collect race-ethnic data, but their collection practices differ, in keeping with state DOJ law that allows departments to modify crime reports to fit local needs, reflecting variations in the local populations that they police. So, for example, Able PD tends to report data following the category names used by the state, whereas Baker and Charlie PDs use different categories on their forms (see Table 5.4). The nineteen categories used by Able PD are reduced to nine categories in Baker and Charlie PDs: Asian, Black, Hispanic, Indian, White, Filipino, Japanese, Other, and Unknown. Where Chinese, Cambodian, Guamanian, Korean, Laotian, Pacific Islander, Samoan, Hawaiian, Vietnamese, or Asian Indian persons would be identified separately on Able PD's report, those ten would all appear as "Asian" in Baker and Charlie PDs' reports.

The nineteen categories in use in Able are the state categories. But when the state reports crime data, it aggregates the nineteen into four: White (not Hispanic), Hispanic, Black, and Other (see Table 5.5). According to a research analyst at the state DOJ Bureau of Criminal Statistics, this is done to improve the statistical significance in cross-group comparative analyses, as well as to streamline the reports. Furthermore, when the FBI reports crime statistics collected from the fifty states, it uses four categories for race: White, Black, Asian, and Other (Hispanic data are tabulated separately).

Assuming for the moment that data collection under field conditions is accurate, that means that the federal and state governments' reports reflect different interests in the identification of the groups committing crimes. Where the California state data system makes distinctions among "Asian" groups—as

Table 5.2

Nineteen Race-Ethnic Codes and Their Definitions Used in the California Law Enforcement Telecommunications System (CLETS)

The basic racial and ethnic codes and definitions for statistical reporting are as follows:

A	Other Asian	Any person who may be Asian but where the specific ethnic origin is not known or declared. Also, where none of the other Asian codes apply. This allows for "sight identification" by officers in the field.
B	Black	A person having origins in any of the black racial groups of Africa.
C	Chinese	A person having origin in China.
D	Cambodian	A person having origin in Cambodia.
F	Filipino	A person having origin in any of the Philippine Islands.
G	Guamanian	A person having origin in Guam.
H	Hispanic	A person of Mexican, Puerto Rican, Cuban, Central or South American or other Spanish culture or origin, regardless of race.
I	Indian	(American Indian or Alaskan Native) A person having origins in any of the original peoples of North America, and who maintains cultural identification through tribal affiliation or community recognition.
J	Japanese	A person having origin in Japan.
K	Korean	A person having origin in Korea.
L	Laotian	A person having origins in Laos.
O	Other	Any person who cannot be linked to any of the general or specific racial/ethnic groups listed on the JUS 750 form.
P	Pacific Islander	Any person who cannot be identified as belonging to one of the listed Pacific Island racial-ethnic groups such as Samoan, Guamanian, Hawaiian, etc.
S	Samoan	Any person having origin in Samoa.
U	Hawaiian	Any person having origins in Hawaii.
V	Vietnamese	Any person having origin in Vietnam.
W	White	A person having origins in any of the original peoples of Europe, North Africa, or the Middle East.
X	Unknown	
Z	Asian Indian	Any person who can be identified as belonging to one of the listed Asian/Eastern Indian racial/ethnic groups, such as Pakistani, Bangladeshi, Nepali, Ceylonese, Afghanistani, etc.

Table 5.3

Sample Report Form Requiring Identification by Race

MISSING PERSON REPORTING FORM
(See Reverse for Instructions)

| 4) **RECORD TYPE** |
| *(Check type which best describes)* |

1) *Check One:* ☐ ADULT   ☐ JUVENILE

2) Reporting Agency _____   3) ORI _____

☐ Runaway Juvenile
☐ Voluntary Missing Adult
☐ Parental/Family Abduction
☐ Non-Family Abduction
☐ Stranger Abduction
☐ Dependent Adult
☐ Lost
☐ Catastrophe
☐ Unknown Circumstances

5) Case # _____

6) DOJ # _____   7) NCIC # _____

8) CATEGORY: ☐ At Risk   ☐ Prior Missing   ☐ Sexual Exploitation Suspected

9) Name _____   Date/Time Missing _____

10) Alias 1 _____   Alias 2 _____

11) GENDER	12) RACE	13) HGT.	14) WGT.	15) EYE COLOR	16) HAIR COLOR/LENGTH	17) DATE OF BIRTH
☐ Male ☐ Female ☐ Unknown	☐ W ☐ C ☐ H ☐ J ☐ B ☐ F ☐ I ☐ O ☐ X			☐ BLK ☐ HAZ ☐ BLU ☐ MAR ☐ BRO ☐ PNK ☐ GRY ☐ MUL ☐ GRN ☐ XXX	☐ BLK ☐ RED ☐ BLN ☐ SDY ☐ BRO ☐ WHT ☐ GRY ☐ XXX Length _____	

18) Residence Address _____   City _____

19) Location Last Seen _____   Probable Destination _____

20) Known Associates _____

21) Mental Condition _____

22) SS # _____   CII# _____   FBI # _____   DL # _____

23) Photo Available: ☐ Yes   ☐ No   Age in Photo _____   Photo/X-Ray Waiver Release Signed ☐ Yes   ☐ No
(Attach Photo and Signed SS 8567 Waiver Release Form)

24) Scars/Marks/Tattoos (locate/describe) _____

25) Skeletal X-Rays Available: ☐ Yes   ☐ No;   Broken Bones/Missing Organs: _____

26) Dental X-Rays Available: ☐ Yes   ☐ No;   (Attach Chart and X-Rays)   Dentures: ☐ Upper   ☐ Lower   ☐ Full   ☐ Partial

27) Visible Dental Work _____

28) Dentist's Name _____   Phone _____

29) Glasses ☐   Contact Lens ☐   Clothing Description/Size _____

30) Jewelry Description _____

31) If Vehicle Involved: ☐ S   ☐ MP   Lic# _____   Make _____   Model _____   Year _____

32) If abduction, did abduction involve movement of missing person in the commission of a crime?   ☐ Yes   ☐ No

33) Suspect Name _____   DOB _____

34) Relationship to Victim _____   Warrant # _____

35) Reporting Party _____   Phone _____

36) Relationship to Missing Person _____   Date Reported _____

37) Additional Information _____

38) Reporting Officer/Agency Contact _____   Phone _____

Upon completion, please return to: Department of Justice
Bureau of Criminal Statistics and Special Services
P.O. Box 903417
Sacramento, California 94203-4170
Attention: Missing/Unidentified Persons Unit

SS 8568 (R 12/88)

Table 5.4

Three Police Department Category Sets

Category	Able	Baker	Charlie	State	Federal
Other Asian	A	A	A	A	A
Black	B	B	B	B	B
Chinese	C	A	A	C	A
Cambodian	D	A	A	D	A
Filipino	F	F	F	F	A
Guamanian	G	A	A	G	A
Hispanic/Latin Hispanic	H	H	H	H	A
American Indian	I	I	I	I	W
Japanese	J	J	J	J	A
Korean	K	A	A	K	A
Laotian	L	A	A	L	A
Other	O	O	O	O	U
Pacific Islander	P	A	A	P	A
Samoan	S	A	A	S	A
Hawaiian	U	A	A	U	A
Vietnamese	V	A	A	V	A
White	W	W	W	W	W
Unknown	X	X	X	X	U
Asian Indian	Z	A	A	Z	A

Note: Able's reporting codes are the state reporting codes (A to Z, not inclusive, assigned according to the order in this list). The other two cities use some combination of the state codes and federal reporting codes (A, B, W, U).

with birth records, no subcategorical distinctions are made for other groups—the federal government is interested only in "Asians" as a collective. Curiously, in the state reports "Asians" (i.e., the collective, umbrella term) disappears entirely. We might expect local PD reports to be far more nuanced, reflecting an interest in data on the specific groups represented in the local community; and we might also expect such an interest to persist similarly at the state level, since such statistics are likely to be used to develop state law enforcement policies. But here, three neighboring cities, with similar populations, have chosen to report under different category schemes. Moreover, different agencies within the same state use different race-ethnic categories, as shown in Table 5.6.

Field conditions, however, do not always allow accurate race-ethnic identification. Suspects being apprehended are not always the most cooperative. Asked, "What is your race?" a suspect may well reply, "What do I look like, a Martian?" Race-ethnic identity has usually not been a subject of training (in general or in the three PDs examined here). The assumptions discussed in chapters 1 and 4 are enacted here in field and reporting practices: that

Table 5.5

Sample California State-Level Race-Ethnic Reporting

Category and offense	Number							Percent						
	Total	Gender		Race/ethnic group				Total	Gender		Race/ethnic group			
		Male	Female	White	Hispanic	Black	Other		Male	Female	White	Hispanic	Black	Other
Total	581,264	486,383	94,881	215,248	202,152	136,149	27,715	100.0	83.7	16.3	37.0	34.8	23.4	4.8
Violent offenses	154,138	135,128	19,010	47,915	58,803	39,065	8,355	100.0	87.7	12.3	31.1	38.1	25.3	5.4
Homicide	2,963	2,709	254	675	1,175	850	263	100.0	91.4	8.6	22.8	39.7	20.7	8.9
Forcible rape	3,305	3,287	18	825	1,249	1,072	159	100.0	99.5	.5	25.0	37.8	32.4	4.8
Robbery	27,984	25,225	2,759	4,575	10,340	11,659	1,410	100.0	90.1	9.9	16.3	36.9	41.7	5.0
Assault	117,654	101,969	15,685	41,159	45,140	24,943	6,412	100.0	86.7	13.3	35.0	38.4	21.2	5.4
Kidnapping	2,232	1,938	294	681	899	541	111	100.0	86.8	13.2	30.5	40.3	24.2	5.0
Property offenses	188,903	152,548	36,355	67,292	65,816	44,081	11,714	100.0	80.8	19.2	35.6	34.8	23.3	6.2
Burglary	69,441	57,023	12,418	24,310	25,637	14,950	4,544	100.0	82.1	17.9	35.0	36.9	21.5	6.5
Theft	62,011	49,184	12,827	23,828	19,594	15,097	3,492	100.0	79.3	20.7	38.4	31.6	24.3	6.6
Motor vehicle theft	39,698	34,657	5,041	11,563	16,530	9,115	2,490	100.0	87.3	12.7	29.1	41.6	23.0	6.3
Forgery, checks, access cards	15,544	9,758	5,786	6,443	3,470	4,560	1,071	100.0	62.8	37.2	41.5	22.3	29.3	6.9
Arson	2,209	1,926	283	1,148	585	359	117	100.0	87.2	12.8	52.0	26.5	16.3	5.3
Drug offenses	155,175	126,251	28,924	65,860	51,177	34,408	3,730	100.0	81.4	18.6	42.4	33.0	22.2	2.4
Narcotics	72,317	60,576	11,741	12,828	29,801	28,230	1,458	100.0	83.8	16.2	17.7	41.2	39.0	2.0
Marijuana	14,668	13,095	1,573	5,599	5,498	3,189	382	100.0	89.3	10.7	38.2	37.5	21.7	2.6
Dangerous drugs	65,660	50,778	14,882	45,879	15,264	2,697	1,820	100.0	77.3	22.7	69.9	23.2	4.1	2.8
Other	2,530	1,802	728	1,554	614	292	70	100.0	71.2	28.8	61.4	24.3	11.5	2.8
Sex offenses	7,390	7,141	249	2,838	2,981	1,198	373	100.0	96.6	3.4	38.4	40.3	16.2	5.0
Lewd or lascivious	4,537	4,415	122	1,782	1,954	611	190	100.0	97.3	2.7	39.3	43.1	13.5	4.2
Other	2,853	2,726	127	1,056	1,027	587	183	100.0	95.5	4.5	37.0	36.0	20.6	6.4
Driving offenses	9,226	8,232	994	3,629	4,367	741	489	100.0	89.2	10.8	39.3	47.3	8.0	5.3
Driving under the influence	7,567	6,783	784	3,114	3,502	591	360	100.0	89.6	10.4	41.2	46.3	7.8	4.8
Hit-and-run	1,659	1,449	210	515	865	150	129	100.0	87.3	12.7	31.0	52.1	9.0	7.8
All other	66,432	57,083	9,349	27,714	19,008	16,656	3,054	100.0	85.9	14.1	41.7	28.6	25.1	4.6
Weapons	23,562	22,175	1,387	8,804	8,716	4,756	1,286	100.0	94.1	5.9	37.4	37.0	20.2	5.5
Escape	654	569	85	332	212	84	26	100.0	87.0	13.0	50.8	32.4	12.8	4.0
Bookmaking	187	146	41	108	9	44	26	100.0	78.1	21.9	57.8	4.8	23.5	13.9
Other	42,029	34,193	7,836	18,470	10,071	11,772	1,716	100.0	81.4	18.6	43.9	24.0	28.0	4.1

Note: Percents may not add to 100.0 because of independent rounding.

Table 5.6

A Comparison of Race-Ethnic Classifications Used in California

California Department of Justice
Division of Law Enforcement
Bureau of Criminal Statistics and Special Services (BCS/SS)

Race Classifications Used by State and Federal Data Collection Agencies (March 1983)

Agency by Classification Used[1] and Groups Included

California Department of Justice BCS/SS, Bureau of Criminal Investigation	California Department of Justice Bureau of Organized Crime and Criminal Intelligence	California Department of Corrections	California Youth Authority	Standardized Crime Reporting System (SCRS)	California Department of Finance,[2] California Department of Health Services,[3] U.S. Census Bureau
White	White	White	White	White	White
Caucasian	Caucasian	Caucasian	Caucasian	(Not of Indian, Asian, Black, or Hispanic origin)	Caucasian
European	European	European	European		European
White	White	White	White		White
Spanish		Spanish-American			
Spanish/American		Portuguese			
Portuguese		Puerto Rican			
		Cuban			
		Hindu			
		West Indian			

Negro	Black	Black	Black	Black or Negro
Black Negro Mulatto	Black Negro (Coded according to appearance as reported by resident institution)	Black Negro Mulatto African Abyssinian	Black Negro Mulatto (Must not be of Hispanic origin)	Black Negro Mulatto
Mexican/Latin American Mexican/American Latin Latin-American	**Mexican/American** Mexican Mexican/American Latin Latin/American	**Spanish-speaking surname** Mexican Mexican/American Central or South American Puerto Rican Cuban Other Spanish culture	**Hispanic** Mexican Mexican/American Central or South American Puerto Rican Cuban Other Spanish culture	**Spanish/Hispanic origin** Mexican Mexican/American Central or South American Puerto Rican Cuban Other Spanish culture
Hispanic Latin/American Puerto Rican Cuban Other Spanish culture				
Indian American Indian	**Native American** American Indian Eskimo	**American Indian** American Indian	**Indian** American Indian Native Indian Eskimo Alaskan Native	**American Indian** American Indian
American Indian American Indian Native Indian				
Chinese **Japanese**	**Chinese** **Japanese**	**Asian** Chinese Japanese Korean Manchurian Burmese Siamese Indochinese	**Asian** Chinese Japanese Korean	**Chinese** **Japanese**

(continued)

Table 5.6 *(continued)*

Agency by Classification Used[1] and Groups Included

California Department of Justice BCS/SS, Bureau of Criminal Investigation	California Department of Justice Bureau of Organized Crime and Criminal Intelligence	California Department of Corrections	California Youth Authority	Standardized Crime Reporting System (SCRS)	California Department of Finance,[2] California Department of Health Services,[3] U.S. Census Bureau
				Filipino	
				Other Asian	
				Other Pacific Islander	
Filipino	Not used	Filipino	Filipino	Not used	Filipino
Other	Other	All other	Other	Not used	Other
Hawaiian	Hawaiian	Hawaiian	Hawaiian		Hawaiian
Samoan			Samoan		Samoan
Guamanian					Guamanian
East Indian					Asian Indian
Indonesian					
Cuban					
Puerto Rican					
Eskimo	Eskimo				Eskimo
Alaskan	Alaskan				Aleut
Eurasian					
Turkish					
Creole					
Other Oriental					

All other

All other

Polynesian
Guatemalan
Aborigine
All other

Korean
Vietnamese

Notes:
1. Underlined names are major classifications used by agency.
2. California Department of Finance–Population Unit.
3. California Department of Health Services–Vital Statistics Section.

race-ethnicity is a factor of appearance alone; that the categories are clear, discrete, bounded, scientifically grounded, and existing in nature, in the "real" world; that race-ethnic identity is self-evident. Mixed race is not a possibility: police officers have been instructed to fill in only one category for each person reported on; incomplete reports are returned to the originating department. A senior law enforcement consultant for the California Police Officers and Standards Commission, who trains police officers in coding information for the CLETS program, said that he encourages the use of "Unknown" for mixed-race persons (or when the officer is unsure of the person's race). One of the Charlie PD officers interviewed said that he indicates "the race the suspect most wants to identify with." The police chief in Baker marks "Other" or "Unknown" in the case of a suspect who self-identifies as belonging to two or more groups.

In all three cities' PDs, if a suspect refuses to identify him- or herself by race-ethnicity, police officers fill in the category based on the suspect's physical appearance—typically, skin color, hair texture, and other facial features, or accent in the case of Hispanics. Two officers interviewed from Charlie PD said that if a suspect gives one race-ethnic identity but looks like a different one, they will mark the category that corresponds with appearance—hence, the sort of situation in which a single individual is variously identified on different occasions.

Race-ethnic crime data are used both for statistical analyses of criminal activity and for descriptive purposes for the apprehension of suspects or for locating missing persons. This is undeniably important, for humanitarian as well as protective reasons. But using only the broader, lumpier categories requires that identification rest on the central prototype of each category. The missing "White" child has blond hair and blue eyes; the "Hispanic" suspect has dark hair, eyes, and skin and speaks accented English. To judge from the categories they use, law enforcement "Adams" in California, like their hospital counterparts, have a far more nuanced experience of people of Asian origins than of other groups. But what police reports reflect are data based on appearance, not race or ethnicity, when that does not necessarily match self-identification and at a time when the standard categories are increasingly less viable shorthand surrogates for appearance.

Race-ethnic data collection in PDs serves a third purpose, in addition to numerical tracking and description. The data are used to develop local or statewide services or programs. When data indicate a higher prevalence of a particular sort of crime within one population (see, e.g., Table 5.5), officers can be trained to target those specifics, both in terms of community awareness programs and PD prevention practices and apprehension. Categorical lumpiness—the creation and perception of superficial similarities—can create problems here, however, of the sort in the "Asian" crime problem described at the beginning of the chapter.

The data are also used for internal tracking, both to monitor and to protect police officers. Charlie PD uses the data to make sure that its officers are not unfairly arresting particular groups based on race-ethnicity (the problem of "racial profiling"). Baker PD uses the data to evaluate the community's charges of arrests provoked by racism. The data allow police administrators to determine whether officers are targeting a category of crime or a particular geographic area, or whether, indeed, members of a specific race-ethnic group are being disproportionately arrested. Here is where crimes against a specific group—so-called hate crimes or bias crimes—would not show up if only the lumpy categories are used.

The drug investigation report form that follows in Table 5.7 suggests a way to think about observer-based descriptions that are not necessarily linked to race-ethnic-based descriptions. They are highly detailed—too much so, probably, for a routine suspect apprehension under "normal" (i.e., highly stressful) field conditions (although less problematic, perhaps, for missing persons searches). But they suggest appearance and behavior-related categories that could be useful in quickly forming an accurate image of suspect or victim—with more accuracy than current "eyeballing" practices. And they point toward a way of thinking about the wider set of problems, by addressing the question, "What is it that we want or need to know?"—ironically more specific a question than "What is the subject's race-ethnicity?"

The Human and Statistical Costs of Identity Practices: Identifying Job Trainees

One of the Charlie PD officers indicated that he felt very uncomfortable with the whole classification problem and with making racial determinations on report forms. "We tend not to look at that information too closely," he said, because the city's nine categories are reduced to four in the state report. Training in race-ethnic identification would be difficult, he said, because it is such a charged subject.

Race-ethnic data collection practices were also troublesome for personnel implementing the federal Job Training and Partnership Act (JTPA) of 1975, which replaced the Comprehensive Employment and Training Act (CETA). It provides job training for several categories of individuals, administered through local service providers.[10] There are three areas of eligibility for program services: General (requiring proof of legal state residence and citizenship status); Economic (requiring proofs of income, welfare

Table 5.7

Descriptive Details on Drug Reports

11550 H & S INVESTIGATION REPORT			CASE NUMBER	DATE
REASON FOR CONTACT:				

THE SUSPECT EXHIBITED THE FOLLOWING OBJECTIVE SYMPTOMS:

EYES	PUPIL SIZE/REACTIVITY			PUPIL RESPONSE		
☐ WATERY	SUSPECT	AT SCENE	AT FACILITY	SUSPECT	REACTION	OFFICER
☐ GLASSY	INITIAL SIZE	___ mm	___ mm	☐	SLUGGISH	☐
☐ BLOODSHOT	REACTED TO	___ mm	___ mm	☐	JERKY	☐
☐ DROOPY	COMPARISON SUBJECT	NAME:	NAME:	☐	IRRITATED	☐
☐ YELLOWISH	INITIAL SIZE	___ mm	___ mm	☐	SMOOTH	☐
☐ FOCUSED	REACTED TO	___ mm	___ mm	☐	RAPID	☐
☐ UNFOCUSED	☐ GLASSES ☐ CONTACTS ☐ OTHER___			☐	HIPUS	☐
☐ IRRITATED				☐	NOT VISIBLE	☐

NYSTAGMUS

LEFT: ☐ HORIZONTAL ☐ VERTICAL   RIGHT: ☐ HORIZONTAL ☐ VERTICAL ☐ NONE

EXAMINATION BY:_____WITNESSED BY:_____

LOCATION:_____LIGHTING:_____

MECHANICAL AIDS: FLASHLIGHT/TYPE_____ ☐ PUPILOMETER ☐ MAGNIFER

DEMEANOR	SPEECH	SKIN	BALANCE/COORDINATION
☐ COOPERATIVE	☐ NORMAL	☐ NORMAL	☐ NORMAL
☐ DEPRESSED	☐ THICK	☐ SCABS	☐ SWAYS
☐ DISORIENTED	☐ SLURRED	☐ COLD-CLAMMY	☐ STAGGERS
☐ ARGUMENTATIVE	☐ EXCITED	☐ SCRATCHING	☐ UNABLE TO STAND
☐ NERVOUS	☐ INCOHERENT	☐ SWEATING	☐ DELIBERATE
☐ DOCILE	☐ SLOW	☐ BAD COMPLEXION	☐ LETHARGIC
☐ VIOLENT	☐ DELIBERATE	☐ OPEN SORES	☐ RIGID
☐ AGGRESSIVE	☐ REPETITIVE	☐ ABSCESSES	☐ UNCOORDINATED
☐ NONRESPONSIVE	☐ DISJOINTED	☐ VISIBLE "TRACKS"	☐ ABNORMAL

PHOTOGRAPHS TAKEN: ☐ YES ☐ NO   TAKEN BY_____   TIME/DATE_____

REPORTING OFFICER	ID#	DATE AND TIME OF REPORT	APPROVED BY	DATE

Table 5.8

Eligibility Verification Checklist for JTPA Services

TITLE II ELIGIBILITY VERIFICATION CHECKLIST

Participant's Name_____   Social Security Number_____

GENERAL ELIGIBILITY

_____Residence   _____Selective Service
                                                 Registrant
_____Age   (only males born on or after Jan. 1, 1960)
                                       ( ) 708-688-6888 No._____
_____Citizen Alien Status

ECONOMIC ELIGIBILITY

_____Cash Welfare   _____Family Income

_____Family Size   _____Family Member's Income

_____Food Stamps   _____Homeless Persons or
                                                 Run-away Youth
_____Supported Foster Child   _____Individual with a
                                                 Disability
_____Eligibility for Free Meals   _____Participating in Compensatory
                                                 Education Program
_____10% Exception/Special Rule

HARD TO SERVE

_____Basic Skills   _____Behind Grade level

_____Pregnant or Parenting   _____School Dropout

_____Recipients of Cash Welfare   _____Offender

_____Individual With a Disability _____Homeless Persons or
                                                 Run-away Youth
_____SDA Designated Category

TITLE II PROGRAMS ELIGIBLE FOR

___II-A (Adult)   ___II-A (Older Individual)   ___II-B (SYETP)

___II-C (In-School)   ___II-C (Out of School)   ___II 8% (Education)

_____   _____
Signature of Intake Worker   Date Completed

The eligibility verification checklist can serve a variety of purposes. It can serve as a desk aid to assure that all appropriate Title II eligibility criteria are discussed, as a file contents list, and as a summary of a clients eligibility. Eligibility criteria that were satisfied can be checked, dated or the type of documentation in the client's file can be written in.

SDA's may find the checklist to be a useful starting point for developing a more useful tool of their own.

Table 5.9

California JTPA Registration Form (revised 7/93)

EDD Serving the People of California

Application Number
3343491

1 Social Security Number

JTPA REGISTRATION FORM

ELIGIBILITY INFORMATION

2 Application Date	3 Component ID	4 Last Name		First	Middle

5 Street Address	6 Residence City	7 Residence ZIP	8 Residence Telephone
			( )

9 Mailing Address	10 Mailing City, State ZIP	11 Message Phone	12 Geo Code
		( )	

13 Citizen	14 Document #	15 Gender	16 Birthdate	17 Age	18 Sel Svc Reg	19 Homeless	20 Veteran Type	21 Separation Date
1 Yes					1 Yes	1 Yes	1 Vietnam Era	
2 Eligible Non-citizen		1 Male			2 No	2 No	2 Recently Separated	
3 Ineligible Non-citizen		2 Female			3 NA		3 Disabled	
					4 Exempt		4 Other	
							X Not Applicable	

22 Number in Family	24 Family Status (Min. Fam Size)	25 Annualized Family Income	26 Foster Child	27 Family GA	28 Family SSI/SSP	33 Applicant is on Welfare Grant:
	1 Single Head of Household with Dependent Children (2)	$	1 Yes	1 Yes	1 Yes	1 AFDC
23 Dependents Under Age 18	2 Single Head of Household (2)	29 Income Elig	30 Family AFDC	31 Family RCA	32 Food Stamps	2 GA
	3 Parent in Two-Parent Family (3)	1 Yes	2 No	1 Yes	2 No	1 Eligible	3 SSI
	4 Family Member (2)	2 No		2 No		2 Receiving	4 RCA
	5 Non-Dependent (1)					3 No	5 SSP
						6 Not Applicable

34 Long Term AFDC	35 GAIN/JOBS	36 School Lunch	37 Economically Disadvantaged		38 Dislocated Worker
1 Yes	1 Yes	1 Yes	1 Yes Public Assistance Family Homeless		1 Terminated or Laid off
2 No	2 No	2 No	2 No Food Stamp Recipient Income Eligible		2 Laid off due to plant closure
			Foster Child		3 Long Term Unemployed
39 Disabled	40 Comp Ed Prog Participant	41 Not Economically Disadvantaged			4 Not Applicable
1 Yes - Voc Rehab	1 Yes	1 YES 10% "Window" Factors			5 Self-Employed
2 Yes - Other	2 No	2 No for Non-Economically Disadvantaged:			6 Additional Dislocated Worker
3 No					(Displaced Homemaker)
		Limited English Lang Prof Offender			
42 Title V OAA Eligible	43 School-Wide Project Attendee	44 Farmworker	Dropout Older Worker		45 Dislocated Worker Hourly Wage (Title III Only)
1 Yes	1 Yes	1 Migrant	Pregnant / Parenting Youth Veteran		
2 No	2 No	2 Seasonal	Disabled Displaced Homemaker		
		3 No	Substance Abuse Other (Specify)		

46 Redeemed CCE	48 Ethnicity			49 Eligible	D Title IIA /OAA
1 Yes	1 White - Not Hispanic	6.2 Cambodian	6.8 Korean	A Title IIA	E Title IVC
2 No	2 Black - Not Hispanic	6.3 Chinese	6.9 Laotian	B Title IIB	F Title IIC
	3 Hispanic	6.4 Filipino	6.10 Samoan	C Title III	X Not Eligible
47 Issued CCE	4 American Indian/ Alaskan Native	6.5 Guamanian	6.11 Vietnamese	50 Date of Eligibility Determination	
1 Yes	6.1 Asian Indian	6.6 Hawaiian	6.12 Other Asian/		
2 No		6.7 Japanese	Pacific Islander		

DEMOGRAPHIC INFORMATION

1 Read Grade	2 Reading Score	3 Reading Test	4 Reading Form	5 Math Grade	6 Math Score	7 Math Test	8 Math Form

9 Reading Below 7th Grade	10 Math Below 7th Grade	11 Basic Skills Deficient	12 Below Grade Level
1 Yes 2 No	1 Yes 2 No	1 Yes 2 No	1 Yes 2 No
3 Not Available	3 Not Available	3 Not Available	3 Not Available

13 Runaway	14 Potential Dropout	15 Pregnant Youth	16 Parenting Youth
1 Yes 2 No	1 Yes 2 No	1 Yes 2 No	1 Yes 2 No

17 Substance Abuse	18 Limited English	19 Offender	20 Lacks Work History
1 Yes 2 No	1 Yes 2 No	1 Yes - Non-Felon 2 Yes - Felon	1 Yes 2 No
		3 No	

21 Displaced Homemaker	22 SDA-Defined Barrier	23 Multiple Barriers	24 Highest Grade Completed
1 Yes 2 No	1 Yes 2 No	1 Yes 2 No	

25 Education Status	26 School Type	27 In School	28 School Attendance
1 School Dropout	4 Post HS	1 Elementary 5 4-yr College/Univ	1 Yes	1 Full-Time
2 Student	5 College Grad &	2 Secondary 6 Not Applicable	2 No	2 Part-Time
3 HS Grad or Equiv	Above	3 Trade/Tech/Voc 7 Alternative	3 Not Applicable	3 Not Applicable
		4 Junior/Com College		

29 Target Group	30 Labor Force Status	31 Date Became Unemployed	32 Weeks Unemployed	33 Hourly Wage Last 26 Weeks
1 Adult 3 Yth-Out-Sch	1 Employed Full Time 3 Unemployed			
2 Yth-In-Sch 4 NA	2 Employed Part Time 4 Not in Labor Force			

34 Job Code	35 Employed	36 Unemployment Insurance	Application Exp Date
	1 Below Skill Potential	1 Current 5 Claimant - Pending	
	2 At Entry, Semi/Unskilled Job	2 Not Eligible Determination	
Job Title	3 With No Advance Opportunity	3 Exhausted 6 Not Filed	Level of Need
	4 Not Employed/Not Applicable	4 Claimant 7 Not Applicable	

Client Certification: My signature below indicates that I have been informed of and understand the information contained on this form. I certify under penalty of perjury that all of the above information is true and complete. I agree that any information I have supplied is subject to verification. I understand that falsification of any item is grounds for termination for the JTPA program and may result in action to recover any moneys paid to me while participating.

Signature of Client	Date	Signature of Parent or Guardian	Date

Signature of Interviewer	Staff Code	Date	Signature of Reviewer	Staff Code	Date

Note: See Item 48, Ethnicity.

supports, family size, homelessness, or disability); and Hard to Serve (a "multiple barrier population," combining prior schooling levels with welfare support, disability, pregnancy and/or parenting status, and other information; see Table 5.8). Race-ethnicity was dropped as an eligibility criterion in 1993, but race-ethnic information is still tracked at county and state levels to comply with the 1964 Civil Rights Act (see Table 5.9). The Department of Labor's Employment Development Training, Job Training Division allocates funds to local service delivery areas based on these statistics.

According to the JTPA data analysis manager in one California county, there has been no significant problem with applicants completing the race-ethnic portion of the form. An incomplete form cannot be processed. If race-ethnic identity is missing, "We either choose an identity based on their name, or we ask the eligibility specialist to complete it" on the basis of observer identification. This forces the employee-observer to act as an ad hoc member of the applicant's "community" for the administrative purpose of assessing how the applicant would be perceived by actual members of that community.

The street-level bureaucrats and their managers in the service agencies are troubled by this state of affairs. A manager at one of the service-providing agencies said:

> The higher-ups may not see this issue as a big deal, but the question has come up as to what if somebody doesn't fit into one category or another? Basically, you are one or the other. Occasionally you get somebody that says, "Well, I am not Black and I am not Hispanic"; or "I'm color blind"; or "I'm a child of the universe, and so I do not want to choose." Then you do the best you can. It's a tricky issue.
>
> My response to that would be, "I understand where you are coming from, but I have got to fill the form out and you have to choose one of these. If you want to get through this process, let's just make it easy and choose one." Usually at that point a person says, "All right, I guess if I have to choose, I am this."

He added:

> This is real and it does happen, and it seems like a minor thing; but it puts administrators and supervisors in an awkward position. What do you do if a person does not want to fill this out? There is no real answer at this time.

An Intake and Eligibility Specialist at the service agency agreed:

> Even though sometimes I know what a person's ethnicity is, I still have to ask, and I usually say, "What is your ethnicity?" The only times that I find

that there is a question is when a person's mother or father is from a different background than the other [parent].

Asked what she did then, she answered:

I don't tell them what to choose. If they are of mixed heritage, I just ask them which one they choose or identify with most often, or if they fill out other forms, which one they pick.[11]

For most of the agency's employees, the issue of race-ethnic identity is merely a matter of filling out a form to comply with JTPA regulations. For some former trainees, being asked to identify themselves by race or ethnicity is also routine. For others, it provokes pause. A woman who completed training as a legal secretary, who identifies herself as Hispanic, said:

At first I wanted to know what this was being used for and why they wanted to classify me in a certain category. On employment applications I feel intimidated, because I wonder if I mark something or if I decide not to choose, what will that do to my chances of getting a job? I also think that it is interesting that on almost all of the forms that ask about race, "White" is always at the top.

Another woman, born in the Philippines, said she had always checked "Other" until someone told her that "Other" was never counted. She wondered why there was no separate Filipino category:

I have always been confused when I have to check a box about my heritage. I am not Asian or Pacific Islander, and I am not Hispanic. I just don't fit in. Then I was told to check "Asian" when I was looking for a job. It doesn't bother me to check Asian, but I still wonder why.

She has also thought about this issue in another context because her son's father, her first husband, was Caucasian. Asked how she identifies her son when asked to fill out forms, she said: "I check 'White.' He is an American, born in the United States, and he is an American, so that is White." Her son is often confused, she said: children at his school call him "Chinese" because of his complexion, and that upsets him. He has asked her, "Mom, what am I?" She tells him, "You are an American. Your father was White and I am Filipino." He has become even more confused, she says, because she is now married to a man of Mexican heritage.

The problem of identifying individuals based on their appearance has arisen in other policy and administrative contexts as well, including in legislative debates during the crafting of the Immigration Reform and Control Act (IRCA) of 1986. The bill required employers to establish that prospective employees are in the United States legally. Opponents argued that this would result in legal immigrants who looked "like foreigners" or who spoke with accents—the concern was primarily with Latino/a Americans—being treated as if they were illegal residents. Indeed, the Government Accounting Office, in a 1990 report, established that after IRCA passed, "891,000 employers began discriminating against US citizens who appear [to be] or are foreign-born, among whom Latinos and Asians number disproportionately" (Haney López 1994, p. 4, n. 11).

Blood Versus Culture: Adoption

Infant and child adoption is a policy and administrative area in which identification and category-making practices are brought into sharp relief, as they affect the feelings of administrators and adult and young clients (or program participants) alike.

Anecdotal evidence suggests that categorizing practices can, at times, be convoluted. One new mother reported:

> Baby J's birth mother is of Scandinavian descent. Her birth father is of Spanish and Guatemalan descent. She . . . is being brought up by a New York Ashkenazi Jew [i.e., of Eastern European heritage] living in a [Northeastern] university town with Latin American influence on child-rearing [practices deriving from] and based on my [research].
>
> A friend keeps trying to insist she's [the baby] a "person of color." . . . I, on the other hand, insist [that] that is a racialization of culture, and [that] she is not. How should she fill out the census?
>
> An African-American friend . . . independently agreed with me that she [the baby] goes down as my ethnicity, because culturally she is [my ethnicity]. . . . If she were clearly Guatemalan indigenous looking, that would be different.
>
> . . . Another interesting addendum here is that on some papers he filled out, her birth father self-identifies his, his parents', and his kids' race variously as Hispanic, white, [or] European.[12]

The mother goes on to note that she will be getting a new birth certificate identifying her as the mother. She remarks on the extent to which that change, the baby's upbringing, and her physiognomy will allow her to escape "color prejudices," in that they will mask her birth identity.

Here, too, we see the limits of statistical data. It is also an example of passing when the choice is made by a parent for a child too young to make that choice herself (see also Isaacs 1995). Other adoption narratives, whether by those adopted or by their parents, indicate similar convolutions in fitting complex race-ethnic heritages into contemporary American categories, and ensuing issues concerning self-perception, self-understanding, and sense making. But the example also illustrates some of the central features in current debates over adoption policies, particularly the matter of adoption across race-ethnic lines.

The Multi-Ethnic Placement Act—Interethnic Adoption Provisions (MEPA-IAP) of 1996 (an amended version of MEPA 1994) was intended to address the fact that a large percentage of the adoptable children dependent on the federal welfare system are non-White, and their wait until adoption is much longer than that of White children.[13] MEPA 1996 extends Title VI (of the Civil Rights Acts of 1964) protections to prospective adopters and prospective adopted children. The act prohibits states and other agencies receiving federal moneys from limiting foster care or adoption, in either recruitment or placement, on the basis of the prospective parent's or the child's "race, color or national origin." Beginning in the late 1960s, people involved in adoption proceedings, among them many African-Americans (in particular, the National Association of Black Social Workers) and Native Americans, argued that allowing White adults to adopt Black and Indian children harmed or even destroyed their "racial" identity and amounted to "cultural genocide" (see Egan 1993). By the late 1980s–early 1990s, the practice of "race matching"—placing children with adoptive parents of the same race-ethnic identity—was seen as the reason that large numbers of Black and other non-White children were not being adopted. There were many more prospective White parents than there were White children available for adoption. The 1996 provisions made it illegal to restrict adoption to same-race-ethnic matches.

"Race matching" and cultural preservation are set up, in this debate, as complementary values, the one implicating the other. But contemporary American race-ethnic practices can actually set them up as opposing forces. The implication, for example, of grouping individuals within reified, lumpy categories could bring about a situation under race matching in which an Asian-American child of Indian birth parents could be placed with an Asian-American family of Japanese heritage. Even though that would not be, under American category rules, cross-race placement, it could very well still create conditions for possible "cultural genocide." The implications of assigning race-ethnic identity by visual markers, thereby privileging "color" (physiognomy) over "culture" (heritage), could have exactly the opposite effect on preserving race-ethnic ties. If "race matching" depends on establishing a physical resemblance based on skin color, one might pass a child into the race-ethnicity that he or she most matches—for example, placing a Pilipino child who looks Chinese with Chinese-American parents, or a very light-skinned Black child with a White family. But this transracial color matching also potentially creates conditions for possible "cultural genocide."

Social workers and the agencies implementing MEPA-IAP are committed to making adoption placements in the best interests of the child. The disagreements arise over what those are. They are seen most clearly when debate treats race-ethnic identity as a surrogate for class. Are non-White children's best interests served better when they are allowed to remain in the family or community of their race-ethnic heritage, or are they better served when children are adopted into White—which usually means, in these cases, middle class or higher, societally dominant—families? Or, are they better served when they are placed with a willing parent, whatever that parent's race-ethnic (or class) background, rather than allowed to languish in a series of foster homes or other temporary locations? Since White prospective parents and non-White prospective adoptees outnumber others, such placement almost certainly entails creating cross-racial families and an uncertain future for the child's non-White heritage. Should parental, societal, and state efforts—and, by extension, the efforts of the social workers and other street-level bureaucrats representing and implementing state policy—be to ensure that all children have the chance of escaping the burdens and limitations of "color prejudice"? Does that of necessity imply cross-racial placements?

We are faced here with seemingly incommensurable values that are able to escape notice or masquerade beneath other concerns in other policy issues, but in this arena are brought into high relief: the desire to preserve ties to a cultural heritage, while escaping discriminations associated with some of those heritages that attach to physiognomy and/or accent. It is in adoption debates that "race" and "ethnicity"—in the sense of "blood" or "color" and "culture," both intersecting with country or continent of origin—are most closely melded into a "race-ethnic" identity.

Service Provision and Lumpy, Reified Categories

Dear Back Fence:
. . . So I went to the [public] school [to register my son]. . . .
When I was asked if he was white, black, Asian, Hispanic
or other, I put "other." He is an American.
School staff told me I can't put that because they don't have that
as a qualifier. Because my last name is of Spanish origin,
they put down Hispanic. I'm of every ethnic background—
Heinz 57. I was born here and so was my child,

but because I have a Spanish surname, he was labeled Hispanic.
. . . I guess this shows that our schools aren't looking out
for the basics but a quota on educational funding.
                            —Upset about labeling
                            (*Orange County Register*, September 29, 1996)

Many policy choices and administrative actions reflect the characteristics of category making and identity construction: reified concepts, "lumpy" categories, a presumed "essence" that enables visual identification. Policy makers and implementors inherit and are party to category logic and the problems associated with it, which were identified in chapter 1 and illustrated in chapter 3: they act as though they were dealing with a fixed set of categories that are readily apparent, unambiguous, and scientifically sound. This diverts attention from the fact that choices are being made, including policy choices, in the treatment of race and ethnicity and in the creation of race-ethnic categories. The politics of problem definition, in other words, play out in the creation of labels antecedent, cognitively, to the perception of policy problems.

Reification and "lumpiness" interact in interesting ways. The treatment of race-ethnic categories as scientific entities allows agencies to mandate "objective" supervisory identification of "clients" (patients, students, victims, suspects, and so on) without inquiring into those individuals' self-identification. The lumpiness of the categories enables the treatment of people marked by differences as if they were alike, without attending to the problems and errors that might arise in doing so, under the assumption that these actions are scientifically grounded.

Categorical lumpiness directs attention away from ways in which members assigned to each category are not alike; yet such differences may be important in the provision of services. Many universities recruiting underrepresented students, for example, have counted large numbers of "Asian-Americans" in their student bodies, disproportionate to their presence in the surrounding population. University Affirmative Action officers see that "Asian-Americans" are adequately represented, leading them to curtail outreach efforts, scholarship funds, and other sources of aid directed to "Asian-Americans." Many "Asian-Americans," on the other hand, see themselves as comprising highly differentiated groups. In their view, few Vietnamese, Pilipino, Thai, and other "Asian"-origin peoples are enrolled in universities. Nearly 60 percent of (Asian) Indians in the United States and 40 percent of Chinese have at least a B.A., whereas the numbers for Cambodians and Hmong are 6 percent and 3 percent, respectively (Sengupta 1997). From this perspective, continued and differentiated efforts to recruit members of these underrepresented groups are still necessary (see, e.g., Magner 1993), but a program directed at "Asian-Americans" is unlikely to accomplish this.

The story with which this chapter began is another example of this set of problems. A key question needed to be asked and, seemingly, was not: What is the specific Asian-American (or Oriental) community involved (e.g., Hmong, Thai, Chinese from Beijing)? In identifying the crime problem as an "Asian-American" problem, the police department seemingly paid no attention to incompatibilities and conflicts that might arise if the new hire were from an Asian background other than the local one. For one, physical features and nonverbal behavior (such as gestures and posture) differ from one Asian-origin group to another. An Indian from Bombay or a Pilipino would be no more accepted (let alone succeed undercover) in a Chinese community than an Irish- or African-American. Nor would a Japanese-American officer be successful at infiltrating a Korean-American community, because of physical and cultural differences, let alone historical hostilities, between Japanese and Koreans.[14] Even if the new hire were from the same ethnic community, but of a different social class, she or he might be equally as unsuccessful as any non-Asian. The conceptual error of thought in this case is similar to the actual error that sent a Chinese-speaking elementary school student in Oakland to a bilingual class studying in English and Vietnamese (Sengupta 1997, pp. 1, 17).

The naming "Adam" in both cases saw only "Asian-Americans," whereas many "Asian-Americans" see meaningful differences among themselves.[15] If city officials in Milpitas, California—the first "majority-Asian" city in the region, at 55 percent of the population by the Census 2000 count—were to design programs for an "Asian" population, thinking that they were addressing the "cultural diversity" of their residents, without attending to its internally differentiated composition of highly educated Chinese and Indians, including Sikhs, and blue-collar Pilipinos and Vietnamese, it is likely that the programs would not address the interests or needs of the different groups. Some also see differences within subcategories, as in the following example from an academic research project. In 1979–80 a team of researchers set out to explore how various Boston-area neighborhoods resolved disputes out of court. Preliminary research had found that members of older generations often mediated neighborhood disputes that otherwise would likely have ended up on court dockets. The researchers chose Chinatown as one research site because one member of the team was Chinese-American. After several weeks of unsuccessful efforts to get local residents to speak with him about their disputes, that researcher advised the principal investigators to choose another site. He had discovered that his access to community members was blocked because, coming from another city and state in the United States, he and his family were unknown to the local Chinese community. Moreover, his parents came from a different part of China than the ancestors of the Boston community, and the "Bostonians" were unwilling to disclose private matters to someone they therefore perceived as a stranger. He thought it was also possible that he was too "Americanized"—his Chinese was American-accented, he could not use chopsticks—for the older generation he was attempting to interview.

The preceding cases, especially the birth and police identification ones, highlight the role played by the needs of statistical analysis in determining race-ethnic practices. The problems of comparability of data across countings and the lumpiness of categories intersected in the 1990 census. The Census Bureau itself has not been consistent in its decisions about statistical comparability across time. The bureau had decided to use a different set of API listings in 1990 from those used in the 1980 census. Asian-Americans successfully protested the decision. One of their central arguments was that community service funding depended on the categories that had been established in 1980, and a different set of categories would affect ongoing program funding.

Another problem arose as well. The bureau had indicated, separately, that it might not provide a tabulation for the subgroups at all. The National Coalition for Accurate Count of Asian Pacific Americans called for detailed information: to do otherwise, the coalition said, will "exacerbate the undercount of Asians and Pacific Islanders, diminish the ability of social service providers to target services to the needy, and undermine the aspirations of Asians and Pacific Islanders for fair, adequate political representation." The executive director of San Francisco's Chinese for Affirmative Action, Henry Der, wrote in a letter dated December 9, 1987, to Mr. Ed Hatcher in the office of Congressman Robert Matsui (D-Sacramento) that the lack of a 100 percent head count of API subgroups would affect implementation of affirmative action programs in California for unlisted and untabulated groups. Furthermore, "the federal Voting Rights Act requires that the provision of bilingual election coverage can only be triggered by separate, distinct racial/linguistic minority groups. Asian American populations cannot be lumped together in order to determine federal Voting Rights Act coverage." Der remarked, "Recent immigrants from Vietnam do not view themselves as Asian Americans" (Chin 1988, p. A16). California's provision of bilingual services, he noted, is also dependent on a "threshold percentage of specific racial/linguistic groups" as determined by the census. Furthermore, such lumping would not capture the socioeconomic distinctions among different API subgroups. For example, the mean annual income for Vietnamese males was $11,303; for Japanese, $21,466. The percentage of families below the poverty line ranged from 35 percent for Vietnamese; 13 percent for Koreans; 6 percent for Filipinos; to 4 percent for Japanese. According to Der, lumping of census data into a single category would affect the provision of social services to these various population groups (*San Francisco Examiner,* 3/16/88). An unsigned editorial in the *Examiner* (4/7/88) observed, "Socially, a lack of information contributes to stereotypes. A census that gathers information including the number of homes with air conditioners and TV sets surely can take the time to determine who we are and where we come from."

In the end, the bureau decided to use the same subcategories it had used in the 1980 census, with a provision for writing in a specific other API subgroup. But in the postcensus count, the issue arose in a different form: Asians and Pacific Islanders were to be counted together with Whites and American Indians not on reservations in the follow-up analysis adjusting for undercounted populations, as their numbers were not statistically significant on their own. After further negotiations, the bureau agreed to use separate categories in cities or regions where Asian-Americans constituted a sufficiently sizable proportion of the population.

Undifferentiated practices devolving from a perception and working definition of American race-ethnicities as undifferentiated, lumpy categories exist within other groups as well, including "Whites." In the tabulation of "hate crimes," for one example, administrative effectiveness is undermined by categorical lumpiness. Arab-Americans experience attacks of various sorts for reasons that can only be called "racial," in this context. But because they are counted as "Whites," community leaders suspect that anti-Arab attacks are unlikely to show up in tabulations of racially motivated hate crimes (Samhan 1993). Federal law enforcement agencies do not include "White" as a group that might be targeted as a race. Hence, police departments investigating attacks on mosques or community centers, for example, are not likely to have a category available on report forms for these incidents.[16]

Medical and related research is also subject to the conceptual limitations created by categorical lumpiness. The National Institute of Child Health and Human Development, for example, issued a Request For Proposals for awards to study "traditional beliefs, values, and responses to mental retardation and developmental disability of ethnic groups, formal and informal support systems that are most likely to be used by families in these groups, and the impact of ethnicity on families' interactions with various types of service agencies." The "ethnic minority populations" to be studied were listed as "African-American; Hispanic; Asian-American; and American-Indian" ("NIH

Guide for Grants and Contracts" 6/11/93, p. 11). The variety of different cultural practices within each of these lumpy categories suggests that findings for families of one subgroup might not readily generalize to others within each category.

Americans are being "colored" with a broad brush in a kind of "painting by numbers" in which the state assigns individuals and groups to categories in ways that are increasingly at odds with their self-perceptions, with outcomes that do not always achieve social justice ends. Social science research and its applications to public policy and administration bolster these state practices.

Notes

1. Contacts in the city and its police department requested that they and the city not be identified.

2. In my notes from the conference at which this essay was first presented, I recorded Segal as having identified his daughter as "Jewess" in the hospital records. Whether she was the first "Jewess" or the first "human" to be born in California is, of course, moot, but the story grounds the administrative practice in lived experience.

3. The NCHS is part of the Centers for Disease Control and Prevention within the Public Health Service of the U.S. Department of Health and Human Services.

4. I thank Lanamaria Smallwood for bringing this matrix to my attention.

5. It is clear that gender plays a role in the practice of identifying infants (broadly speaking) by their fathers' race-ethnic classification, but I have been unable to ascertain the reasoning behind it. It is certainly not universal practice to assign infants' identity in this way. Lott (1992–93) provides one historical clue when he notes that mid-seventeenth-century legislation in Virginia "stipulated that children born of a black woman would inherit her status, even when the father was white" (p. 185, n. 56). Census Bureau instructions to enumerators follow similar patterns (see chapter 3). According to Haney López (1994, p. 1), the legal determination of slave-free status established as long ago as 1806 followed the mother: "[a] person born to a slave woman was a slave, and a person born to a free woman was free." American Indian tribes vary in their membership practices, some requiring patrilineality, others, matrilineality (Wilson 1992, p. 121). Patrilineal designation, in other words, has not been uniform practice in the United States. And certainly, health issues argue more strongly in favor of identifying infants by their mother, as the NCHS came to see. In some cultures, children are seen as the property of the father; but I have been unable to establish this as the underlying principle here. I note that one custom among some Americans appears to follow this sense of ownership: the practice of a man asking his intended's father's permission for her "hand" in marriage, and the father "giving" the bride "away" at the wedding.

6. This possible explanation was first suggested to me by Professor Miguel Mendes, then at Stanford Law School. I have been unable to find written support for this in agency or governmental documents, or any agency official who can explain it, but it is supported by Jaimes's (1995, p. 141) example of Hawaiians in her discussion of blood quantum.

7. The technical appendix to this report notes that "deaths are classified by race—white, black, American Indian, Chinese, Hawaiian, Japanese, Filipino, Other Asian or Pacific Islander, and other." The white category includes Mexican, Puerto Rican, Cuban, and all other Caucasians. American Indian includes American, Alaskan, Canadian, Eskimo, and Aleut. A white/nonwhite mixture is "coded to the appropriate other race." Other mixtures are coded to the first race listed, except for any mixture including Hawaiian, which is coded as Hawaiian (U.S. Department of Health and Human Services 1994a, p. 25).

8. Gershon (n.d.b) notes the use of colonial censuses—her case is the German and Australian administrations of Papua New Guinea—to control "reproductive capabilities" (p. 5). Certainly, the U.S. census has been used, as all censuses have, to track the potential size of the country's military and labor forces, and following infant birth and death rates fits into such an estimation. I am not prepared to argue that American Indian birth rates are being intentionally suppressed in order to minimize tax redistribution to the state of California, although the California matrix does keep the "White" race "pure." But such an argument could well fit with the point she develops there, resting on Foucault's notions of "population" and control.

9. I am indebted to Barry Kalar and Amy Brown for research assistance on the three police departments discussed here. Because it is not my intention to analyze a single department, but rather to use their cases to illustrate a broader set of issues, I will not use the actual names of persons or departments. Interviews were conducted in February 1996 with the police chiefs of two of the cities, two officers responsible for data collection and reports in the third, and three people responsible for data collection, analysis, and training at the state level. One of the researchers was a participant-observer in one of the city PDs; analysis also included various local, state, and federal reports and departmental memos.

10. I thank Kelly Sherman for research assistance on the JTPA. Unless otherwise identified, the quotes in the following section come from interviews conducted on February 15 and 20, 1996.

11. In an interview, an Affirmative Action Officer at an area transit agency said that she would assign ethnicity to a mixed-race person, counting a "half Black, half White" person as African-American for statistical purposes, because the race codes are "used to determine if you are underrepresented by a certain race."

12. Personal communications by e-mail, August 4 and 5, 1998. I have chosen not to identify the mother. She also notes that she and the birth mother chose to mark the father's race-ethnic identity as unknown—although that apparently was not the case.

13. My thanks to Teresa O'Leary for research assistance in this area.

14. This is not the only area in which such "pairings" may not be thought out. Apparently, an ad developed for New York Life Insurance Co. oriented toward Koreans backfired—the model was Chinese (S. Johnson 1992).

15. A story about California rice production makes the same point in the context of trade relations. It seems that in 1993, Japan had a disastrous rice-growing season, brought on by excessive rains. This was seen as an opening by California rice growers, who had long been trying to overcome trade barriers. The first 7,560 tons of the 1.1 million-ton rice shipment, however, was the "wrong" variety of rice: seemingly in ignorance, they did not load the short-grain rice known to growers as M-401—a brand Japanese tourists take home as souvenirs—but rather a tasteless short-grain of pasty consistency (Noguchi 1993). From outside the community, rice, it would seem, is rice.

16. I thank Charles Friedman for bringing this to my attention.

6

Constructing Race-Ethnicity Through Social Science Research: Managing Workplace Diversity

Do You Have a Japanese American Parent
and a European American (White) Parent?

A dissertation study is being conducted for the purpose
of understanding how interracial parents relate with their
biracial children, and how ethnic identity develops.
If you are the first-born in your family, are 20–45 years old,
your parents were born in the United States,
and your Japanese American parent is either a second (Nisei)
or third (Sansei) generation Japanese American,
please consider participating in this study.

—University bulletin board, 1999[1]

Federal policies and their implementing agencies are not alone in constructing notions of race and ethnicity and American race-ethnic categories. Social scientists who study race-ethnicity in various contexts also play a role in constructing and reflecting current conceptions of these entities, as their published work often shapes the ways that public discourse develops, within the classroom and beyond. This is particularly the case for "applied" social science: those areas of research that are oriented toward applications of psychology, social psychology, and other fields to various areas of professional practice, such as public administration, management and organizational studies, and public policy analysis. Such research is often published in journals oriented toward practitioners, rather than for an academic readership alone. And it is often conducted by researchers who themselves are involved in the world of practice (such as organizational or management consulting), rather than following academic careers.

As an example of the ways in which scholarly work constructs the concepts and categories of race-ethnicity, Chock (1995b), in analyzing the entries in the Harvard *Encyclopedia of American Ethnic Groups,* found that the editors tended to provide more descriptive detail for those groups closer to their own race-ethnicity, while not making that identity explicit. She found that white ethnic groups were described as having "an abundance of cultures and therefore many differences among them. . .; [whereas] non-white ethnic groups [were seen as having] fewer cultures, hence fewer differences" (p. 308).* Such differential treatment has taken place even outside the social sciences. A major review of published papers in epidemiology found that although reference to "race" rose steadily from 1975 on, it was not matched by a parallel increase in "nonwhite" subjects: research was being based on predominantly "white" study populations (Jones, LaVeist, and Lillie-Blanton 1991).

When such taxonomic and experimental research achieves a nonacademic audience—through newspaper accounts, television and radio reports, and magazine articles, for example—it is accorded "scientific" status by virtue of its origins in the academy and the academy's publishing outlets, with their own standards of peer review. The standing of "Science" in contemporary society as a concept and as a practice, represented by these academic affiliations, lends weight to the concepts of race and ethnicity and their associated categories, thereby contributing to the reality-making social construction process. Race and ethnicity come to seem more and more natural, even though most scientists (both social and natural) now consider them socially constructed concepts; their attendant American categories have also come, in this fashion, to acquire a more fixed and objective ontological character. Academic research has contributed to the construction of contemporary race-ethnic categories and identities, implicitly and perhaps tacitly contributing to the maintenance of those categories and race-ethnic concepts as if they were scientific. Treating social constructions as if they were objectively and factually scientific, while forgetting or ignoring this "as if" quality, has important implications for research and administrative practices. It follows from an assumption that "race" and "ethnicity" are scientific concepts that the category names for race-ethnic groups also

---

*Throughout this chapter race-ethnic names are used as given in the research cited (e.g., "white" in the previous sentence rather than "White"). Where not citing others' research, I have used the names preferred currently by the group in question (e.g., "Asian-American" rather than "Oriental"), where this is known and common practice.

embody scientific reality. This can be seen particularly in research articles published in both academic and practitioner journals oriented toward interventions (e.g., through training programs) in what has been called "workplace cultural diversity" and its management. Their presumed scientific character explains the lack of analytic reflection in the articles on race-ethnic concepts.

My intention here, as elsewhere in this book, is not to claim that "race" and "ethnicity" *are* terms that capture unambiguously distinct features of the human population and that researchers should be more careful not to mix them. Rather, I wish to show that whereas these are social constructions reflecting particular historical arguments of the times of their creation and use, they are being used in these articles *as if* they were ahistorical, unambiguous, scientifically grounded terms. In a circular, hermeneutic process, the articles assume the natural, scientific character of the categories and concepts. In turn, through their publication in scientific and practitioner-oriented journals, adhering to the criteria for scientific writing (including the use of citations and footnotes, methods statements, quotes from interview subjects and experts in the field, and so on), they further contribute to the maintenance of the idea of that scientific character.[2] The analysis in this chapter is an approach to the study of science that seeks to explore what it is that scientists actually do, including in their writings. As the focus is social science applied to everyday practices, I am also exploring the implications of those acts for public discourse, including public policy and administration.[3]

Organizational researchers collect and use race-ethnic data in two administrative areas. Employee demographic data are collected to comply with federal Affirmative Action/Equal Employment Office (AA/EEO) legislation, as well as to respond to communal and societal demands to diversify the workforce—to add women and members of non-White race-ethnic groups. In addition to this human resource management function, many agencies collect race-ethnic data on their clients for service and programmatic reasons, usually to comply with federal regulations, as we saw in the previous chapter. This chapter looks at articles published in both academic and practitioner journals on the changing race-ethnic character of agency personnel, showing how they reflect the contemporary understanding of race, ethnicity, and the standard categories. As these articles become the basis for training and development programs and are read by students in professional degree programs preparing for administrative and other careers, the perceptions of American race-ethnicities embedded in them in turn further shape, sustain, and potentially change those understandings among an audience wider than academic social scientists.

Workplace Diversity

Impending race-ethnic demographic changes in the U.S. population became a central concern for administrative practices in the late 1980s–early 1990s under the rubric of "managing workplace diversity" or "valuing cultural diversity." Many reports pointed to the growing diversity of the population along race-ethnic lines, citing the Hudson Institute's *Workforce 2000* report and often using California as the example of what awaits the rest of the nation. (Although "cultural diversity" is often used to refer also to gender, sexuality, physical ability, and other traits, they are not the focus here.) In 1991–92 for the first time, people of Asian heritage constituted the largest group of new students admitted to the University of California at Berkeley (those of European heritage were the second largest group). For the country as a whole, the Labor Department estimated that in the 1990s "women, minorities and immigrants [would] constitute 84% of the new entrants to the American work force. Already, white men make up less than a majority of American workers, a milestone passed in the first half of the 1980s" (Schachter 1988, p. 1:1). In California, in 2000, hitherto numerical minorities taken together comprised the majority of the population, surpassing the total of European-Americans.

It has been argued by many, including both academic researchers and human resource professionals, that these demographic changes in the workforce require new skills on the part of managers. Rather than see this increasing diversity of race-ethnicity as a drawback interfering with productivity and efficiency, managers and executives have been encouraged to see it as adding new ideas and creativity. While studies of the private sector argue for the competitive advantage of a diverse workforce (see, e.g., Cox and Blake 1991; Loden and Loeser 1991) affecting marketing, consumers, and international trade (Foster et al. 1988), public sector studies praise the promotion of workplace diversity as a social justice issue and for its promise to enhance representative administration (see, e.g., Kellough 1990; Schmidt 1988), although some articles published in public administration journals also emphasize standard business criteria, such as "performance effectiveness and competitive profits" (Coleman 1990, p. 2).[4]

This chapter explores the characteristics of race, ethnicity, and the race-ethnic categories revealed through a close reading of the language, methods, and other rhetorical devices used by authors of articles published at the height of attention to managing cultural diversity in the workplace. How have articles on workplace and workforce diversity defined these population groups? What criteria were used to select the race-ethnic groups under study? How is "diversity" being defined? What are the implications of the foregoing for "managing cultural diversity" programs?

Accessing Data: The Journals

The analysis is based on a study of selected public administration (PA), organizational and management theory (OMT), and personnel/human resource management (HRM) journals published between 1987 and 1993, the period during which attention to workplace diversity exploded. I searched academic journals in these fields, as well as those taking a practitioner focus, looking for articles that used "race," "ethnicity," "diversity" (by itself or in such phrases as "managing diversity," "cultural diversity," "workplace diversity," "managing workforce diversity"), or any race-ethnic category name (e.g., "Hispanics") in the title, the abstract, or index keywords. OMT journals were selected that had published public sector–related research. The search also included political science journals to see how more purely theoretical articles might treat the nature of race and ethnicity, as well as international journals for comparative purposes. The research question in all of these was whether cultural diversity researchers begin their reports with explicit definitions of population variables.

No attempt was made to make an exhaustive search of all academic and practitioner journals in these fields. For example, PA journals that focus primarily on finance, budgeting, international development, accounting, and so forth were not included. Only those journals that were most likely to publish articles on so-called "diversity issues" with a workplace emphasis were reviewed.

I searched a total of thirty-six journals: twelve in PA, eleven in OMT, eight in HRM, and five in political science. These include international journals for PA (2), OMT (2), and HRM (1). Except for the political science and international journals, the other fields were divided between academic journals (fifteen in total) and those that focus on practitioners (eleven in total). The academic journals in HRM were further divided between general subject journals (1) and those specific to public personnel/HR management (2). These are listed in Table 6.1.

Accessing Data: The Articles

The search yielded a total of ninety-four articles that were directly relevant to the subject of race-ethnic diversity in the workplace: thirty-three in PA (four in academic journals, including one in an international journal, and twenty-nine in practitioner journals); seventeen in OMT (twelve in academic journals and five in practitioner journals); and forty-four in HRM journals (two in general academic journals, four in public sector–oriented academic journals, and thirty-eight in practitioner journals). In all, twenty-two articles

Table 6.1

List of Journals Searched

Category I. Public Administration—academic
Administration and Society
American Review of Public Administration
Journal of Public Administration Research and Theory
Journal of Policy Analysis and Management
Public Administration Quarterly
Public Administration Review

Public Administration—practitioner focus
American City and County
The Bureaucrat/The Public Manager
Public Management
Western City

Category II. Organizational and Management Theory—academic
Academy of Management Journal
Academy of Management Review
Administrative Science Quarterly
Human Relations
Journal of Applied Behavioral Sciences
Organization Science

Organizational and Management Theory—practitioner focus
Academy of Management Executive
California Management Review
Harvard Business Review

Category III. Personnel/HRM—academic, public focus
Public Personnel Management
Review of Public Personnel Administration

Personnel/HRM—academic, general
Human Resource Management

Personnel/HRM—practitioner focus
HR Magazine
HR Focus (Personnel)
Personnel Journal
Training and Development Journal

Category IV. Political Science—academic
American Journal of Political Science
American Political Science Review
Journal of Politics
Polity
Political Research Quarterly (Western Political Quarterly)

Category V. Public Administration—international
International Journal of Public Administration
International Review of Administrative Sciences

Organizational and Management Theory—international
International Studies of Management and Organization
Organization Studies

Personnel/HRM—international
Personnel Management

appeared between 1987 and 1993 in the academic journals searched, seventy-two in the practitioner-oriented journals. The journals containing relevant articles are listed in Table 6.2; the figures are summarized in Table 6.3.

I eliminated articles that did not deal directly with the workplace or workforce. So, for example, an article that explored questions of merit and equity in employment testing and another on fire chiefs' attitudes toward affirmative action were not included since neither directly addressed changing workplace dynamics in the face of changing workforce demographics. Another article explored diversity (and its lack) in the student populations of programs accredited by the National Association of Schools of Public Affairs and Administration (NASPAA). Although this article raises a concern that is of central importance to recruiting a more diverse workforce, it does not directly address workplace issues and was, therefore, also not included. Lastly, articles exploring inter- or cross-cultural management and training issues were not included because they address Americans overseas.

Cox and Nkomo (1990) found a falling off of published research analyzing "race effects" in the workplace for the period they studied, 1964–1989, from 11.7 per year in the 1970s to 3.6 from 1985–1989. I expected to find that the extensive public attention given to the *Workforce 2000* report had spurred further publication of research on cultural diversity in the workplace. What these tables show is that practitioner-oriented journals were publishing more articles on workplace diversity and its concerns than the academic journals: seventy-two articles appear in the former as compared with twenty-two in the latter. This is perhaps not surprising, given that the subject itself is of central concern to administrative practice, had been highly visible in that context in many daily events, and had been widely discussed in newspapers and the popular press (e.g., such magazines as *Time, Newsweek, Working Woman*). As might be expected given this attention, there was a steady increase in the overall numbers of articles published in the journals reviewed, growing from one in 1987 to twenty-seven in 1992, although the number fell to sixteen in 1993. Most of the growth, however, was in practitioner journals, rather than academic ones. Despite all the public attention to present and/or impending changes in the workforce, still not much academic research has been published on race-ethnicity in the workplace.[5] Table 6.4 documents this pattern.

Given the orientation of both public administration and OMT as academic fields to matters of practice, it is surprising that only four articles appeared in academic PA journals (out of eight journals searched), as compared with eleven in academic OMT journals (out of eight searched). On the other hand, these data show that practitioner PA journals published twenty-nine articles (out of four journals), as compared with five in the practitioner OMT journals

Table 6.2

Journals with Articles Relating to Workplace Cultural Diversity

Category/title	Number of articles
Category I. **Public Administration—academic**	
American Review of Public Administration	1
Public Administration Review	2
Public Administration—practitioner focus	
The Bureaucrat/The Public Manager	11
Public Management	13
Western City	5
Category II. **Organizational and Management Theory—academic**	
Academy of Management Journal	5
Academy of Management Review	2
Administrative Science Quarterly	2
Human Relations	2
Journal of Applied Behavioral Science	1
Organizational and Management Theory—practitioner focus	
Academy of Management Executive	2
California Management Review	1
Harvard Business Review	2
Category III. **Personnel/HRM—academic, public focus**	
Public Personnel Management	4
Personnel/HRM—academic, general	
Human Resources Management	2
Personnel/HRM—practitioner focus	
HR Magazine	7
Personnel/HR Focus	8
Personnel Journal	14
Training and Development Journal	9
Category V. **Public Administration—international**	
International Journal of Public Administration	1
Total	94

Note: One article appears in two different journals. No Category IV journal published an article.

searched (three journals). This discrepancy might be attributed to the choice of practitioner OMT journals as contrasted with practitioner PA journals: the *Academy of Management Executive, California Management Review,* and *Harvard Business Review* target a narrower management segment than the PA journals searched. A more comparable selection of OMT journals might have included *Business Week* and the like, in which one might expect to find more articles on workplace diversity.

Table 6.3

Distribution of Articles by Field

Field	Academic	Practitioner
Public administration	3	29*
Organizational and management theory	11	5**
Personnel/HRM	6	38***
Political science	0	n/r
International (PA)	1	n/r
	—	—
Totals	21	72

*Six of these are in 1 special issue; 2 are in a "series" in another single issue; 9 are in a series spread across 9 issues; 1 appears in 2 journals, and I have counted it only once here (hence, a total of 93).

**Includes two *Harvard Business Review* pieces treated as one: a personal essay and responses that appear in the subsequent issue.

***Five of these are in a "special section" of one issue; 3 are in a single issue's "cover story."

Table 6.4

Distribution of Articles by Year of Publication

	1987	1988	1989	1990	1991	1992	1993
Pub. ad.							
Academic				1	1		1
Practitioner	1		4	2	5	15*	2
OM theory							
Academic				3	1	4	3
Practitioner			1	1	2	1	
Personnel/HRM							
Acad., public				1	1		2
Acad., general			1			1	
Practitioner		3	5	6	10	6	8
International							
Pub. ad.			1				
	—	—	—	—	—	—	—
Totals	1	3	12	14	20	27	16

*Six of these were in a single special issue; 9 were in a series. The twice published article is counted only once.

This points to one of the limitations of inducing too much from a statistical evaluation of these data. In general, we may conclude that the issue was being addressed more in the pages of practitioner journals than in academic journals, more in PA practitioner journals than in OMT practitioner journals, and more in academic OMT journals than in academic PA journals. But the numbers very much reflect the quantity and character of journals chosen in each area, and the research was not designed to be exhaustive of all journals in each category. Rather, the intention was to investigate the character of research discourse about race-ethnicity in the workforce and the workplace, by exploring how published articles defined and used race-ethnic terms and categories. The articles analyzed here do not constitute, in other words, a representative sample drawn for purposes of statistical analysis. They are, instead, a purposive collection intended to discover how researchers, both academic and practitioner, publishing in a directed range of journals, framed the subject—workplace diversity. Data analysis drew on a variety of hermeneutic methods used to understand texts.[6]

Language Data and Analysis

The second phase of the research moved from identifying the articles to a close reading of the texts, in order to analyze their use of the concepts "race," "ethnicity," "culture," and "diversity" and their treatment of race-ethnic categories. As with research on the census and other policy and agency practices, analysis focused on the meanings implicit in category names and in their usage.

Analysis began with the expectation that given the professional culture of research, which encourages reflective consideration of research questions and methodologies, "applied," practitioner-oriented as well as academic social scientists researching and writing about race-ethnicity would begin by defining their variables—in this case, race, ethnicity, and/or race-ethnic categories—or reflecting on the meanings of the terms and on their usages (e.g., their socially constructed character) and limitations. Few did. What these articles reveal, on the whole, is the frequent usage of "race" and "ethnicity" as interchangeable concepts; a treatment of race-ethnic categories as if they were naturally occurring, scientifically grounded facts; and a working definition of "diversity" in its racial and/or ethnic element that actively negates or is ignorant of American race-ethnic history prior to the 1990s.

Authors of the articles reviewed here use two different systems of classification to characterize human diversity. Most of the ninety-four articles characterize human diversity solely according to membership in a race-ethnic group. Group names used are typically variations on the five categories stipulated by the version of OMB No. 15 in effect through the 1990s. As used in these articles, these categories appear to be discrete and unambiguous: the possibility of membership in more than one category (i.e., mixed race) does not appear. And what defines membership in each group is presented as if it were clear and unambiguous: category names suggest an internal uniformity that is not supported by experiential and analytic evidence. I will consider these points in order and at length, turning to the second classificatory system toward the end of the chapter.

1. Race = Ethnicity?

Almost none of the ninety-four articles begin with a definition or discussion of the terms "race" and "ethnicity." The authors use "race" and "ethnicity" in their commonsense meanings, corresponding respectively to the "physical traits" and "cultural traits" taken to characterize different groups and demarcate between and among them. In this view, the two terms mean different things and refer to different human groupings. So, for example, one author writes about humans' ancient and "inherent tendency to classify individuals within the collective society." Making such classifications is easy with respect to some criteria, she continues, noting "race/ethnicity" as one type of classification that is "easily measured" (Hughes 1991–92, p. 23). What makes such a statement conceptually possible is the assumption that the two terms are objective measurements of clearly definable and distinct traits. Under these conditions, for example, a "Black" person could never pass for a "White": that would make the classificatory system less "easily" measurable.

But the separation of race traits from ethnic traits is not uniform, even within the same article. This author's statement also points to a different problem with the measurement or categorization she discusses: her use of "race/ethnicity" as a compound indicator suggests that race and ethnicity are not separate categories after all. Some researchers believe that they should be. Cox and Nkomo (1990), for example, observed that nearly all of the published management research they looked at "treats these *distinct dimensions of group identity* as though there were 100% overlap" (emphasis added)—that is, as though "race" and "ethnicity" referred to the same set of features, whereas in Cox and Nkomo's view, they do not, and the management researchers are wrong to have treated them this way.

The reviewed articles tend to use the terms in various ways, at times with distinct meanings, at times interchangeably. For example, one set of researchers uses "ethnic group" to refer to the "cultural norms" of Anglo-Americans, Asians, Hispanics, and Black Americans. They define the "ethnic" group "Anglos" as "racially white and of European descent" (Cox, Lobel, and McLeod 1991, p. 828, n. 1). This makes "race" a component of ethnicity, while not specifying what comprises the cultural content; the usage treats "Asians" and "Black Americans"—continent- and color-based categories— as ethnicities having cultural norms, rather than as races (racially Asian, racially Black). There is a tension between usage and definition. Another article describes the characteristic feature of the group here called "Anglos" as "based in European traditions," which eliminates the racial component and makes them a cultural or ethnic group only, albeit with a broad and unspecified cultural content (Europeans having many languages, foods, histories, etc.).

Other authors, in reporting on a laboratory experiment, define "a cultur-ally diverse group" as having both ethnic and national differences (Watson, Kumar, and Michaelsen 1993, p. 591). This definition makes no reference to race, nor does it explore how ethnicity and nationality at times overlap and at times are distinct. It posits a distinction between ethnicity and nationality (national origins cannot define an ethnic identity in this usage) at the same time that it stipulates by definitional logic that groups are culturally diverse in only those two ways. The ethnic and national differences represented in the lab groups were white American, black American, Hispanic American, and foreign national (from Asia, Latin America, Africa, and the Middle East). This treats whites and blacks as ethnicities, rather than as races.

Another author defines "majority" as a non-Hispanic white male or fe-male. He cites U.S. census categories as his basis for definitions of "minor-ity," although the census does not use that term. Minorities, he says, "seem to be clearly defined by the US Census. We know that Blacks, Hispanics, Asians, and Native Americans are considered minorities. They are rather distinct *ethnic groups* and can be *effectively separated* from non-Hispanic whites" (Rich 1989, p. 654; emphases added). Once again, groups that in other contexts are identified as "races" are here treated as ethnicities, al-though the ethnic components—shared language, religion, customs, and so forth—that would "effectively" separate each from the others are not identi-fied. Without such specification, it is also not entirely clear which groups Black-Hispanics, Asian-Hispanics, and mestizos would belong to.

Cox (1990, pp. 6–7) is one of the few to begin with a discussion of what "race" and "ethnicity" mean, noting their historical usage to distinguish be-tween biological and cultural differences. He adds that there has been a ten-dency to use "race" in reference to whites and blacks, and "ethnicity" in reference to Hispanics and Asians. The overwhelming majority of the ar-ticles reviewed here use race and ethnicity as if they were ahistorical, unam-biguous, empirically grounded, scientific terms.

2. Categorical Logic and Lumpiness in Research Categories

In these articles, every employee is treated as if she or he fit into one and only one category. The categories as they are used allow no room for people of mixed race-ethnic heritage. They are presented as discrete groupings; no article entertained the possibility of membership in multiple categories or of an "Other" category.

Membership criteria for each category are also assumed to be clear and unambiguous, yet this assumption becomes problematic in usage. For ex-ample, two articles note that it is the use of the Spanish language that makes

"Hispanics" different from other peoples. This omits Portuguese-speakers (included in the OMB definition), speakers of Indian languages (e.g., from the Oaxacan area of Mexico), and many second- and later-generation Hispanics who do not speak Spanish—at the same time that it includes Spanish-speaking Pilipinos. Another article observed that what makes African-Americans different is their history. This is precisely the argument made by Afro-Caribbeans, for example, yet they are not mentioned here as a separate grouping; nor is shared history a demarcation unique to African-Americans.

Moreover, not only are criteria for membership assumed to be clear and unambiguous, but authors rarely treat the five categories as anything other than internally homogeneous groupings. To take "Hispanic" as one example, only six of the ninety-four articles noted the existence of Mexican-Americans as a distinct group; Cubans were mentioned three times, Puerto Ricans twice, and one article included Central and South Americans as having potentially different customs, beliefs, and practices (Matthes 1992). One article notes generational differences between recently immigrated "Mexican-Americans" and "Chicanos" of second and later generations (Kavanaugh and Retish 1993). One mentions the existence of heterogeneity among Cubans, Mexicans, and Puerto Ricans; but without exploring the point further, the author describes Hispanics as a seemingly unified group (Sisneros 1993). Another notes internal differences among "Latins," but without specifying them. Yet another author writes that "Hispanic" and "Latino" "refer to a variety of distinct cultures" and are not synonyms, the latter term not including European Hispanics. Her recommendation: use a term derived from the person's country of origin—"Peruvian," for example, instead of "Hispanic" or "Latino" (or, she adds, tribal affiliation instead of "Native American"; Petrini 1993a).

No author noted the existence of variety among Native Americans. In fact, Native Americans are all but "disappeared" in this research. More subgroups were listed in the articles for Asian-Americans than for any other of the five groups: two each mentioned Chinese-Americans, Vietnamese, and Filipinos; people from Japan, Taiwan, Cambodia, Laos, Korea, Pakistan, India, and Hong Kong were each mentioned once; but few articles made their internal variety an explicit point.

Internal differences among African-Americans were noted in only one article. The category name would be an inappropriate reference, the author notes, for "employees of African descent [who] are not American citizens" (Petrini 1993a, p. 36)—that is, legally resident citizens of African or other countries. Only two articles noted any cultural differences among Caucasian- or European-Americans. Both noted that White Americans are assumed to be culturally homogeneous, and one author remarked on a training session

participant's surprise at learning the range of diversity among the white participants (Watson, Kumar, and Michaelsen 1993; Ossolinski 1992). Such
assumptions of homogeneity create the "categorical lumpiness" discussed in
chapter 3.

The articles also reflect the instability of category names. For example,
the most common names used in the articles for "nonminorities" are White,
Caucasian, and European-American. Two articles used "white American,"
and four others called the group "Anglo-Americans." By contrast, an article
describing workplace diversity in Australia used "Anglo-Celtic" to refer to
the same "racial" group (Ho 1990).[7] "African-American" and "Black" are
both used. "Native American" is more widely used, but "American Indian"
also appears in the articles. "Asian-American" is predominantly used, although "Orientals" appears at times.

One author who does not treat the categories as internally homogeneous
writes, "Within any designated category of employees, there is enormous
diversity. For example, blacks, whites, Hispanics, and Asians differ among
themselves significantly" (Thomas 1991–92, p. 21). Yet none of the articles
identified in this research explicitly discussed category definitions or the
reason for using the particular categories that were chosen. Researchers might,
for example, have supported their choices of categories "in an effort to comply with government definitions of ethnic groups," as did the authors of an
article not part of the data pool for this research (Kirnan et al. 1989).

3. Statistical Lumpiness: Generalizing from Limited Data

Not only do the authors not define the race-ethnic categories they use. Many
extrapolate from research on one or two non-White groups to all non-White
groups, as if the traits and/or experiences of one were identical for all. Many
authors, for example, suggest by their titles and introductory arguments that
they are going to discuss races and/or ethnicities in the plural, but their research is based on Blacks and Whites only. One article, for instance, re-
searched Black and White managers but presents the research as the "effect
of race" in general (Shenhav 1992). The title of another refers to "minorities"; the author notes that the argument "applies to most minorities, but is
especially applicable to black Americans who have experienced many of the
situations mentioned" (Washington 1987, p. 30). The author appears to be
saying that although his data come from Black Americans' experiences, his
findings can be generalized to most "minorities" because those experiences
are shared—but it is an argument by assertion alone. Others talk about "race
differences" but mention only Blacks and Whites (e.g., Greenhaus,
Parasuraman, and Wormley 1990; Veres, Green, and Boyles 1991). This is in

keeping with Cox and Nkomo's (1990) finding that 100 out of 140 empirical studies of race-ethnic issues published between 1964 and 1989 focused on Blacks alone as the "Other" race-ethnic group; Hispanics were included in only 17 of the 140.

Few authors explicitly reflect on this limitation of their research. Those who do often give statistical reasons for it, noting that they had too few members of other groups (typically, Asian-Americans and Native Americans) to produce statistically significant findings about them. For example, an article that refers to "Minority . . . Employment" in its subtitle is based on data about Blacks and Hispanics, as well as an "overall measure of racial/ethnic integration" derived from data on "all minority groups targeted for affirmative action." In an endnote, the author adds: "The representation of Native Americans and Asians is generally low and lacks sufficient variation among agencies to permit meaningful analysis of those two groups separately" (Kellough 1990, p. 565). The authors of another article are explicit about grouping all minorities in a single category because the numbers for the different groups were too small to treat them separately (Fine, Johnson, and Ryan 1990). Cox and Nkomo (1990) found a version of such generalization in their study of race-ethnic research in the fields of organizational behavior and human resource management (OBHRM): "If no obvious main effects [of race on the organizational component studied] were found, the researcher typically concluded that race was not an important variable [for *any* aspect of organizational life] and that, indeed, OBHRM theories are applicable to *all* employee race groups" (emphasis added).

Two of the ninety-four articles discussed this problem of generalizing to nonresearch subjects. Cox (1990, p. 7) emphasizes that he had little data on Asians, Hispanics, and Native Americans because of their underrepresentation in his field of research. He writes: ". . . I am most confident of [my arguments'] veracity for research on blacks and whites. I recognize that their applicability to other racioethnic groups is open to question."[8] And Ibarra (1993), in the conclusion to an essay that discusses whites and "racial minorities" but that primarily examines blacks, notes the possibility of differences across racial groups and the dearth of research on other than African-Americans.

While it has been, unfortunately, the case that race-ethnic groups other than African- and European-Americans have been subjects in workplace research projects in too few numbers to yield statistically significant findings, "disappearing" them into an all-encompassing non-White group or generalizing to them from research based on Blacks violates the canons of statistical science to no less a degree than claiming findings from too small a sample size. Such a practice is made conceptually thinkable by categorical logic similar to that which constrains a White "Adam" from seeing difference among non-White groups, one that emphasizes binomial oppositional thinking.[9]

4. Some Are More Different Than Others: "Managing" Race-Ethnic "Diversity"

Statistical and categorical lumpiness shape the ways in which cultural diversity and its valuation or management have been conceptualized. Programmatic and personnel choices are often made on the basis of these categorical assumptions of internal homogeneity that are misleading, resulting often in administrative policies and practices that are destined to mismatch or fall short of their intended and desired results. Much in the workplace programs for managing "cultural diversity" plays on the prototypes imagined for each race-ethnic group.

One of the consequences of reifying the race-ethnic categories-in-use—of considering them to be natural and unchangeable and internally uniform—is a conception of race-ethnic "diversity" only in terms of those lumpy groups and a consequent privileging of continent-based difference. This leads to discussions that do not fit the historical record. With rare exception, those writing about workplace or workforce diversity at the end of the 1980s and early 1990s wrote as if race-ethnic diversity were new, as if the workforce had been race-ethnically homogeneous until then. Such an approach negates labor and social history, at the same time that it reinforces the inclination to restrict the notion of "diversity" to a single feature. So, for example, one author writes: "Our human diversity is greater in the 1990s than it has been at any time in our history" (Hawkins 1992, p. 33), without any context or rationale for the statement.

By contrast, Foster et al. (1988) place late-twentieth-century race-ethnic diversity in a historical context, in one of the few articles to do so. They write: "Employee diversity has been an ongoing theme in American industry for many years; the only aspect that changes is the groups toward which companies have directed diversity activities" (p. 41). They note that from "around 1870 to about 1924," the "outsiders" were Italian, Polish, Irish, and Russian men—those "white ethnics" considered to be "inferior" immigrants; and that Jews weren't accepted even as customers in the insurance industry until the 1940s, at which time they still could not build careers in insurance and banking. It was not until the 1960s, they write, that the "white protestant" work force accepted these others into the workplace, creating the "white, male-oriented world of American commerce as we know it today" which is faced with incorporating "cultural and racial minorities and women of all races." Dominguez (1991–92, p. 16) is another exception, remarking that it is possible to talk about a new diversity without discounting history.

While researchers need not give a history of race and ethnicity in every article (and, certainly, those writing for practitioner journals typically do not have room to do so), ignoring that history has serious implications for the training programs and other solutions that are proposed. The more common, ahistorical account of workforce diversity leads writers to assume that present managers have no prior experience in "managing" diversity. Coupled with the treatment of race-ethnic categories as homogeneous groupings, it also appears to assume that all managers are White and, therefore, ignorant of diversity or without culture themselves. Thinking seemingly follows this logic:

- The current workforce is now race-ethnically diverse, whereas before it had been homogeneous;
- This "new" state of affairs implies that different skills are required than those used in supervising an earlier, presumedly not-diverse workforce;
- "Diverse" means "minority" or "non-White";
- A "diverse workforce," then, implies that managers are "nondiverse," that is, "nonminority," White;
- By implication, then, (only) Whites need training to manage non-Whites.

The identification of Whites as a racial group alone and the imputed distinction between race and ethnicity implies that Whites lack cultural traits. In these articles, by and large, only non-"Americans" and nonmanagers are diverse and have cultural traits. This leads to the assumption that only Whites need training in managing "culturally diverse" people (which is to say, people unlike themselves). The research project described in the chapter's epigraph departs from the same point of view: the Japanese-American parent is described in detail, by generation as well as by race-ethnic subcategory, whereas the White parent is just that. While "cultural" clashes between employees do take place, and educating people in cultures not their own may ease such tensions, this logic, informed by the understanding of race-ethnicity discussed above, frequently leads writers to recommend training programs based on stereotypic assumptions about the traits characterizing each race-ethnic group, to the detriment of Whites and non-Whites both. It is a return to the ancient, medieval, and nineteenth- to mid-twentieth-century linkage of race-ethnicity with behavioral traits.

Even when Whites are referred to as an ethnic group, there is little or no discussion of what their shared cultural traits might be. Identifying Whites as an ethnicity implies that all Whites share the same cultural heritage (religion, food, language, customs, etc.), one of the characteristics of categorical lumpiness. One article, for example, says that "Religion-inspired values [held by Blacks and other minorities] . . . are likely to conflict with values of nonminority coworkers . . ." (Washington 1987, pp. 30–31)—as if one of the traits that characterizes "nonminorities" as a group is the absence of a religious background or perhaps an antireligious stance. Another recommends: "The first step is to implement a training program for . . . the American white male [managers] to operate in and facilitate team work in a multicultural society" (Foxman and Polsky 1989). One cultural diversity consultant writes, "The majority of today's managers are white males who grew up with little exposure to people from other cultures . . ." (Copeland 1988, p. 45)—a very broad generalization, without supporting data. Another writes about both elected and appointed local government leaders: "Since most local government officials are European-Americans, they need to step outside their traditional comfort zones. They must learn about different cultures and ethnic groups, attend cultural festivals and visit the homes and businesses of the various ethnic groups in the community" (Benest 1991, p. 4).

Analysis of the articles reveals other assumptions about who is doing the managing and, therefore, in need of training, and who is being managed. Many write about "American managers" appreciating, valuing, or managing culturally diverse workers, suggesting that "culturally diverse workers" are not American as well as that the managers are culturally homogeneous, neither of which is supported by empirical research or by the articles themselves. In one otherwise excellent essay, the author uses the phrase "American men" to make a point about how managers and employees are feeling in today's demographically changing workplace (Solomon 1991). To be "American" is to be "White." Most of the "managing cultural diversity" programs outlined in the articles reviewed here target White males alone for training.

Implying that Whites are the only race-ethnic group that cannot manage culturally diverse employees without training shortchanges both Whites and the "culturally diverse." Differences among Whites that result in discriminatory practices—Italian-Americans are still a protected class in New York in 1993, as noted in chapter 3—are ignored. The construction of the "White" or "European-American" category as internally uniform and cultureless facilitates stereotyping of White managers' abilities. One author, for example, writes, "You have to be careful about stereotypes [of nonwhite Others]. . . . So what do you do about that? You do what is often hard for whites and for men in particular. . . .You watch and you listen, and let the other people show where they are coming from. A white person doesn't have to be dominant. A white person has to learn to live with ambiguity" (Copeland 1989a, p. 20). The advice inadvertently stereotypes White persons, and White men in particular.

Stipulating that European-Americans are the only ones who need to learn how to manage a diverse workforce (e.g., Benest 1991, p. 5; Galagan 1993) implies that Americans from the other categories already know how to manage people different from themselves. This stereotypes them as well as Whites, while treating them as not-Americans and not-managers. It assumes that non-White managers are naturally knowledgeable about and comfortable in cultures not their own, or that they have had exposure to cultures other than their own and the dominant American culture. While many Whites, especially those from suburbs, smaller towns, and rural areas, may well have grown up in race-ethnically homogeneous communities, and while most non-Whites and non-Protestants learn to be bicultural, navigating both their own and the dominant culture, it has not been demonstrably shown that African, Asian-, Hispanic, Native, and other non-WASP Americans have been exposed to one another's cultures to any great extent, especially with regard to picking up cross-cultural managerial skills. Non-Whites are assumed not to need training in how to manage White workers or workers from different non-White categories: they are treated as innately knowing how to manage people (assumed to be) not like themselves. Non-White managers are thereby deprived of training in potentially needed skills and denied avenues toward promotion that could accrue to Whites who are targeted for additional training. Understanding diversity as a central management concern for all is subverted.

This reasoning about "managing diversity" entails several testable hypotheses, among them (1) that there are identifiable skills required to supervise diverse people (in general or as currently constituted) and (2) that White (male) managers lack these skills. None of the articles investigated reported on research designed to test these assumptions. "Common management techniques are not as effective with culturally diverse work groups," writes one author. He continues: "To manage diverse work groups you should:

> Know thyself. Let others know how you work best.
> Share work goals and expectations.
> Help others to be clear about their job functions.
> Communicate work priorities and criteria.
> Invest time in coaching subordinates.
> Delegate responsibilities based on others' interests and abilities.
> Set and communicate performance criteria.
> Provide on-going performance feedback.
> Encourage two-way communication.
> Empower others. (Coleman 1990, pp. 2, 3)

The list seems to be sound advice—about techniques for good management practices in general. The focus on lumpy, discrete categories "orientalizes" difference, to adopt Said's term (1978): it emphasizes difference and makes it seem exotic. At the same time, it essentializes race-ethnic differences, and it directs management development efforts toward generating trait lists for each race-ethnic group—in the process, maintaining stereotypes—and training for "trait competencies" (Dobbins and Skillings 1991, p. 37). Diversity training films instruct managers that Asians don't make eye contact, Hispanics can be volatile in making oral presentations, and so on. Other programs schedule annual set-aside times for the different foods, musics, dance forms, religious-cultural observances, clothing, literature, and history—the "legitimating tokens of culture" (Segal and Handler n.d., p. 11)—of each represented group. This "trait list" approach to each lumpy group ignores the fact that at least American-born Chinese-Americans make eye contact like other Americans, and immigrants from India have no difficulty making eye contact at all.

"Mixed race" is not considered because it would upset the clarity that discrete, bounded, categorical essences putatively have. By positioning difference solely among workers, these articles cede the power of defining diversity and who is diverse to managers, who themselves are treated as uniform, not-diverse, "normal." They also reproduce—extend, sustain, further reify—the existing race-ethnic categorical structure, in its boundedness, rather than modifying or supplanting it. In this they also set the stage for the "fundamental attribution error" (Kopelman 1994; Ross 1977; see also Litvin 1997), in which individuals explain others' behavior in light of their ascribed attributes (in this case, presumed race-ethnic traits), rather than structural elements of the situation.

Varieties of Diversity: A Second Approach to Classification

Diversity research toward the end of the 1987–1993 period appears to shift toward a more complex understanding of what "diversity" and difference mean. Although the main focus largely continues to be on race-ethnicity and gender, a greater variety of diversity traits is considered in some articles. These constitute a second system of classifying human diversity, identifying people by demographic traits more broadly cast. The list of traits considered begins with the categories protected by federal law:

- *Race, color, religion or creed, national origins* or *nationality, gender* or *sex* (the language from President Franklin D. Roosevelt's Executive Order 8802 and from Title VII of the Civil Rights Act of 1964);
- *Age* (from the Age Discrimination in Employment Act of 1967, which extended Title VII protections to persons over forty);

- *Physical (dis)ability* (from the Rehabilitation Act of 1973 and the Americans with Disabilities Act of 1990).

But increasingly since 1990, other sources of "difference" were included as characteristics of workforce diversity, going, in some cases, far beyond the law-based, commonsense usage of "workplace diversity" in reference to race-ethnic groups and women. The articles used the following language to describe these sources of individual difference:

sexual orientation, sexual preference
people from other countries; immigrants
mental characteristics
language [spoken]
single parents
work styles—regional, functional, professional (as well as ethnic)
skill levels; skill deficits in reading, writing, grammar
philosophy
culture
politics
attitude, social attitude
personal [attributes]
values
socioeconomic [background]; class
lifestyle
aptitudes
outlooks
backgrounds
learning styles

This list underscores one of the characteristics of the race-ethnic diversity discourse: it largely focuses on a small subset of the ways in which humans differ from one another; "race" and "ethnicity," in this context, are just two among many categories. One writer asks: "Have we been defining diversity too narrowly?" (Solomon 1991, p. 90). Another defines diversity as the "inclusion of all races, ethnic groups, and cultural backgrounds" but later adds age, ability, and gender (Skinner 1991, p. 29). Others include addressing the special needs of "even non-minority males" (Nobile 1991; see also Petrini 1993b). Several articles quoted Thomas's analogy of a jar of red jelly beans into which yellow and green ones are put. "Everyday language labels the yellow and green beans as 'diversity,' but managing diversity views the mixture of yellow, green, and red jelly beans to be 'diversity.' It recognizes further that the beans can differ in ways other than color, such as taste, age, weight, and time in the jar. Even among all red beans there can be substantial diversity." In this view, diversity is broader than race and gender. It is not about "white males managing minorities and women, but rather about any manager managing whoever is in his/her work force" (Thomas 1991–92, p. 20). In this approach "managing" cultural diversity comes to mean providing a work environment in which each employee can work to his or her best (Reynolds 1992).[10]

Understandings of "diversity" have also changed to reflect a growing understanding of "culture" and its sources and dynamics. The traditional management view held that the individual must adapt to the workplace. It is an assimilationist, Anglo-dominant, melting-pot view: there is one way to be "American," and that entails speaking one language at home and in public, one way of dress, one cuisine, one set of holidays, and so forth.[11] This view is based on assumptions about the need or desire for homogeneity, all individuals' cultural identities melting into the single, "American" pot, with no hyphenated cultural residuals. In this assimilationist view, "different" meant (and means) something negative (Hanamura 1989) or inferior, and equality meant (means) identical, the same, the perceived "normal" or unmarked state. The trait list above suggests the range of characteristics that individuals might bring with them to the workplace. Any aberration in any of these areas from the dominant norm was to be submerged, kept in the realm of private expression beyond public viewing.

"Culture," in this view, was a source of identity that lay outside the workplace and was to be kept there. Bringing one's own culture inside the organization was seen as complicating the "real" mission of work (Dubinskas 1992). Culture and cultural diversity need, in this view, to be "managed" in order to minimize the differences that would presumably conflict with or detract from this mission. In the workplace this also meant the creation of and adherence to a single identity, a single organizational "culture." To this end, white males also suppressed their diversity (R. Roosevelt Thomas, Jr., quoted in Solomon 1991, p. 91) to blend in with the unspoken but implied and tacitly known norm.

The shift in general public discourse from seeing the United States as a "melting pot" to the metaphors of "mosaic" or "tossed salad" may account, at least in part, for the broadening of vision in organizational contexts with respect to cultural diversity. In this sense, managing "diversity" becomes, conceptually, the opposite of managing "uniformity." The view that this broader approach to "managing cultural diversity" offers is, in the words of one of its main practitioners, "to seize the benefits that differences bring" (Copeland 1989b, p. 9). This expansion of what constitutes diversity requires a reframing of the meaning of "difference" in U.S. society, to a more positive consideration (see also Minow 1990 on this point).

One can also read in these changing notions of cultural diversity a history of the heritage of AA/EEO policies. In keeping with assimilationist assumptions, AA/EEO focused exclusively on increasing the numbers of underrepresented groups, without regard to the impact of their presence on interpersonal or group dynamics. The burden of accommodation and change is on newcomers to the organization. In the "managing cultural diversity" approach, acculturation is no longer seen as change in one direction alone, organizations or corporate cultures socializing "minority" individuals to the existing culture. Rather, the organization is also seen as changing, in a process of mutual adjustment and adaptation (Goldstein and Leopold 1990; Thomas 1991–92).[12]

Seeing the workplace as adapting to a changing workforce emphasizes a "mosaic" or "salad" view: Uniformity is not required; there can be moral and economic strength in diversity. Two mutually influencing forces are at work in this view: the bidirectional interchange between the workforce (employees) and the workplace (the organization), and that between the workplace and the family/community. It is a view that no longer isolates the workplace from the society in which it resides. In the words of Santa Ana, California, city manager David Ream, "The primary assets of a modern corporation leave the workplace each night to go home for dinner . . ." (quoted in *Public Management,* December 1992, p. 17).

Research in organizational culture adds yet another dimension to an understanding of "cultural diversity." Cultural differences are seen as arising from structural features of life within organizations, and not only from individual traits. These features include professional or technical styles within an organization (e.g., research vs. managerial vs. engineering cultures; see Dubinskas 1992); organizational level or position and type of enterprise (Phillips and Sackmann 1991); tenure within the organization or union membership (R. Roosevelt Thomas, Jr., cited in Solomon 1991). These compound sources of diversity caution against making "a priori assumptions about a single domain of culture being the primary or exclusively dominant influence" over individual action (Dubinskas 1992, p. 9). To the extent that these approaches to diversity move beyond considering race-ethnicity alone, they also escape the conceptual problems and limitations that those terms bring.

The Role of "Science" in Constructing Race-Ethnicity

"With the triumph of the reform movements [in professionalizing public administration, e.g., the Progressive Movement] in American cities, the intellectual mainstream of public administration was forged in the belief that the implementation of public policy could safely and rightly ignore ethnic group diversity" (Schmidt 1988, p. 191). This attitude was so strongly entrenched that it has been an effort to bring management, both public and private, to the view that race-ethnic difference did not need to be parked at the front door or otherwise submerged. From this point of view, it is a step forward to have workforce diversity of any sort recognized explicitly. Yet the conceptualizations of race-ethnicity entailed in most of the articles discussed here appear still to be efforts to contain and control difference based on old fears of it.

Researchers and the journals publishing their articles play a role in the construction of contemporary notions of race and ethnicity, although few appear cognizant of their role in reifying race, ethnicity, and the categories. As noted in chapter 1, categorizing processes in everyday life are typically not made explicit. But this is precisely the work that social scientists should, and do, take on.

What makes it conceivable to use these terms in an unreflective fashion is the underlying presumption that they are scientifically grounded and capture some reality that exists in the social world. Under the assumption that race-ethnic categories are scientific "facts," there is no need to begin an empirical research article or a practice-oriented report by defining those categories. "African-American," "Asian-American," "Native American," "Hispanic," and "White" are assumed to be commonly understood, unproblematic refer-ents to known groups with uniformly shared physical and cultural traits. Each time a category is used, it is reified—given the sense of a fixed, unambigu-ous, objectively, factually real entity.[13] As these research reports are read and cited, each race-ethnic group is re-created as an entity, and the presump-tion of its scientific reality is reinforced. In both their usage of race and ethnicity and in their unreflective usage of race-ethnic categories, these au-thors participate in and contribute to the contemporary creation of American race-ethnic identities. As a consequence, managers and employees of all race-ethnic backgrounds are being shortchanged.

By using race-ethnic categories as if they were discrete and unambigu-ous, researchers ascribe an objective, factual reality to them that diverts at-tention from the human acts that created them. Given this inclination to reify the categories and the distinctions among them, it is particularly odd to find some groups at times amalgamated in these articles into a single category. For statistical reasons, Native Americans become "Asian," or Native Ameri-cans, Asians, and Hispanics become "African-American," or all four be-come a single, uniform "minority" group whose members share in common not being White. At the same time, "White" and "minority" are often paired as opposites and used in practice to mean White-Black. By extension, "race" comes to mean Black and White only, or to mean "minority," which is used to mean Black (see, e.g., Shenhav 1992). Generalizing beyond the database conceptually negates race-ethnic differences. This is a statistics-driven categorical lumpiness paralleling the conceptual lumpiness that portrays each of the standard categories as internally uniform.

Such lumping for statistical reasons parallels OMB policy requiring summary distinctions between Whites and "All Other Races," or between a non-White category and "All Other Races" including Whites. It echoes the statistically driven attempt to count Asians as Whites in processing the 1990 census data, successfully protested at the time (mentioned in chapter 5). It also underscores the Eastern seaboard view of racial tensions underlying contemporary practices, where "Black" is still seen as the principal minority race, as compared, for example, with the view from the Southwest or California, where Hispanic-Latino/a and/or Asian-American populations dominate and where, in some situations, "White" is no longer the numerical majority. This Black/White view of American race-ethnicity came to the fore publicly in responses to newspaper coverage of the O.J. Simpson trial. "Seeing only black and white misses a lot" (the headline on an op-ed essay by Richard Rodriguez, *San Jose Mercury News* 10/29/95, pp. 1F, 4F) and "Beyond black and white and O.J." (the title of a personal view column under the editorials by Sharon Noguchi, *San Jose Mercury News* 10/13/95) are two examples of the feelings of exclusion experienced by Latino/a- and Asian-Americans on seeing the United States reduced in public discourse to a biracial society.

These practices have important implications for thinking about diversity programs. The repetitions of the five categories in research reports focus attention on physiognomy and skin color (and possibly language) as the essence of what makes people different, much as the usage of "race" and "ethnicity" focuses on color, country of origin, and culture. Such definitions-in-use of race-ethnic categories reflect the sorts of understanding of what "race" and "ethnicity" mean discussed in chapters 3 and 4. They have the conceptual effect of narrowing thinking about managerial training and other programs.

Expanding the concept of diversity by bringing many other traits into consideration might appear to stretch it to meaninglessness. Regarding diversity in the training classroom, for example, a trainer lists as types or sources of diversity "different knowledge levels; desires for varying amounts of detail; different levels of commitment; conflicting agendas; different levels of responsibility and influence in the organization; different thinking patterns; preferences for different styles of learning; different cultural and ethnic backgrounds" (Marda N. Steffey, in Petrini 1993b, p. 22). Such a list could be generated with respect to any classroom and any work site. "Managing cultural diversity" in this sense becomes synonymous with good management practices in general.

Perhaps it should: perhaps this reflects a move toward a state where race-ethnic differences will take their place among other differences as simply that, without "difference" carrying a pejorative judgment of shortfall from some implied but unstated norm. Normative assumptions about the desirability of homogeneity are, however, ironically, seemingly being displaced onto the standard race-ethnic categories, in their definition and treatment as internally homogeneous groups. One piece of empirical research that focused on race-ethnic differences concluded that the experimental groups "could have had many other diversity elements affecting their problem-solving . . ." (Watson, Kumar, and Michaelsen 1993, p. 601). These researchers assume that it is common-sense knowledge that ethnic and nation-of-origin differences entail "cultural diversity." Yet this assumption seemingly prevented them from seeking to define cultural diversity or its components in framing their research question or from reflecting on ethnicity or the nature of difference. Does race-ethnic diversity determine the greatest differences in problem solving observed among their experimental groups?

Comparative analysis could contribute greatly to broadening the ways in which we conceive of diversity in the United States. For example, diversity in Australia includes 140 ethnic groups, 90 languages, 80 religions (Ho 1990). The EEO policy statement of Lower Hutt City in New Zealand protects "sex, marital status, religious or ethical belief *or its absence*, colour, race, ethnic or national origins, health status, disability, age, sexual orientation, pregnancy, *political opinion*, *employee association involvement*, employment status, beneficiary status, family status, identity of partner or relative" (De Vito 1992, p. 17; emphases added). Seeing what "race," "ethnicity," and "diversity" mean in other national contexts might underscore the extent to which these terms are bound by time and historical circumstance, as well as how varied human "diversity" can be. Research of the sort examined here contributes both to constructing notions of race, ethnicity, and diversity and to silencing reflective discourse on its own role in these processes.

Notes

1. This is the opening text of a fuschia-colored flyer (with tearable tabs with the researcher's contact information) that was posted on several of the bulletin boards at California State University, Hayward, in the fall of 1999.

2. Chock (1989, p. 178) also notes that "[s]cholarly discourses on ethnicity in the United States . . . infuse them [popular notions of ethnicity] with authority derived . . . from the diverse institutional centers of power where scholars write and speak." And Ferber (1995, pp. 157–163) points to the role played by social scientists in "reproducing categories of identity as normative" (p. 161). Attention to the rhetorical devices used in social scientific writing to persuade audiences has grown in recent years. See, for example, Golden-Biddle and Locke (1993, 1997) on rhetorical devices in organizational studies and McCloskey (1985) on the rhetoric of economics.

3. Such an approach is in keeping with work in the sociology of science exemplified by Latour (1987).

4. Thomas (1991–92, p. 19), however, argues that this is precisely the point of difference between "managing diversity" and "affirmative action": while the latter is driven by social justice concerns (through legal means), "managing diversity" is motivated by business concerns—the uses of human resources to competitive advantage within the organization, while addressing external diversity among clients or customers.

5. Cox (1990) suggests various reasons why this might be so. The taboos that he noted against researching and writing about race, and associated difficulties with promotion and tenure, apparently continued to exist through 1993, in PA as well as in schools and departments of business administration. Anecdotal evidence from the Academy of Management's Gender and Diversity in Organizations division and from female doctoral students in business and management schools and programs more generally suggests that this is still the case.

6. These include frame analysis, category analysis, metaphor analysis, and semiotic analysis looking for oppositional meanings, among others. See, for example, Chock (1995a), Feldman (1995), Golden-Biddle and Locke (1993, 1997), Gusfield (1976), Lakoff and Johnson (1980), Linder (1995), Miller (1982, 1985), Rein and Schön (1977), Schön and Rein (1994), Yanow (2000a).

7. When gender is included as a factor, group members are usually referred to as "white males" or, in one article, "non-minority males." One article referred to the "dominant anglo-male culture" (Kennedy and Everest 1991).

8. Part of Cox's article discusses sample size and other methodological obstacles limiting research on race-ethnic issues.

9. On a methodological note, I would say that this is an example of methods driving research questions and, hence, limiting what can be explored and, potentially, learned. The answer to the problem presented here is, in my view, to abandon statistical analysis, which clearly does not fit the circumstances, and, instead, opt for a method that is more suitable to the situation—such as some combination of observation and in-depth interviewing.

10. Others have also analyzed the changing notions of multiculturalism and what it means to manage it in the workplace. See, for example, Nemetz and Christensen (1995) and Choudhury (1995). I have restricted my analysis, however, to the uses of the terms made by authors of the ninety-four articles reviewed here, rather than attempting a meta-analysis of others' analyses.

11. It is in this context that the "English-only" movement and its legislative efforts are related policy topics.

12. At least one set of researchers argues that such mutuality of influence in socialization or acculturation processes is a hallmark of organizational learning (Cook and Yanow 1993).

13. This is akin to the process that Berger and Luckmann (1966, Part II) describe, attempting to explain how socially constructed human realities acquire a seemingly objective, factual quality.

Part IV
Telling Identities:
The Contemporary Legacy

If, indeed, "race," "ethnicity," and their categories are not scientific entities, why are they still so widely used and accepted in U.S. public policies and administrative practices in ways that presuppose or suggest that they had a scientific basis, and what are the consequences of this use?

There are (at least) two answers, one ideational/conceptual, the other instrumental. Science, as a practice, is a cultural system. Two of its components are facts and theories; and elements presented as facts within a given scientific practice owe their constitution as such to some underlying theory.[*] The policy and administrative practices in use in the U.S. concerning race-ethnicity continue to be enacted as if they were scientifically grounded, and the elements of that putatively scientific system continue to undergird these race-ethnic practices, not only making them possible but also wielding the full weight of "Science" as presently constituted to make them persuasive. The race-ethnic categories, which are treated as facts, presuppose a theory about the world. That theory is embedded in the concepts of "race" and "ethnicity" and in the five predominant categories. These continue to be central to contemporary identity discourse in part because they carry the heritage of old ideas that are still, in some way, compelling. They occlude other forms of identity and other moral-political ideologies and logics.

Chapter 7 offers a conceptual treatment of the tenacity of these practices, in exploring how these concepts and categories enable a collective account of, and accounting for, American identities and origins. Instead of engaging in debates about the veracity and utility of the concepts and categories, and seeking to refine the latter to ever more finite levels of distinction, we should be critically, reflectively engaging the identity narratives they enable, asking

---

*These points have been argued and illustrated at length by sociologists and philosophers of science. See, for example, the writings of Geertz (1983a, 1983b), Kuhn (1970), and Latour (1987).

ourselves—in communal and national, public discourse—whether these are the identity stories we want, or need, to be telling. For example, if "race" and "ethnicity" are used in these policy and administrative practices with inter-changeable meanings, why not just drop the "race" question from the census and other instruments? Or drop both and, instead, ask about ancestral ori-gins? We would still get interesting data about what countries (in the plural) we or our ancestors (again, in the plural) come or came from, what lan-guages we speak, and so on, from other, already existing questions. And at the same time, we might begin to dilute and diffuse the present focus on color. Perhaps we should be asking, What do "race" data tell us about our-selves—that we are Blacks from England, Japanese from Brazil? How does that knowledge help us—with taxation, military service, the labor pool, or with underservice, redistribution, and social justice? In this view, we cannot eradicate "racial profiling" without eliminating the significance we attach to "race"—something that the daily policy and administrative usages of the categories and concepts do not allow.

And yet, there are strong instrumental arguments against dispensing with race-ethnic categories, along these very lines of making our society a more just one. Chapter 8 looks at the practical entailments—the categories and their counts have become the basis for redistributing the nation's wealth through many social policy programs—and explores questions for changing our (ac)counting practices raised by these administrative and policy practices.

Categorical practices—whether in the form of affixing plant taxonomies or assessing anthropological divisions or deciding legal determinations or enacting policy implementation—require making interpretations and judg-ments: Is "this" a "that"? Perhaps there is always a conundrum, whatever the context, between the desire to eliminate categories that, over the life span of their use, have become so reified and inflexible that they no longer accom-modate lived experience, and the recognition that in order to accomplish certain ends, the categories cannot be eliminated—just yet. David Rosenhan, in two groundbreaking essays (1973, 1975), pointed to this very tension in the context of psychiatric diagnosis. Clearly, he argued in the first essay, the categories are context-specific, rather than "scientifically" objective and universal. And just as clearly, he maintained in the second essay, in situa-tions of practice where decisions are made that allocate resources and affect people's lives, we cannot do other than to use the very categories that, in a critically reflective mode, we reject. But he added a caveat: as long as the use of these categories does not wrong the people they are designed to aid.

This is the question we should be exploring in the context of race-ethnicity and its categories.

7

Public Policies as Identity Stories: American Race-Ethnic Discourse

We have a great desire to be supremely American.
—Calvin Coolidge, 1925
(quoted in Star 1997)

My name is Arturo Madrid. I am a citizen
of the United States, as are my parents and as were
my grandparents and my great-grandparents.
My ancestors' presence in what is now the United States
antedates Plymouth Rock, even without taking
into account any American Indian heritage
I may have.

I do not, however, fit those mental sets that
define America and Americans. My physical
appearance, my speech patterns, my name,
my profession (a professor of Spanish)
create a text that confuses the reader.
My normal experience is to be asked,
"And where are *you* from?"
—quoted in Haney López (1993, p. 122)

Everyone is acquainted with dogs and horses
since they are seen daily.
To reproduce their likeness is very difficult.
On the other hand,
since demons and spiritual beings have no definite form
and since no one has ever seen them
they are easy to execute.

—Old Chinese treatise,
paraphrased by Gombrich
(quoted in Edelman 1995, p. 18)

President Franklin D. Roosevelt's Executive Order 8802, signed on June 25, 1941, offered the categorical language of "race, creed, color, or national origin" for nondiscrimination in employment in industries receiving defense contracts (U.S. Equal Employment Opportunity Commission 1968, p. 2). Title VII of the Civil Rights Act of 1964 refashioned the categories as "race, color, religion, country of origin, and sex." Contemporary daily language names race and ethnicity, multiculturalism, managing cultural diversity in the workplace, and, currently, five American race-ethnic groups; "mixed race" may soon join them. If, in fact, the categories themselves, as well as the concepts "race" and "ethnicity" and the distinction between them, are social constructions not supported in the natural world, why do Americans continue to frame public policy and administrative (not to mention general) discourse in those terms?

While these common usages may reflect a "folk wisdom" about race, it is important to understand what this folk wisdom entails, as it undergirds an ongoing engagement with concepts and categories that can no longer claim scientific support. To understand why this is so—why American public policy and administrative practices continue to invoke putatively scientific categories and concepts—requires a perception of public policies as more than instrumentally rational entities. They are also, both in their written form and in their enactment, expressive entities: modes of narrative through which we recite, publicly, various beliefs about who we are as "Americans," to ourselves and to other audiences. In the use of race, ethnicity, and their categories, Americans are telling stories, stories about national identity and group identity—we "tell" both of these as we use the categories—and about national origins, which we "tell" in using the concepts "race" and "ethnicity" the way that we do.

Practices of "Race" and "Ethnicity"

The concepts and the categories *as they are used* mix race/color, ethnicity/ culture, and nationality/country of one's own or of some ancestor's origin. Even in the language of Roosevelt's Order and of Title VII, "race" is used to mean something other than "color" (as both terms are included in the list). Since both religion/creed (i.e., "cultural" concepts) and country of/national origin are also named, however, it is not clear what the residual meaning left for "race" might be.

The various race-ethnic policy, administrative, and research practices explored in previous chapters enable and are part of a story that is being told about who "Americans" are. The story being told at the moment at the national level is that Americans come in five basic varieties: African-, Asian-,

European-, Latino/a-, and Native American (despite the 1997 OMB revisions, Pacific Islanders are still encompassed by the "Asian-" category in daily speech and media reports; I have seen as yet no reference to "Pacific Islander–Americans" or to "mixed race–Americans"). Each of these varieties, according to this story, is internally homogeneous: differences of generation of immigration, of economic class, of religion, or of physical, linguistic or cultural nuance are not recognized. At state and/or local levels, the latter may vary, if California police practices are any indication, but the national story does not. These "gross," five-part differences call attention to continent of personal or ancestral origin and to skin color and physiognomy of the most general sort, from the point of view of the presumed and usually unspoken norm and as contrasted with it. The race-ethnic categories create and institutionalize a public memory. Their link to scientific practices invests them with the authority carried by science in the United States of the late nineteenth to twenty-first centuries.

The reification of the five "lumpy" American race-ethnic categories and their treatment as scientifically grounded entities directs attention away from the similarities within the human species, the socially constructed (and hence, theoretically flexible and changing) character of the categories, and the possibility of categorizing humans according to other sorts of differences. Boundary maintenance between lumpy categories depends on social choices to measure blood (or some other bodily fluid), accent, or (ancestral) geographic origins as the indices of within-group similarity and between-group difference, while within each lumpy category ignoring other, equally strong points of difference. No effort is made to find out about the fish whose parable opens this book—about characteristics of subgroup differences. Like the first speaker in that parable, present usage of the categories presumes common knowledge about what characterizes the fish swimming in the river, without reflecting on or inquiring into these assumptions.

The implicit logic of one category name invokes and implicates others; they "speak" one another into existence. Color requires color; countries and continents require complementary companions. "Black" requires "White." These two colors are often treated as sufficient unto themselves: conceptually (within American English, at least, as well as in other languages), they are treated as forming a complete picture. This is reflected in much contemporary discourse, especially emanating from the Eastern seaboard to Chicago range. But the linguistic structure of "African-American" and "Native American" requires "Asian-American" and "Hispanic (or Latino/a-) American," and these call "European-American" into being. Much in the way that Native Americans are expected to fit the (constructed) image of "tribe" (McCulloch and Wilkins 1995) and new nation-states are expected to mirror the patterns of older ones (Löfgren 1993), race-ethnic categories must fit within the constructed logic of an overall schema. In the conceptual logic of this schema is embedded the fuller story of contemporary American identity.

It is not only the five categories that are treated as if they were "real," scientifically grounded, objectively factual mirrors of human experience. The concepts "race" and "ethnicity" are also treated in the same way: they are endowed with meaning and a time-specific significance, yet treated as if they were timeless, universal variables generated by scientific observation; and the power and standing of science in the modern world is used to bolster that reality status. The ongoing usage of "race" and "ethnicity" in everyday practices—even in their amalgamation of meanings—continues to institutionalize a sense of difference based on and reflecting a valuative hierarchy.

These categories and concepts are "practical" narratives, creating public understanding, memory, and silences, structuring metanarratives of social identity and thereby of individual identity, invested with authority and legitimacy deriving not only from their putatively scientific character, but also by virtue of their being state practices.

National Identity Stories: –American

One of the objections raised to attending to race-ethnic distinctions at all is that it diverts attention from what unifies Americans, away from the "unum" and toward the "pluribus." The fear is often expressed in terms of a balkanization of the country, that Americans are becoming "a nation of people afraid of a national 'we'" (Rodriguez 1990b). "Hyphenated Americans"—in identifying a piece of the geographic area of an American's (ancestors') origin—are a manifestation of this feared balkanization, somehow "less than" real Americans. So, Haney López (1994, p. 7, n. 28) could write, the "American" appended as a suffix "only adds to the sense of exclusion by generating an impression of domesticated foreignness."

This fear points to one aspect of American race-ethnic discourse: the categories narrate how to be American, as well as reflecting a struggle over who gets to define what an American is. The taxation, military, and labor concerns of the earliest censuses are no longer our primary concerns. Beginning in the late 1800s and increasingly into the 1900s, the census has reflected a growing preoccupation with national identity. And race-ethnic components have come to be seen as the central, if not exclusive, feature of that identity. Why?

By lumping at a high level of aggregation—making, for example, "Asian-Americans" out of people from such varied backgrounds as Pakistan and Korea—we accomplish an "ethnic deracination," bleaching all members of each lumpy category of cultural marks. This aggregated lumpiness reflects a

profound indifference on the part of the defining Adams, vested in the category names and their overarching structure, to the sorts of things that are
meaningful to some of their members. Lumping at this level of aggregation
appears to deny any but the most superficial cultural identity to all groups:
one can be an "Asian-American," but not a "Pakistani-American" or "Korean-American"—let alone a Pashtun- or Hazara-American—according to
this category structure. To be an American, the categories seem to say, requires a hyphenated identity—but only at a highly aggregated, continental
level. This is part of the narrative plot that is condensed within the categories
by their structural logic: it enables both a nod to difference—although in
name only, devoid of cultural substance—and the preservation of the "we" on
the other side of the hyphen. Lumpy hyphenization thereby accommodates
linguistically a national phobia toward difference and the fear of splintering
like Yugoslavia or the former Soviet Union.[1] The lumpy categories erase the
threat that difference represents: the orderliness of the bounded categories naturalizes and normalizes difference, rendering it as no difference at all.

Until September 11, 2001, I would have said that Americans had lost a
sense of this "we" and that as a nation feared and mourned this loss. Contemporary hyphenization has been as much an attempt to counter this lost
sense of national identity through its proliferating –American side as it has
been a reflection of diversity within it, as narrated by the hyphen's left side.
The (upper) class consciousness of the Reagan and Bush-père administrations further eroded the sense of national identity, whose loss began with the
Kennedy and King assassinations and grew through the divided responses to
the Vietnam War and Watergate, a fissure that President Carter was unable to
counteract and that played out in the dynamics of the Clinton and early Bush-
fils administrations. This sense of identity lost was exacerbated by the fall of
the Soviet "evil empire": when Americans feared Communists under our
beds, we had an oppositional category against which to define ourselves.
Saddam Hussein has sporadically served the same purpose, but discontinu-
ously and, hence, more weakly.

The events of 9/11 dramatically and suddenly changed all this: in the face
of external attack and horrendous loss of life, seen or heard far and wide as
airplanes crashed and towers collapsed, Americans pulled together as a nation. Osama bin Laden and fundamentalist-inspired terrorism catapulted into
the oppositional void, serving to account initially, also, for subsequent an-
thrax poisoning and a fatal plane crash (later explained as mechanical failure). National values were articulated and defended, in the media, in places
of worship, in local as well as nationally broadcasted gatherings—and invoked
also to forfend and castigate attacks on Arab- and Moslem-Americans, their
mosques and shops, and Sikhs. The hyphenization of "Moslem-American"

or "Arab-American" illuminates both aspects of this experience: the fear of splintering on the left side; the national identity underscored on the right. But even these experiences were cast in light of the prior erosion of national unity: the responses to the newfound unity reflected amazement that the sense of national identity was still there, along with wonder at how long it would continue to be in evidence. The fear that it will, once again, be lost lingers.

Interestingly, Fuchs (1990, p. 23) shows that subgroup identity manifestation was not always perceived as a threat to American national identity: "The civic culture, with its principles of separation of church and state and the right of free speech and assembly, facilitated and protected the expression of ancestral cultural values and sensibilities," he writes, "and, in so doing, sanctioned the system of voluntary pluralism by which ethnic groups could mobilize their economic and political interests." He notes as one example German cultural celebrations as long ago as the 1830s and 1840s (long before wars would make a German-identity problematic).

Race-ethnic, class, or geographic identity could substitute for lost national identity. Americans fear them all. Past race-ethnic divides were controlled through slavery and other economic, labor, immigration, and citizenship policies. The power of "culture" to compel group ties is perceived as potentially pulling away from national loyalty. Even the separation of church and state can be read as an effort to circumscribe and delimit a potentially divisive force. But the perceived power of race-ethnicity is emasculated by the lumpy categories: it will take a long time to forge a strong political force across the differences within each lumpy category; "sub"-groups—Afro-Caribbeans, Mexicanos, Arab-Americans—continue to contest their submergence into "their" larger group, and this contestation diverts energy that otherwise might cohere into a powerful political force. The effort to meld smaller entities into larger, but lumpier, categories may also divert attention from the kinds of geographic or class differences that provided potential sources of power for the Independence and Civil Wars, thereby prolonging the time separatist forces would need in order to develop.[2]

One argument that counters the perceived centrifugal force of race-ethnic attention is that it allows Americans to identify with both sides of the hyphen, as Africans, Hispanics, Asians, Europeans, Natives, as well as Americans. In this view, race-ethnic identity helps people "to overcome the isolation of modern life, while paradoxically also allowing a sense of uniqueness" (Duster 1991). This, however, points to one of the difficulties of categorical lumpiness: how many Italian- or Irish- or Egyptian-Americans identify with "Europe"? Trinidadians with "Africa"? Argentineans with "Hispania"?

In these categorical constructions, we seem preoccupied with a concern for locating origins in some distant and unbounded time horizon of heritage and descent, as if an ancient mooring in ancestral time will anchor us more firmly in our Americanness. Greenblatt (1996, p. 12) tells the story of a fellow student from a 1960s language course, a wealthy aristocratic Spaniard. One day, changing for swimming, he noticed that Javier was wearing an undershirt with fringes attached to the sides. When asked about it, he explained, "'An old family custom, the oldest son wears one of these.'"

Recognizing the article as a Jewish ritual object, Greenblatt said, "'So your family must have been Marranos.'"[3]

"'Don't be absurd. There are cardinals and bishops in my family going back for centuries.'"

"Where is the Jewish history or memory in such an exchange?" writes Greenblatt. Further, commenting on author James Shapiro's characterization of a group of suspected-Jews arrested in England in 1541 as Jews "of Italian descent," Greenblatt asks how far back their "Italian descent" should be traced: "Why should they not be called Italians, of Jewish descent? Or Christians, of Sephardic (or Spanish or Portuguese) ancestry?" This tracing of suspect ancestry back to some oppositional category—Jews, not Anglicans; Jews, not Englishmen; in this effort to clarify through opposition, Italian is not presented as a relevant category (Italian vs. English)—echoes in the U.S. census heritage/ancestry question and in the OMB definitions. But how far back in time to locate "origins" is a murky business. In the absence of a clear yardstick, blood has become the Occam's razor, in the blood quantum requirements imposed by the state on American Indians—through the federal Bureau of Indian Affairs—and on African-Americans—through the courts' adjudication of one-drop rule applications. The narrative embraces a tension between "original peoplehood" that implies a rootedness in its native earth, with attendant humors and behavioral traits and collective history and memory, and its transplantation to American soil and American values. The oppositional identity is captured within the hyphenated construction: the "not-American" lacks the right side of the hyphen.

According to Greenblatt, the English were obsessed by the question of Jewish identity in the sixteenth and seventeenth centuries because they "were engaged in a momentous, prolonged process of racial, religious and national self-definition" that raised concerns about the "Hebraic origins of Christianity." This parallels Segal's (1991) view of colonial Americans' juxtaposing of their emergent national identity against the English. In analyzing colonial practices, Segal suggests that the early settlers established a conceptual syllogism between "American" and "English folks" as figures of identity. After severing ties with England, colonialists could no longer identify themselves politically as "English." To mark themselves as a political entity, they developed an identity that rendered them equal to their image of the English—equally "free" and equally an independent people. It was along the lines of racial purity, he argues, that this syllogism was established: the construction of "(northern) European" as a category and its equation with "free" (not-slave) labor, and the construction of "African" as not-free (slave). To be "American" meant to be free and racially "pure," like the English.[4] The categorical logic became problematic in the 1800s: Chinese, Japanese, and Mexicans were categorical anomalies, "free" but not "European." Their visibility as "category mistakes" challenged the category logic and the self-perception of the socioculturally dominant majority—"Americans"—as a free, racially pure people. These "others" were depicted as resembling the contemporaneous characterization of "Negroes"—shifty, lazy, lustful—as were Native Americans and many "European ethnics."[5] "All Others"—including Irish, Jews, and the like—were incorporated into the non-European side of the European-African opposition.

This dichotomy maintains the sense of two groups, White and Black, vested still in much contemporary race-ethnic discourse. The categorical division of Americans in two entails an imputed conceptual parity—of numbers or of parties to a conflict, if not of class or status (northern Europeans' sense of the latter made such parity conceptually impossible). Kusmer (1996) reads Jacob Riis's popular book *How the Other Half Lives*, published in 1890, along these lines. Had Riis counted more accurately, he notes, he would have titled the book *How the Other Three-quarters Live*. Moreover, the "other"-ness in the title maintains not only the separateness of the Protestant middle class but also their hierarchical elevation, as he notes: the "other" portion is the marked, "lesser," inferior population. If Segal's analysis is correct, the American national identity narrative—the definition of the "good" citizen—is inherently race-ethnic-based. The "good" American—the non–"other" half—historically has been an English person or its later Dutch or other northern European equivalent: lumping began early, with all the associated cultural trappings. This is the definitional and categorical heritage that is now being broken down. It is another aspect of the condensed identity plot narrated through the five major category labels.

Since the first national census in 1790, "all other" has become progressively more refined. Such refinement is one of the elements of the analytic story presented here: the Other is seemingly becoming more domesticated, less strange. And yet, we are not really coming to know her. As Gombrich's Chinese treatise (the third epigraph at the beginning of this chapter) indicates, nuanced identification requires familiarity: paradoxically, it is far easier to paint a picture of someone one has never seen, or does not know intimately, and categorical lumpiness holds the Other at arm's length. It lets us know only superficial differences: certain physical differences that define identity only in the visual gaze of the other, as when the EEOC mandates that an employer documenting workplace racial composition use "visual surveys" and appearances or when the Census Bureau opts not to tabulate or publish self-identifications that are at variance with its pre-established categories. These and other practices enact a story line about national identity that acknowledges differences among Americans in the names of their continents of (ancestral) origin, but minimizes any difference in cultural substance.

The entrenchment of the five categories in public policy and administrative practices implies that being an American today requires membership in one of the categories. No longer is anyone "just" an American. The melting pot works differently than envisioned: it produces hyphenated Americans, rather than "just" Americans. Even the English and the Dutch are, in this view, "ethnics." The category structure "naturalizes" difference as part of American identity.

Group Identity Stories: The Five Categories

The five categories tell us not only how to be American, but also how to be a member of the group one "must" be hyphenated into. The primary hallmark of contemporary American ethnogenesis is the lumpiness of the categories currently in use. The melting pot forges disparate peoples together within each hyphenated identity. All are jointly "othered" by the dominant culture—which they perceptually congeal and "other" in return as "White" and monolithic—as well as through interactions with the other groups. There is still resistance within each lumpy group to the externally imposed unification: for example, most Indians, according to Wilson (1992, p. 116), "still posit their identification tribally and only secondarily as Indian"; and the Mexica (pronounced "m'-SHEE-ka") Movement, of Aztec-, Mayan-, and other indigenous Mexican- and Central American–Americans, based in East Los Angeles, seeks to establish an identity against what some call the "ethnocide" that melds its members into a Hispanic or Latino/a group identity (Arrillaga 2001). It is unclear how the forces of "melting" and resistance will play out in the long run: as Fuchs (personal correspondence, 2001) notes, such ethnogenesis has occurred in the past, as Ilocano and Tagalog immigrants to the United States became Filipinos (now Pilipinos), and Sicilians and Italians united under one group name.

Our limited understanding of cultural identity is "dilute[d] and sanitize[d]" (Hymowitz 1993) by categorical lumping. It creates the illusion of sameness; but it is a superficial sameness. Aside from its broad-brush treatment of geography and physiognomy, this lumping treats culture as folklore—collections of foods, songs, dances, special outfits, and so forth:

an anthropological "trait list"—rather than as the deeply entrenched values, beliefs, feelings, and other aspects of meaningfulness that are powerful enough to compel group ties. The creation of the five categories rests on the successful creation of a prototype for each, what Gershon (n.d.a, p. 20) called "cultural horoscopes" in reference to stereotypes developed by New Zealand government officials of Pacific Islanders (Maori, Samoans, Cook Islanders): "rough guidelines for how a group of people might behave" comprising individual behavioral characteristics (such as shyness, generosity, or aggressiveness). Because their reference point is so general and covers such a vast range of elements, the prototypes often capture the most common stereotypes of each lumpy group, often to the point of caricature for one familiar with group members at a more intimate proximity; and these are often misleading, or wrong. Workplace cultural diversity programs illustrate this vividly, in a modern-day version of the older humor-induced behavioral trait lists. Several training videos urge managers not to be insulted when their Asian (–American) employees don't make eye contact. Looking down is a cultural mark, the narrator says, not a mark of disrespect or lack of interest. A possible characteristic (and certainly a major stereotype) of one Asian subgroup is projected onto all "Asians." Other trait lists accomplish the same.

This reinforces the view that language, religion, traditions, and myriad other elements are solely the domain of the group, rather than also components of individual identity, at the same time that it instructs individuals in the behavioral attributes that they must possess and exhibit in order to be seen as belonging to each group. Category membership socializes: Nigerian immigrants learn how to be "Black," Jewish Israelis learn how to be American Jews, "mulatto" or "Indian" Cubans learn how to be Hispanic or Black (Navarro 1997). There is a desire to belong, to be a "real" American, but it can only be fulfilled through the particulars of one of the five categories, which carry the message that one is different, not in individual terms, but in the identity terms of one's group.

Kusmer (1996, p. 20) observed that in his 1916 and 1933 writings, Madison Grant, a racial nativist, "saw no need to categorize or rank" the nonwhite races, "because he assumed their abysmal inferiority." Unfortunately, there is a sense in this undifferentiated lumpiness of a similar attitude on the part of those doing the naming. The lumpiness of the five categories is in the mold of Glazer and Moynihan's 1963 study of ethnic groups in New York. Each group (*the* Negroes, *the* Puerto Ricans, the Jews, the Italians, the Irish) is treated as if it were singular and uniform, with distinctive name, attributes, and interests (Chock 1989, p. 166), without internal differences. The prominence accorded to the language of "cultural diversity" suggests that race-ethnic group membership is an expression of *cultural* identity and that

Americans are diverse only or predominantly with respect to race-ethnicity in its cultural sense. This is a limited, indeed, impoverished, notion of identity: it provides an understanding of the diversity of identity that is restricted not only to dimensions of race-ethnicity, but to a small number of categories of very broad character; and it thereby limits the story that can be told. The Census Bureau, OMB, EEOC, and other agencies are, on the one hand, enabling storytelling by providing categories for membership but, at the same time, forcing individuals to constrain their stories to a narrow range of externally determined, state-provided language.

To be without a race-ethnic group identity in the United States today is to be without identity. In many contexts—from schools and universities to employment to health care to housing—often several times a year, one must be able to tell a race-ethnic group identity story: "I am a _____–American." Being unable to do so calls into question one's membership in American society. Individuals who cannot find their identity in the available categories become invisible, in a sense: without a label, without a vocabulary, their stories are untellable and they themselves are unnarratable.[6] Much of the struggle to include a "mixed race" category in Census 2000 was just that: an effort to make a personal story narratable, to make visible and to accord legitimacy to a social identity and the individuals holding it who have been silenced and "disappeared."[7] Forced to choose one among several ancestral origins—Cherokee, Irish, Black, and Chinese, for example—they have faced Arturo Madrid's problem (the second epigraph of the chapter) in even more complex ways.

"Unnarratability" has material consequences. As Levitt and Nass (1994, p. 239) point out, "nonpersons do not have the legitimacy to make ... claims." The social contract reflected in contemporary race-ethnic discourse lies not between the state and individuals, but between the state and race-ethnic groups. To the extent that membership in one of the five (or six) race-ethnic groups is required to make claims under various social policies, not belonging to one of them costs the individual the right to claim governmental attention and benefits in those areas.[8] As noted in chapter 4, individual identity within society reflects social rules for personhood and its substantive content. Identity is narratively established according to state-mandated terms. Invoking character traits other than those attributed to one of these groups means the individual's personhood cannot be empirically verified: the claim can be deemed false or irrelevant. Levitt and Nass cite the example of Shylock in *The Merchant of Venice,* among others in literature, who lists his general human traits in an effort to lay claim to humanness, to no avail.

A letter to the *New York Times* (4/9/93) underscores how this limited notion of identity works in practice. It seems that the newspaper headlined an article on two nominees for positions as U.S. Attorneys with the words "Woman and a Black." The letter writers point out that this categorization marginalizes women and Blacks, and Black women doubly, by implicitly distinguishing them from "normal" people. The headline's categories also imply that women are not Black and Blacks are only men, or that Blacks have no gender and women have no race, as the writers note. The headline could equally well have said "Mother and Father" or "Gardener and Pianist" or "Two Legal Scholars." A similar point is made by the book title, *All the Women Are White, All the Blacks Are Men, But Some of Us Are Brave* (Hull, Scott, and Smith 1981).

People who do not fit the category scheme—category "mistakes" who cross the boundaries: "mixed"-race people, for example—have long been conceptually troubling. The conceptual need for categorical purity (played out in the context of race-ethnicity as blood purity) is exceptionally strong, as Douglas (1966) argues in linking violations of such purity with perceptions of danger[9]: proximity can lead to contagion and contamination. Some of the prohibitions seem, however, to have been overcome (at least in law if not in practice), in the enactment of antimiscegenation and anti-housing and -loan discrimination laws, and the like. And yet, purity is entrenched in the five categories. Public narratives are only now beginning to become available to such category "mistakes," as OMB and the Census Bureau enable self-identification through more than one race-ethnic box.

The creation of "Other" and "Mixed race" categories is a recognition of change. But like "Pacific Islander–Americans," they are not yet on par with the five "regular" categories. They are still seen as exceptions. The conceptual power of bounded categories and the danger of crossing boundaries renders members of these extracategorical exceptions "impure," out of place.[10] Group identity stories may begin to make room for multiple prototypes within each category—the 1990 census named more than thirty different ethnic designations, and the Census Bureau announced that it will tabulate sixty-three race-ethnic identities in the 2000 census analysis—although this runs counter to categorical thinking. Through the proliferation of group identity narratives, the central case is slowly dissolving: the prototypical American is now hyphenated, marked; perhaps the five central prototypes will also dissipate. Passing is another way in which the categories are challenged, but people who pass are not precisely category mistakes: their acts of border crossing are intentional. Nor is theirs a nonstory: their silence is chosen; "passers" merge their identity stories with the absorbing group. But the circumstances that bring people to make these choices and the paths they follow have still not been fully told.

Category maintenance requires vigilance not only over group belonging and membership, but also over boundaries. "Halfway passing" is not allowed, because it entails enacting membership rites and adopting traits that violate group identity and membership criteria. It is policed as much, perhaps even more, by subdominant group members as by members of the groups passed into: "Oreos," "bananas," "Uncle Toms," and "Uncle Jakes" are roundly condemned because they adopt membership attributes of categories to which they do not perceptibly belong.[11]

There is yet another group of people who find that present category construction makes it difficult for them to narrate their identities. These are the people who identify themselves as "just American." Many who are predominantly of European extraction explain that they have no particular heritage other than American, that they are all "mutts" (a word used by many of them in self-description)—mixtures of many (usually European) origins. They are often the descendants of European immigrants who gave up speaking their parents' language(s) of birth, along with most other cultural markers, to become "true" Americans and who married across "ethnic"-nation-state lines. Often, these descendants grew up in highly homogeneous towns, knowing only the cultural practices of the dominant, Protestant-European group. They have no hyphenated group identity story; and if to be an American today means being hyphenated, they are without a national identity story as well. They could lay claim to European-American, but the "European" part contains no identity markers that are meaningful for them. It is as artificial an identity as claiming to be Native American would be.

In the United States, group identity continues over time (unless you "pass"), for some: marked identities tend to remain marked. An African-, Asian-, Hispanic, or Native American who moves from Atlanta to Oakland remains so (assuming she is not making the choice to pass into "Whiteland" [Scales-Trent 1995]), no matter how long she stays there. But a Caucasian-European-White eventually becomes a "Californian," especially as traces of the Atlanta accent disappear. This is not the case for others: a Madrileño who moves to Barcelona does not become a Catalunyan; the Yemenite from Jerusalem is still a Yerushalmi (and a Yemenite) after relocating to Beer Sheba.

An alternative to these group identity stories would be others similarly geographically based: Bostonian, New Yorker. . . . We might choose to create an indigenous, place-based, intersubjective set of meanings and practices, including language and accent, modes of dress, posture, and so on, as a set of American race-ethnicities. We might have Boston Blacks along with Boston Jews or Boston Chinese, or plain Californians and New Yorkers. The left side of the traditional hyphen refers to cultural history that, in some cases, continues to inform. But in many respects we could be growing our own hyphenated groups and attendant identity stories, without reference to color or to some geographical or cultural location external to our own borders. Color, country, and culture can be domesticated.

National Origin Stories: "Race" and "Ethnicity"

But the discussion so far only begs the question that prompted it. Since most people know themselves in more than just this one dimension, why are identity stories largely confined to race-ethnic terms, especially when those terms are not "real"? To put the matter bluntly, if it were truly "racial" differences that concerned us, wouldn't we have instituted as formal categories the destigmatized "Red" and "Yellow" to accompany the "Black" and "White"? That would obviate the need for subcategories (except for "mixed race," which could increase the range of the color spectrum, from Pink to Grey); but it sharply asks what the point of public discourse is.

We are telling origin stories. Categorical lumpiness and the reification of race and ethnicity maintain one of the classic areas of silence in American society: the notion of class. Presenting race-ethnicity as the central component of American national identity maintains the founding story that the United States is a classless society—but that story does not tell "where" Americans come from: it does not account for our collective origins as a people.

Neither does a story in "color" terms alone. The ancient color story originated in geographic locationing, as noted in chapter 1: people behaved differently from one another because (supposedly) they were nurtured by different air, water, sun, and earth; these (again, supposedly) caused the production of bodily fluids in different strengths and presences: blood (red), phlegm (white), and bile (yellow and black); and these, in turn, were understood to occasion different temperaments: nobility, calm, agitation, laziness. Begging for the moment the narrow limitation of human skin terms to these four absolute shades, color stories explain nothing without their associated bodily fluids ("humors") and behavioral attributions, and these have, thankfully, been roundly debunked (although, as I have argued here, echoes remain). But that, too, leaves us without a narrative that grounds (literally and figuratively) our national origins.

We are clearest that "our" national ancestors, the Pilgrims, came in search of freedom from persecution. This is the cultural component of the American origins story. It is celebrated at the Thanksgiving holiday (which used to, at least, have an overlay of giving thanks for refuge and freedom, in addition to its harvest context), and it has been extended to include other groups and other hardships—inscribed on the Statue of Liberty and in schoolbooks and television programs, enshrined in the refuge sections of U.S. immigration policy (which offer safe harbor to those fleeing adverse political and religious regimes, as long as that adversity is also recognized by U.S. foreign policy), increasingly institutionalized in museums and memorials, particularly those on the national mall in Washington, DC.[12] We are coming, over time, to narrate the story in African-American terms, through the life of Martin Luther King, Jr., and the civil rights movement, for example; we are still struggling, I think, to find its Native American form—it is hard to celebrate refuge and foreign origins for those who were already here and suffered at the hands of the nation-building European refugees; Cesar Chavez Day is now a state holiday in California; and the detention camp at Manzanar to which Japanese-Americans were relocated during World War II has been made a national monument.

Yet the refuge/freedom narrative is incomplete. The color-based origins story has been replaced with one told through geographic terms alone. Even if these labels have become euphemistic placeholders for the color scheme, the language itself is explicitly geographic. What makes Americans "American," according to this narrative, is that we all have other places of origin—in space (Europe, Africa, Asia, "Hispania") and in time (Native[13]). This origins narrative creates a link of birth with a place-based, air-earth-sun-water identity that itself links to nationhood. It is not by accident that nation, naturalization (as in "acquired citizenship"), and nature share an etymological root in "birthing": Middle English >> Old French >> Latin: *nātiō,* race, breed; from *nātus,* to be born (*American Heritage Dictionary* 1975, pp. 874–875).[14] Nation—meaning "people"—is distinct in this sense from state—a governmental unit that may or may not be sovereign—and country—a land or region bounded against (*contra*) some other region (Safire 1999). To make automatic citizenship a matter of birthplace or blood is to hark back to those ancient Greek notions that link the state to race-ethnicity. To become "naturalized"—to acquire citizenship other than by birth or descent—is to acquire the "nature" of that state by symbolic conversion (through immigration ceremonies) and "birth" (*natio*) to its people. In this conversion and rebirth, one acquires not only nationhood (of land and genealogy), but also (depending on the state) the identifying marks of ethnicity, culture, clothing, and language that enable participation in public life (see Crossette 1996). This is why for an immigration policy, such as that of the United States, whose symbolic conversion requires the conceptual and legal renunciation of other allegiances, a bicultural immigrant—who travels back and forth from birthplace or country of emigration to the United States—is problematic (for a view of public perceptions of this experience, see Sontag and Dugger 1998).[15] "Americans" are, in the lived experience of many like Arturo Madrid, still understood to be English and northern European Protestants. This is what the instantiation of "European-American" seeks to overthrow, by achieving an equalization of hyphenatedness, of "othering," that creates a shared sense of American origins. "Real" Americans have origins elsewhere as reflected in the left side of the hyphen, and America is made up of all these entangled roots.

Here lies the incommensurability: the knowledge that Americans are immigrants—something we value: a heritage of finding and giving refuge—and the weakness of that origin as a claim to land and nationhood, according to ancient meanings still buried deep within our language. And so we create a national origin story that can narrate an account of our collective heritage—as people with origins elsewhere who nonetheless are also rooted here. It serves as a public myth, to deflect attention from the internal contradictions that might destabilize national identity and cohesion. Ironically, we *need* hyphenated identities, at whatever level of lumpy aggregation, because they preserve American identity—although there is nothing in this logic that requires a limited handful of categories. Acknowledging differences through category language, in other words, preserves national unity by enabling a shared, collective, "American" origins story.

But we deny, in all practical senses, that those ancestors brought a social and economic class structure with them and/or developed one on this soil. And in this denial, in the active embrace of classlessness, Americans deny ourselves a fuller explanation for ongoing status differences and, therefore, of potential policy remedies. The particular form of race-ethnic stories told through contemporary U.S. policies and administrative practices provides this explanation, at the same time that it masks it: the relics of the unnamed White norm and remnants of behavioral connotations of color and country explain status; the five hyphenated categories mask difference. This narrative allows us to maintain the belief that success and failure are in individuals' hands. Counting all Asians and Pacific Islanders in one category (or even in two), thereby reporting a statistic that is an average over all subgroups, diverts attention from those below the poverty line. Treating Blacks without internal differentiation sustains stereotypes that are silent on the existence of a well-established Black middle class. The category structure also obscures the existence of poor Whites—agricultural families, for example, who moved to the small towns of California's Central Valley during Dust Bowl migrations, whose middle-aged children or grandchildren in the 1980s and 1990s were the first generation in their family to go to college.

The notions of race and ethnicity may also constitute a societal myth. It is a myth that arises from the incommensurability of the experienced reality of differential treatment, on the one hand, and the founding belief in equality, on the other hand, despite family or class of birth. We cannot relinquish either of these. The equality is an equality of individuals: if one does not succeed, it is due to personal failure of effort or skill or personality. The perceived difference, however, is a collective difference—the sort that would be explained by a group "success factor" (such as posited by earlier ethnic studies[16]) or a "culture of poverty" argument. But "cultural" differences (including speaking one's "native" language; see Schmidt 1999, p. 5) have been consigned to the private realm, and we maintain public silences about class, thereby depriving ourselves in our public, collective discourse of two possible means of explanation. Focusing on race-ethnicity as a continent-based phenomenon allows us to explain persistent inequalities and discriminatory practices, to talk about them publicly (albeit in a sanitized fashion), when public discourse on some of their components is not publicly sanctioned. It is the current iteration of the Horatio Alger stories: anyone can make it, regardless of institutionalized societal practices that favor certain groups and discriminate against others. Policy and administrative practices such as current census formulations are the rituals enacting this myth, and through them Americans tell ourselves about ourselves.

The choice to make "continental" race-ethnicity the central organizing principle of societal status often puzzles immigrants from countries where class is the more publicly visible and discussable feature. Americans maintain the fiction that we are a classless society by focusing on race-ethnic categories, but empty those categories of substantive meaning, so that there is little to divert energy from the cultivation of a national identity. At the same time, however, attention is diverted from economic sources of power and status in this country.[17] The explanation of national origins—that we come from elsewhere; all Americans are hyphenated-Americans—is thereby extended through this particular story line to include the classless character of national identity. Not that class alone should replace race-ethnicity; but its occlusion constrains the faculty of our collective self-narrative to imagine and generate potentially more capacious social justice remedies.

And Yet . . . : Exploring a Counter-Narrative

What appear today in usage as fixed race-ethnic ideas have actually been changing throughout the history of our country. This is reflected in changing category names: earlier, from free persons to White, for instance; today, in struggles over the five (or six) categories. Census policies seemingly build on past practices, incrementally adjusting the language of questions and categories from one decade to the next, and other policies rest on these Census Bureau decisions and data. For example, until the 1965 bill, all prior twentieth-century immigration legislation invoked quotas based on earlier census counts of national origins. The 1921 law used 1910 census data; the 1924 law reverted to 1890 data; the 1929 amendment returned to 1920 data, and the 1952 McCarran-Walter Act retained that base. The 1965 and subsequent bills abolished country-based quotas enumerated according to the presence of those nationals in the United States and substituted quotas by hemisphere with per country maximums.

If such changes are not new, and if military and foreign policy concerns do not mandate it, do we need to continue to ask about race-ethnic background in each census, in order to have a proportional assessment of the population for some other control purposes? It is time to break this cycle of incrementalism and re-engage the matter of what we want to know, collectively, as a polity, and for what purposes.

The absoluteness of the categories and the longstanding absence of an interracial category reflect a conceptual heritage of the earliest distinctions between free and slave: one could not be both. Labor, taxation, and military service required such absolute knowledge. Between 1790 and 1820 "color" was of little interest. Attitudes and purposes changed over the next fifty years; the categorizing eye began to count subgroup details as "race" became a salient category for the state. The meaning of White was clear—by negation: not African, not American Indian. To be "White by law" meant to be not non-White well into the 1900s (Haney López 1994, p. 28).

What these changes reflect is a reconsideration of the quality of the "man" created equal to all others. This is seen most clearly in 1860: the categories are arranged in descending order of "personhood," from White to free colored to Indian to slave. This heritage of attitudes toward personhood is also carried in current race-ethnic categories: displayed formerly in antimiscegenation laws, it was evident most recently in the struggles against establishing a "mixed race" category.

During this same period in the mid- to late 1800s, the idea became entrenched that each American has a single source of origin. Intermarriage between the Jew and the Catholic who began to arrive in the next decades was of little interest to the state (even though it often created family havoc); but between White and Black it was (and still is, in many places) unthinkable (if no longer illegal), as it was between White and any other, and regulated by the state. That Blacks, Hispanics, and Native Americans are often "racially" mixed (and in the case of Hispanics, often with Asians) has been of little concern to the state (and is only becoming publicly and explicitly recognized now, in the aftermath of the Census 2000 multiple-choice option). This categorical absoluteness is still visible in the language of "ethnic origin" in Census Questions 13 (in 1990) and 10 (2000): the singular noun does not entertain the possibility of multiple heritages.

Today, "Others" and "Mixed race" persons are actively rejecting this either/or approach to race-ethnicity. This attack on categorical purity may do as much as, if not more than, affirmative action policies to break down our conceptions of social status along race-ethnic lines. As policy and administrative uses of census data clash more frequently with individual identities, it is more likely that the silences enabled by these categories will be broken, along with the artificial boundaries between them. Evolving understandings of American democracy may demand that race-ethnic categories capture variation and reflect differences, rather than elide them, with consequent policy and administrative adjustments.

"Racial" discourse is not just descriptive. The establishment of race-ethnic differences entails hierarchies based on what a society or a polity and its state manifestations have deemed sociopolitically important. State-maintained population categorization does not speak of "talent," for example; there is no "race-ethnic" group of pianists or skiers. Difference of another sort lies at the root of race-ethnic identity: it is aggregated group differences based on the criteria that constitute a prototypical citizen, created and maintained by the state and inscribed on the individual. These categories are not experienced or treated by individuals as merely statistical entities, however, which is how they have been treated by the state agencies that have created them. There is a social reality for individuals beyond the categorical boundaries of race-ethnic category membership, beyond the terms of "diversity" accepted in current parlance. It is the need for self-expression, reflecting lived experience, within the bounds of other-defined categories that drives the desire to change the categories, to bring them more clearly in line with personal experience and social reality.

Other stories (or sets of stories) still echo in race and ethnicity discourses. The story linking behavioral traits and race-as-color has largely been broken,[18] but its foundation echoes still in blood (and other bodily "fluids," such as genes) and in soil: race-as-country-of-origin. The valuative hierarchy narrative is ensconced in the conceptual history of the word "race" and invoked every time the term is used. But whereas the code using "race" for assigned hierarchies has been made explicit in public discourse and largely debunked, not so the embedded link to the 2000-year-old theory of fluids and temperaments.

If only for these reasons, we should stop using race-ethnic terms and categories in public policy and administrative practices. We can tell national identity, national origins, and personal identity stories without recourse to the language of race or of ethnicity. It is time to rewrite the story line, to see that we can be Americans, and hold on to cherished meanings, without constantly reinventing race-ethnic questions, without harming either side of the hyphen, and perhaps without asking the questions at all or, at least, without asking them in the reductionist, lumping way that is currently in use.

The five categories imply that Americans are "biracial": both American and something else. The good American is someone who comes from many elsewheres, some more recently, some a long time ago. The argument expounded by Peter Brimelow, the English immigrant whose 1995 book called for a halt to immigration, is wrong, morally, not because of its substance, but because of his effrontery, as someone who comes from somewhere else claiming privilege or priority over others who come from different elsewheres. This is what lies at the heart of cries for valuing diversity, however superficial the practical programs may be: that no elsewhere takes precedence over any other elsewhere. It is a view from both Boston and California: Americans are all relocated, some of us dislocated.

For familial and communal concerns, cultural heritage still matters. Yet, American liberal ideology instructs us to leave group storytelling to the private, communal realm, without making it a matter of state. In this sense, the Census Bureau's announced shift toward sixty-three analytic categories for "race" is potentially generative. It promises to shift the focus away from continental origins and to bring communal stories into the national domain. In this, it goes a long way toward altering the presupposition of categorical purity, and perhaps even toward undermining the categories themselves and the category logic that underlies them.

Zack (1995, p. 301) writes: "I propose that we write ourselves out of race as a means of constructing racelessness or removing the construction of race." Surely, as she notes, language is instrumental in the production and maintenance of these concepts and categories. But changing language alone is not sufficient; practices also need to be changed.

Notes

1. Greenwood (1989, pp. 5, 6) notes that in Spain under Franco, cultural diversity—which there has a regional geographic base—was seen as an attack against the unity of the state. This regionally based ethnogenesis has, in time, become a political identity, and ethnic politics has replaced the politics of social class.

2. Greenwood (1985), examining the Spanish experience, argues that ethnic movements flourish when governmental centers are weak. Extended to the United States, this would mean when there is no strong sense of national purpose or identity, as under the Reagan, the elder Bush, and the Clinton administrations.

3. *Marranos* (lit. "swine"), also known as *conversos* (currently, the preferred usage): Spanish and Portuguese Jews who converted to Catholicism during the Inquisition, living publicly as Catholics while continuing to practice Judaism privately, within the family.

4. Matters of "racial, religious and national self-definition" were preoccupying the English during the sixteenth and seventeenth centuries, according to Stephen Greenblatt (1996), in a review of James Shapiro's *Shakespeare and the Jews* (New York: Columbia University Press). It should not be surprising, then, that emigrants from England should have brought these concerns to the colonies and that their preoccupations with them should have colored founding policy doctrines and administrative practices.

5. See Kusmer (1996) for a fuller treatment of this history.

6. As Taylor (1989, p. 34) also noted, without "some reference to a defining community," identity and "self" cannot be played out.

7. See also Squire-Hakey (1995, p. 225) on silences.

8. Amselle (1995) argued this case within the history of France. French indigenism prior to the Revolution, he said, consisted of three ethnicities: a German nation in the area of Alsace, a Portuguese nation in the southwest (around Bordeaux), and communities of Jews in Carpentras, Avignon, and surrounding towns (the "Pope's Jews," so-called because of protections extended to them in that region by Pope Clement VI and his successors from 1274–1791). The creation of the first two groups meant that a Jewish identity needed to be created. But all of these group identities needed to disappear in order for their members to become "Frenchmen": the traditional French notion of citizenship depends on assimilation, and a citizen made claims on the state as an individual, not as a member of an ethnic group. Amselle suggests that this tradition is currently under assault with the creation of French ethnic groups.

9. See, for example, Naomi Zack's account (1992) of her mother's shame as a Jew over her relationship with her father, whom she identifies as an African-American whose mother was Sioux. She speaks there of breaking her own long-term silence, echoing themes presented by Scales-Trent (1995). This reluctance to recognize the existence of mixed race-ethnic heritage or to grant it standing equal to "pure" race-ethnic lines echoes what Douglas (1966) identified as pollution taboos protecting societal classificatory schemes.

10. This is the conceptual situation of "illegals," immigrants who do not fit into a "regular" category and are hence seen as being "out of place" and "dirty" (or impure, in Douglas's [1966] terms).

11. These terms refer to "mixed" identities: "Oreos," like the cookie, are Black on the outside, White on the inside; "bananas" are yellow ("Asian") on the outside, White on the inside; Uncle Toms, after the character in the novel by Harriet Beecher Stowe, are traitors to their African brothers (Black outside, White inside); and Uncle Jakes, named after the model of Uncle Toms, are traitors to their fellow Jews (Jewish outside, White inside).

12. Varenne (1998) notes that diversity in ethnic origin as well as in religion is central to American origin myths.

13. It is curious that we use this term rather than, say, Australia's "aboriginals" or Canada's "First Nations." David Wilkins (personal communication, August 25, 1996) notes that many American Indians reject the label "Native American"—a term created, he thinks, in the academy—but many want to hold on to it in preference to some other label. I am struck that it preserves the syntax and meter of the other hyphenated categories, and this may explain part of its appeal.

14. Even "heritage," used so widely with "ethnic," carries a relation to birth and even to birthright, from the Latin $h\bar{e}r\bar{e}s$ = "heir" (see also heredity, inherit; *American Heritage Dictionary* 1975, pp. 617, 676). Bernard Lewis, writing about the Middle East, notes that "blood," "place," and "faith," three primary human identities, are acquired at birth, although Wheatcroft (2000), in reviewing Lewis's essays, chides him for thinking this limited to only that part of the world.

15. It also may be part of what makes bilingual education in the United States appear to be "unAmerican," and perhaps "Ebonics" (Black vernacular English) as well (see Steele 1997).

The relationship among state and nation, and their associated notions of citizenship, naturalization, language, and religion, is convoluted; and established concepts are under attack and in flux worldwide and very much matters of national and international public discourse, to judge from recent newspaper coverage. The discussions all seem to echo the ancient Greek notions of geography and genealogy.

German notions of *Volk* ("people," "peoplehood") as the basis for nationality seem to rest on stock or an "image of Germany as a blood community" (sociologist Hartmut Esser, quoted in Cohen 1998, affirmed there by Claus Leggewie, another sociologist), rather than on a liberal, republican view of citizenship. Or, at least, this seems to have been the traditional view that remained in West Germany, whereas East Germans under Soviet-Russian influence developed an "ethnic view of identity" (in Leggewie's words). Their experience is supported by the large number of "guest workers" from Turkey and refugees and asylum-seekers from the former Yugoslavia, Italy, Greece, and Eastern European countries staying in Germany, leading to legislative efforts to revise the citizenship laws. These would, among other things, lower the residential requirement for applying for citizenship from fifteen years to eight. In 1997, "more than 60% of legally registered foreigners under 18 were born in [Germany]—what German officials call '*immigration by birth*'" (Cowell 1997, pp. 1, 3). The French, by contrast, would be—at least according to official policy—happy to consider anyone French as long as she or he gave up any sense of other-group identity, learned to speak French, and relinquished all "non-French" customs, such as Moslem women and girls wearing head scarves, an issue in schools in Paris and the south of France.

16. For example, Glazer and Moynihan (1963); see Chock (1989) for one critique of these.

17. See also Steinberg (1989) and Williams (1990) for more extensive analyses of the connections among class, race, and ethnicity.

18. Obviously, not entirely, given the recent publication (1994) of Herrnstein and Murray's *The Bell Curve* and its argument implicating a racial basis for intelligence.

8

Changing (Ac)Counting Practices: Meditation on a Problem

To do my work, I have to get genetic data
from different parts of the world,
and look at differences within groups and between groups,
so it helps to have labels for groups.

—Dr. Alan Rogers,
population geneticist, professor of anthropology,
University of Utah
(quoted in Angier 2000, p. C1)

The American people are infected with racism—that is the peril.
Paradoxically, they are also infected
with democratic ideals—that is the hope.

—Martin Luther King, Jr.
(quoted in Carson 1995, p. 6)

[The power of classificatory systems] is closely tied to [their]
invisibility
and to the assumption that the common classifications
and the cause-effect relationships they imply
are objective and self-evident....
The common classifications obscure the important ways
in which policies in supposedly different categories reinforce each
other....

—Murray Edelman (1995, pp. 131–132)

Q. You've seen the evolution from Negro to black to African-American? What is the best thing for blacks to call themselves?
A. White.

—*Dr. Kenneth B. Clark,*
interviewed by Sam Roberts (1995)

And yet again . . .

It would have been easy to stop at the end of the last chapter: the research and analysis lead me by their logic to the conclusion that the continued invocation of "race," "ethnicity," and the state-defined categories as they are presently used only harms us. There is nothing natural about the concepts or the categories, but various "common sense," everyday practices (re)present and treat them as if they were, thereby making them appear to be so. Because many of these practices involve public policies and their implementation, and because the practices are used, then, for both administrative and identity-expressive purposes, what many individuals experience is the power of the state to construct and constrain identities through the construction of policy and administrative categories. Social scientists are complicitous in this: in adopting, unreflectively, state-constructed categories, their practices reinforce and maintain state practices. The power of the state and the social standing and, hence, power, of "Science" intertwine. Resistance is difficult. Some individuals opt for a passive mode of resistance to the categorizing power of the state (as well as to the experience of lesser status) by passing out of subdominant into dominant groups. The "mixed race" possibility has seemed like another path out, but as it is now sanctioned by the state, it hardly seems like resistance at all. Both of these work within the social reality of the categories. And then there is the question of resistance and social justice.

At the same time that they shape individuals' identities and group members' perceptions of their own and of other groups, these policy and administrative usages—these identity stories—have very practical, material, social justice implications. Specifically, the OMB-defined census categories have become, since 1980,[1] the foundations for the redistribution of wealth in the form of various publicly funded programs and eligibilities for their services, as people qualify and disqualify for participation in governmental actions according to their fit within state-determined categories. Yet we cannot—I cannot conceive of a way in which we can—achieve a socially equalitarian society when we constantly remind ourselves, almost daily, of differences of the sort that are built—conceptually, cognitively, linguistically—into the race-ethnic language that we use. The categories implicitly "sell" concepts of race and ethnicity through dispassionate documents and administrative means that most people would not give a second thought to, but that have material consequences: they encourage and focus a great deal of energy on oft-contentious public discourse over definitional and identity concerns, while diverting attention from other, perhaps equally important, terrains, among them class, age, gender, local geography (in no particular order). It seems to me, in light of the preceding case examples, quite evident that in order to achieve a socially just society, we need to give up these ways of counting ourselves and find others. But to date, most such attempts to rewrite the American story by altering these categories or even dropping them entirely have led, themselves, to resistance in the form of arguments that social justice cannot be served without them.

The census and its categories were not created to allow individuals to express their identities. They had clear instrumental purposes and, as with immigration policy, have reflected contemporary domestic and foreign policy issues throughout the history of their existence. Census tabulations served planning purposes as well as descriptive ones, with policy and administrative implications for the central state. Color, culture, and country were not of uniform interest to the state for the first ten censuses, developing mostly over the last 100 years. The state's interest can be redevised again.

"What now?" concerns need to be argued with passionate humility: the ardent conviction in one's position moderated by the humbling recognition that one may be wrong. In the sway of this stance, I cannot offer certain answers and directions for action. What I can do is point to some entailments of the arguments for and oppositions to tearing down this categorical infrastructure. This is what I undertake to accomplish in this last chapter.

Immutability Versus Challenge: Concerning Agency and Change

One of the hallmarks of this contemporary race-ethnic discourse is our reification of both categories and concepts, without attending to this act. We have lost sight of the "as if" quality of both: commonplace, everyday policy and administrative practices have naturalized the concepts of race and ethnicity and their attendant categories and routinized the acts of assigning people to them. OMB is our modern-day Linnaeus, naming and defining race-ethnic groups; and researchers in the academy and in applied practices exploring workplace cultural diversity are the contemporary incarnations of early twentieth-century anthropologists, identifying group trait lists. Color, country, and culture—to be blunt, blood (there is no "one gene rule") and geography—are, still, the themes underlying these practices. What hurts, mor-

ally, about racial profiling is its conflation of physical traits with social behaviors, in echo, still, of the ancient Greeks and medieval Spain. Even "mixed
race" is an oxymoron: it posits, linguistically, that each of the other race-
ethnic categories or subcategories in current usage is pure. This is hardly the
case: Anglo-Saxons, Italians, Guatemalans, Cambodians—each designation
is, itself, a mixed "race"; the search for a race-ethnically "pure" group is
probably as elusive as the (old) anthropological search for a tribe uncon-
taminated by the modern world—and as outmoded.

That this is the case should not surprise: coming to perceive an external,
objective reality in collective, human constructions, and then forgetting its
artifactual origins, is the very process of constructing the social world. In
this process, human agency becomes blurred: we come to perceive that "the
state" or "the organization" is taking action in a depersonalized way. This is
built into the American policy-making process: through successive hearings
and debates, with input from lobbyists and columnists and town hall meetings, the authorship of category definitions and policy programs becomes
diffused. The consequence for social change is profound: it appears impossible. Without a historical or comparative context, the categories appear to
be natural and stable, and social change appears nonexistent.

This is the danger of seeing reified categories as permanent and unchangeable; we need to shake loose that perception. What historical and
comparative analyses show is that there is more than one way to deal with
"race-ethnic" differences. Policy choices are choices. Human agency has
not been eradicated.

More than that: seeing or treating "race" and "ethnicity" as scientific concepts—not in an academic-intellectual understanding of science as a social
practice, but in the commonsense, everyday view of scientific terms as generated by and reflective of objective, empirical study of the natural and social world—graces them with an ontological reality as independent variables,
thereby masking the power and status contexts within which they were created and within which they have meaning as expressions of group relations.
Treating them as independent, causative explainors diverts attention from
other possible explanatory frames in which the social realities of race-ethnicity
might be of subsidiary significance. As Graves (2001) points out in the context of medical treatment, seeing through race-ethnic membership as the primary diagnostic lens leads physicians to disregard certain diseases, because
the individuals they are examining present as members of groups not known
to carry those diseases.

Again, reading race-ethnic categories in a historical context that demonstrates their mutability highlights the power relationships that they were created to preserve, both domestically (as with respect to slaves and Indians)

and for foreign policy (as with tabulating Mexican-Americans) or immigration policy (e.g., counting Japanese and Chinese). Categorical lumpiness and reification interact: the conceptual uniformity imputed to the five categories blinds us to differences that, were we but aware of them, would keep us from treating these categories as real divisions in the social world; and reification of the lumpy uniformity diverts our attention from differences that might divide us—including the class and geographic differences that we fear because they are part of the historical and ancestral divisions of Americans' collective past.

Concepts and categories of race and ethnicity are dynamic reflections of intergroup relations and/or group-government relations, but their reification as they appear over and over again, in agency questionnaires, media reporting, and elsewhere, in seemingly identical format, makes them seem as if they were not only stable but fixed, unchanging and unchangeable. Argument over the labels accepts the existence of the categorical schema and forestalls further discourse about its artifactual nature. It diverts attention from the possibility of challenging, let alone changing, the schema or even the very concepts of "race" and "ethnicity" altogether. As Starr (1987) notes, these classifications are powerful "cognitive commitments": administrative language shapes action (and vice versa), including individual identity formation as well as that of the state. And yet, the situation is not as binding as Starr would have it. This is, in fact, the practical difference between understanding and treating race, ethnicity, and the categories as socially constructed entities and as natural facts: the former allows both conceptual and actual change, whereas presenting and treating them as if they were reflections of naturally occurring human characteristics and divisions creates and underscores their immutability—at least insofar as human control is concerned.

Moreover, although they were designed as a tool for instrumental purposes, the census's race-ethnic tabulations have more recently come to serve expressive purposes as well, at the same time that those instrumental purposes are changing. Today, race-ethnic categories appear to be expressive statements about identity, including social status and class.[2] But since we continue to maintain a national mythology of classlessness, alluding to class through race-ethnic labels highlights "racial" discourse while it silences public discourse concerning economic (and other) bases of status. Segal and Handler (n.d., p. 20) argue that presenting data for both "race" and "class" (their quotation marks) would undermine the "objectification of America's races," de-factualizing them, while revealing the contingency of each as a classificatory mode. It would most likely be a step toward eliminating the prevalent stereotyping of "all" Whites and Asians as middle or upper class and Blacks, Hispanics, and Native Americans as poor.

"Race" differences are not rooted in class differences: they constitute one way of constructing class differences, whether for economic or social-psychological reasons. They assign one or more groups to lower status and one or more to higher status; the public policies and administrative practices that undergird them enact these assignments; and they appear to reflect the state's interests or those of the ruling class(es) (to the extent that these can be separated). In that sense, the hyphenization of all American groups is a radical egalitarian move, to the extent that the linguistic construction drives status (re)conceptualizations (or draws them in its wake). But socially real cultural and identity differences are masked by continental designations: there is no more a single European culture or identity than there is a sole Asian or African, Latin or Indian one. As a substitute for community ties, continental designations are inadequate: these are impoverished entities, and to the extent that our language, including our categories, shapes our lives, the language of these categories cannot enrich us.

Asking Different Questions: What Do We Want to Know?

But, the counterargument goes, these categories are now entrenched and necessary for allocating federal funds for affirmative action and other redistributive policies and programs. They cannot be changed or abolished without undermining social justice goals and ideals. Hospitals, schools, city planners, banks, public health departments, Fannie Mae, and many other federal, state, county, and local agencies use these categorical data for entitlement and protection programs. In short, we need some method for counting, and the categories in use in the census enable us to do that.

Educational policy maker Harold Hodgkinson (2000) notes the "deeply American irony" of having to keep categories that are considered "a scientific and anthropological joke." "We need the categories," he writes, "in order to eliminate them. Without knowing who our oppressed minorities are, how can we develop remedies so that they will no longer be oppressed?" The most recent expression of this tension is in the context of "racial profiling": in seeking to counter it, we measure its incidence by those same "racial" categories whose use the critique condemns. This debate over the necessity for or the deleterious effect of race-ethnic categorizing and counting has been joined publicly by many scholars, among them Anthony Appiah; Derrick Bell; Stephen Carter; Henry Louis Gates, Jr.; Lani Guinier; Manning Marable; Claude Steele; Shelby Steele; Patricia Williams; William Julius Wilson.[3] Much of this debate has taken place in the context of questions about affirmative action. More recently, researchers engaging the debate from the perspectives of medical practices (see, e.g., Graves 2001) and statistical analysis (Zuberi 2001) have added their voices.

The analysis presented in the preceding chapters leads me to call for a national, public conversation across the widest range of race-ethnic groups, not just on the utility of using state-defined race-ethnic categories, but at a more fundamental level: on the purpose of counting, and on the kinds of traits that need to be counted, and for what ends. Perhaps we do still need to know the potential size of our fighting force, our labor pool, and our tax base (and constitutionally, we are still mandated to enumerate for purposes of representation). But none of these, today, requires us necessarily to count ourselves by race-ethnic group (not that they ever did, except for reasons of state-supported prejudices and discriminations and ruling group control). The research coming out of the Human Genome and Genome Diversity Projects shows that racial categorizing puts artificial boundaries along a continuum: we are genetically far more alike one another than we are different (and those differences are statistically minuscule). "Ethnicity" would seem to allow us to mark cultural differences; but what is being tabulated under the guise of ethnicity is an ahistorical amalgam of place names at varying levels of geographic specificity. If what we are truly interested in is where Americans come or came from, let's ask a different set of questions:

- What continent(s) did your ancestors come from? Specify the generation.
- What country(ies) did your ancestors come from? Specify the generation.
- What region(s) did your ancestors come from? Specify the generation.
- What was the birthplace of your _____ (list family kinship terms, e.g., "mother," "father," "spouse/partner," "first cousin," "mother's mother's mother")?
- What is/are your cultural heritage/s?
- What languages are spoken in your home, and by whom (identify by kinship terms)? What languages do you speak?

In the present age of large-capacity computers, surely the variety of possible answers to these questions can be assembled and tabulated with relative ease. They would replace the "race" question and the "Hispanic/Latino/a" question and transform the ancestry question. But why is such information important as a contemporary census or other administrative category?

It is very important to many of us to achieve social justice, and the redistributive role of the categories is what has been established for this purpose. Yet perhaps it is time to stop using race-ethnicity as a proxy for economic and behavioral problems, lest our very language continue to perpetuate inequality. We need to be more actively and explicitly reflective about the categories we are using today and about the reasons for our categorizing practices, and not unreflectively carry out past practices simply because they are embedded in routines. The twenty-first-century United States—post–Tiger Woods, the O.J. Simpson trial, Rodney King, and the 2000 census figures—

can no longer be seen as just a Black/White world. Whereas what is seen as constituting "White" has changed over the last twenty years or so, what has not changed is the logic underlying the category system. It superimposes a binary White-"raced" opposition over the five- (or six-) part structure. Race-ethnic identity is determined by the enacted definition of White and proximity to or distance from its traits, however they are being defined at the moment.[4] The strength of this binary is made visible in the April 2001 City Council vote in San Diego to declare "minority" an unwanted, discriminatory term and to outlaw its use (Safire 2001).

The cases presented in the preceding chapters show that the scientific basis imputed to the categories we are using is nonexistent. "Race" and "ethnicity" are not precise terms; they do not identify precise categories of meaning. Neither are their categories precise categories. Efforts to make the categories ever more refined will still not render them more accurate reflections of what is a very complex human reality: they are based on a sense of category members being "nearly the same." I have tried to show, however, that their trappings of scientific practices—formal taxonomies, definitions of terms, a heritage of (outdated and hateful) "scientific" usages—serve, by the power accorded to "Science" in contemporary society, supported by the authority of the state that created them, to argue, tacitly, for their possessing scientific character, which itself carries an implication of precision. Even in academic settings, in which it has become more commonplace in the last decade to argue for them as social constructs rather than as externally objective, scientific facts, the use of the concepts and categories as if they were taxonomically clear and unambiguous is largely not challenged—not in administrative practices and not in public policy and administration or business administration textbooks (such as in the area of human resources management). Nor are they challenged in elementary and secondary school curricula exploring "multiculturalism," in which certain groups are selected for inclusion in the curriculum, although typically without public discussion concerning the criteria for choice or for assessing equal treatment.[5] We have not only routinized difference and naturalized it in terms of race-ethnicity, but fossilized what that means, with so many public institutions—from schools to hospitals to banks to police departments—organized by race-ethnic categories. We continue to use the categories because of their narrative power in providing us with ways to answer central identity questions, but also because of their imputed scientific standing.

Category language itself forces race-consciousness. In comparing the ethnicization of Samoans in New Zealand with their racialization in the United States, Gershon (n.d.b) shows how the state, typically through tying identity to fundable program categories but also through substantive programmatic concerns, makes—defines and enacts—race-ethnic groups. In the United States we see this most clearly in the two recent changes in OMB and census procedures. The creation of a new Pacific Islander category is a step toward creating a new American "race." And the argument for the 2000 procedural change that placed the Hispanic question before the race question would be true of all ethnicities, not just Hispanic: the order may allow for a more conscious self-identification as a member of one (or more) racial group. But it is still a "race"-conscious argument. One still cannot identify as a mixed race Italian-Irish-Indian or as Iranian-Lakota or as a Galitzianer-Litvak Jew, and so on, within the preestablished logic of the OMB categories.

What does it avail us to recount our origins, for public policy or administrative purposes, as far back as Lucy? We continue to deal here with inherited, outdated science. It is time to move on. We need to give up these outmoded concepts and categories and to rethink and reframe the problem.

Policy and Administrative Ethics: Do No Harm?

OMB 15 was an effort to standardize data collection in order to eliminate irregularities of reporting local knowledge across multiple agencies, fifty states, and numerous locales. Judged by measures of administrative efficiency, it has worked. But driven by the desire for universal standards, the state has extended a single set of categories to situations in which they may not be appropriate or effective measures. It is not sufficient just to count numbers and analyze them statistically. We need to be aware of the meanings underlying— and, hence, the consequences of—the acts of naming and counting. What the cases explored here show is that the goal of statistical efficiency in standardizing the category names and their definitions has failed—except in the most statistical sense abstracted from the lived experience that is being named and counted. Administrative uniformity at the federal level masks administrative difference at the local level—and the latter is closer to, but often still divorced from, many individuals' lived experiences.

Continuing with the categories as they are out of the sense that changing or dropping them would eliminate our ability to achieve social justice goals means that we allow statistics to drive policy practice and discourse. Foregrounding the problem of comparability of data means allowing a method of analysis to drive policy choices, rather than engaging the policy issues substantively and subordinating the method of data collection and analysis to what it is we want to know.

This would not be the first time in American history that statistical science has played such a determinative role. It was implicated in immigration restrictions in the late 1800s to early 1900s, when statistics and racist ideas kept company. For example, Francis Walker, Census Office Superintendent in 1870 and 1880, theorized about "racial" differences between earlier Northern- and Western-European immigrants—skilled, thrifty, hardworking—and newer immigrants from Southern and Eastern Europe—unskilled, ignorant, predominantly Catholic or Jewish and, hence, potentially unassimilable. His ideas were endorsed by other bureau statisticians, among them a director, an assistant director, and a chief clerk, and led to the National Origins Act of 1924 limiting immigration to 1890 census proportions (Anderson 1988, pp. 137, 143, 147).[6]

The state, through present public policy and administrative practices, is tied to funding and programming categories, and it makes, defines, and enacts race-ethnicity. Census results increasingly form the basis for welfare and social service policies and resource reallocations by group size. Race and ethnicity data, as established under OMB definitions and guidelines, provide ways of naming discriminatory practices and seeking legal redress, and they legitimate and provide credibility for claims for governmental assistance (funds for schools, hospitals, health services, housing, jobs, etc.) and political representation. This is not new. The first time Congress used census numbers to apportion money—$28 million surplus revenue—from the federal government to the states was in 1837 (Holt 1929, p. 26). They were not used again for such purposes for another hundred years, until the passage of the Social Security Act in 1935, a grant-in-aid system administered by the states, in which census data were the basis for grant-making formulas (p. 179).

Controversy over the use of census numbers is not new, either. Debates in 1850 over census revisions raised questions not only about (dis)union, slavery, and the North-South balance of power, but also about the scope of federal power and the centralized collection of data by the federal government: whereas police, health, education, and other data are collected by local agencies and reported up the federal system, census data collection and analyses are conducted by a federal agency alone (albeit for good historical, constitutional reasons). Between 1850 and 1900, the purpose of the census changed, in Anderson's (1988) analysis: "Though still a political apportionment mechanism, the census also became a full-fledged instrument to monitor the overall state of American society," influenced by the professionalization and bureaucratization of the data collectors and paralleling the rise of the "science of statistics" (p. 85). The latter seems to have driven a desire to know in more detail the characteristics of American "popular, economic, and social life" (p. 98).

If we refuse to reconsider the ways in which we base our desired equity outcomes on conceptually flawed categories, the result will be that in our own social reality, we are reconfirming on a daily basis, through administrative and policy usages of the categories and concepts, the very thing that we wish to eradicate, in the name of achieving social justice. This is not a problem of incommensurables: in comparing the values inhering in the preservation of counting by race-ethnicities versus those of our social justice objectives, I suspect that the latter would win out. That is, in the public discourse over the relative merits of retaining race-ethnicity and its categories, proponents argue for their utility, not for some intrinsic value. This raises the Rosenhan question (noted in the introduction to Part IV): Is there harm in these naming and counting practices? I think the answer is yes, on three counts:

- Every time we invoke one of the category names or one of the race-ethnic terms, we sustain through that language the reality status of those things in the world (including the eugenic and classical baggage that they carry and that echo in their usage);
- Every time we use a category name that lumps together several identities, we enforce the characteristics of that lumpier identity in its limited range on those subsumed under the name; and
- Every time we use a race-ethnic term, we impute an importance to those traits that occludes other features, such as class, that might be equally important or even more powerful explainers of the social problem we are trying to solve.

The question is whether the potential for harm outweighs the potential for remedy. Whereas I would not have said so twenty years ago, today I would answer, Yes.

My concerns reflect a sense of the layers of meaning embedded in a word: "race" carries with it ancient valuative hierarchies; it cannot be used in a neutral way, without all those layers riding in on it, in however tacit a fashion. It may be a "dead" metaphor—in the sense that it is no longer seen actively as such—but it is very much alive in carrying tacit knowledge from other sources that shapes perceptions of its subject, in a metaphoric process. Language matters. We know this in terms of the power of "labeling." It is no less true in naming categories and concepts—which we then reinforce by using them in questionnaires and other counting practices for administrative purposes. The power of tacit knowledge in policy and administrative practices is that it shapes action without awareness that that is happening.

Why not proliferate the number of categories reported out in agency analyses? From a narrative point of view, 63 or 163 race-ethnic combinations enable the same sorts of stories. Analysis of a greater number is constrained only by the limits of computing power. But for reasons of state control, the larger number becomes unwieldy: for statisticians in agencies at all levels of government turning out reports, five categories is more manageable.

These are the tensions that are being played out today: between a tool designed for instrumental state purposes and one that has evolved a role in individuals' identity designations; between one assayed for descriptive purposes and its present prescriptive uses; between a desire to know a feature of American life rooted in history and a present use that seems dated and unnecessary. At the moment, we are continuing its use unreflexively, building current practices incrementally on past ones.

Rethinking and Recounting

We seem, then, to be faced with a dilemma: if we ignore the category names and terms, there will be no relief; but if we dwell on them, the stigma is continued.

The formulation of this problem is based on the same assumptions that characterize American race-ethnic discourse in general. How many people answering "other" or "mixed" will it take to entirely subvert not only the categories but the redistributive formulae as well? To push this to its extreme, will the need to shore up the 1980 census's race-ethnic categories— especially in light of the changes in the 2000 census—lead to the perceived need to police race-ethnic identity? Will we need a race-ethnic identity card in order to qualify for benefits, similar to the INS I-9s used to verify citizenship and hence eligibility for employment?

.   The categories serve to establish and maintain a set of ideas about American groups, power, and powerlessness that is at the moment dominant. The categories and the concepts are accepted as factual, descriptive, and scientific even though each of them is a metaphor—a way of seeing one class of things in terms of another, "shap[ing] our definitions of benefits and costs" (Edelman 1985, p. 150); and metaphors are contestable.[7] We should not be locking ourselves into problematic usages because we have come to build redistributive policies and programs on them. As difficult as it will no doubt be, we need to rethink how to get social services to needy and deserving groups without contributing further to the reification of already problematic categories.

Census questions and categories have, in fact, been changing since the beginning. A question about "mother tongue" was added in 1910 to determine the background of immigrants and their children whose "ethnicity" was not the same as their country of birth in order to assess the size of the non–English-speaking population—Jews, for example, who were not so-identified under the church-state separation clause (at a time when "leaders" of the Jewish community were arguing for their standing as a religion, rather than as an ethnic group, in order to garner state protections against discriminatory employment, educational, and other practices), or ethnic minorities from Eastern and Central Europe (Anderson 1988, pp. 123–124). Housing characteristics were added to the 1940 census, which could be combined with such categories as income, immigration rate (by year), fertility, education, occupation, and social security status (Anderson 1988, p. 186) to assess "otherness" from the middle-class, nonimmigrant "American" norm. The first six censuses also tabulated information by household: information on individuals was first collected in 1850, at the same time that a federal-level Office of Statistics was created to tabulate results and publish reports (Anderson 1988, p. 37).[8] Statistical comparability has been impaired since the beginning: categories have been changing since 1790; even 1980, 1990, and 2000 data sets are different.

Part of the deliberation underlying both the social justice claims and the argument for doing away with the five (or six) race-ethnic categories seems to hinge on the meaning of "difference" in American society. In arguing either for treating different people similarly or similar people differently, we have to ask: same and different with respect to what? The Voting Rights Act and the questions about its implementation in Florida during the 2000 presidential election stipulate that all people (or, at least, all voters) are the same and should not be treated differently. On the other hand, access to elementary and secondary education (and, hence, to college education) is entrenched in local communities and neighborhoods, and thereby establishes differential treatment based on economic class and, often, its intersections with race-ethnicity (even busing, which was invented as a policy measure to address this structural situation, was circumvented along race-class lines by parents who could afford to withdraw their children from the public school system and send them to private schools). This is a policy that, while enshrining local community and parental choice for good reasons, establishes treating children who are similar with respect to age, differently. Justice Blackmun, in his dissent to the Bakke case, wrote: "In order to treat some persons equally we must treat them differently"[9] (quoted in Lustig 1997, p. 9). Feminist standpoint theory, phenomenology's emphasis on lived experience, and the more general orientation toward the importance of local knowledge in anthropology and planning all support arguments for particularism.

This line of thinking underscores an argument *against* the universal application of the existing five (or six) categories and suggests a possible avenue out of our present conundrum. The focus on race-ethnicity privileges those characteristics over other traits that characterize individuals. It restricts the kinds of questions that can be asked of their subjects. Instead of enshrining a single set of universal categories—applicable identically to all people, in all places, at all times—we might establish different category sets for program eligibility according to the social justice criteria manifest in each program. There may be aspects other than race-ethnicity that would provide more effective avenues for the prosecution and treatment of inequalities. Perhaps we need to disaggregate policy areas, to use race-ethnic categories for some policies and programs and not for others.

For epidemiological and other health issues, where race-ethnicity seems clearly to be a surrogate for socioeconomic background and attendant dietary, environmental, and other circumstances, and where family genetics seems to play a role much stronger than race-ethnic population genetics, perhaps a category set built on those parameters would be more useful. Indeed, one researcher is exploring the health effects of living in inner-city neighborhoods, suggesting a range of attributes—including gender, encounters with discrimination, and geographic location—other than race-ethnicity tout court (Brainard 2000; see also Graves 2001). For police matters, where race-ethnicity is used as shorthand for behavioral and physical traits, a category set based on more explicit measures, such as that in Table 5.7, could be more effective. Columnist Max Frankel (1998, p. 46), in calling on police artists to render suspect portraits in "truly descriptive shadings," drives the point home with vivid satire: "Think how liberating it would be to read, 'The gunman, a six-foot ocher, fired twice at the frail, russet shopkeeper before two elderly neighbors, one buff, one milky, wrestled him to the ground.' Or, 'Muhammed Jefferson Akeem, the first umber ever elected to the House of Representatives, is being actively wooed by both the Melanic and Earthtone caucuses.'" Community-oriented policing programs are based precisely on an assessment of the importance of local knowledge: a Black man driving a Mercedes in a middle- or upper-class neighborhood (who is not driving erratically or running red lights) is less likely to be arrested by police officers who know that he lives in the neighborhood. For schools and colleges, a complex measure that evaluates intersections of race-ethnicity, class, geographic region, and so on might be more effective in evaluating applicants—much like the one that universities in California, Texas, and elsewhere claim to be using. The University of California system is enacting a new policy of taking a handful of the top graduating seniors from all high schools throughout the state: knowing how schools vary by locale and class (and linking those variables to educational preparation and achievement) enables a policy targeting affirmative action principles, without invoking and reinstantiating the concept of race. One school district outside San Jose, California, has Spanish, Mandarin, Cantonese, Vietnamese, Korean, Farsi, Portuguese, Dari, Hindi, Cambodian, and other language groups among its students—suggesting the possible utility of yet another set of categories. The National Science Foundation proposed using program eligibility criteria that would identify recipients who are "underserved" or "financially needy" (Cordes 1995). For a city grappling with providing fire or other services to new populations of Vietnamese, Cambodians, Russians, and Iranians (Grant 1993; Slavin 1993), race-ethnic categories may still be germane—but they are likely to be better served by categories that reflect these specific groups, rather than the five (or six) lumpier ones.

Such differentiated practices require a judgment of when class, or some other element, is a factor and when it is not. It requires a return to context, asking anew what the problem is, and seeing what the best answer in the specific circumstance is. For that matter, in some policy arenas where the equivalent of the entrenched race-ethnic categories might be useful, a more contemporary set might be entirely place-based—drawing on American places. A column on Hillary Clinton's then-anticipated Senate campaign provides unwitting evidence of one possible future set of American race-ethnic categories. She is described as rooting for the Yankees and buying a very expensive residence, in an attempt to become more like a New Yorker. "But," the columnist continues, "she does not seem to have acquired any ethnicity. ('Protestant?' guessed one supporter at a recent teachers' union rally.) Her campaign spokesman admits he has no idea where Mrs. Clinton's roots lie" (Collins 1999, p. A31). She continues:

> This is not the way we do business here. A New Yorker whose ancestors left Bavaria in 1840 and intermarried with Belgians will still get nostalgic about the Steuben Day Parade, and demand to know what the next U.S. senator is going to do about the Walloon situation. Mrs. Clinton took one small step forward when she discovered that her maternal grandmother's second husband was Jewish. . . .

The columnist, however, has given us a very precise description of Mrs. Clinton's would-be race-ethnicity—New Yorker–American!—in identifying its contemporary attributes in terms of residence and sports-team support.

There is no logical reason, in other words, why we have to maintain the five- (or six-) part category structure that OMB institutionalized in Directive No. 15. Let's multiply the categories we use and create more complex measurement tools. We could do this not just by multiplying the race-ethnic categories in use, but by adding other policy-issue-specific dimensions to our assessment tools, including class, sex, and so on, as relevant. Shifting the public perception of the categories as fixed, scientific entities to an understanding of them as dynamic, social constructions, and making this perception more widespread, would begin to break down the simplicity of the present system.

This is not an argument for substituting class for race-ethnicity, but rather for looking at the interplay between or among whatever traits are significant for a particular policy issue or program. Rather than treating race-ethnicity always as an independent variable, policy analysts, program developers, and other interested parties should look for interactive effects and develop category sets accordingly. The insistence on a single set of universal categories is in keeping with an understanding of race-ethnicity as scientifically grounded: social science informed by a positivist philosophy would carry precisely such criteria. A focus on race-ethnicity as the sole and independent variable is what creates such situations as drug cartels using Whites—"people who look like mild-mannered suburban housewives"—as couriers, drawing on the stereotype that drug addiction is predominantly a Black or Latino issue (Staples 1999, p. A22). Similar evidence comes from the field of espionage. According to Philip B. Heymann, deputy attorney general in the early Clinton administration,

> ... using a suspect's heritage ... is also often a lazy form of stereotyping that can do more to hamper a counterintelligence investigation than help it. ... Motivation and opportunity are the two things you look for. Ethnicity ... can serve as a misleading surrogate for those factors. Ethnicity turns out to be a very difficult factor to use properly. ... There are so many steps between the initial observation of someone's ethnicity and making an intelligent use of it that it's really not worth using. And if you use it to focus too quickly on a narrow category of people, you're giving a pass to other people in other categories. (Lewis 2000, pp. 4, 6)

A more widespread understanding that race-ethnicity and its categories do not today emerge from empirical scientific research might open the door to a more diverse approach to programmatic indicators and a view of them as dynamic, collective, human creations.

The alternative, which is to continue using the same five (or six) categories for the statistical sake of continuity, creates the kinds of administrative and implementation problems identified in chapter 5. Most importantly, it masks the differential experiences (whether underachievement, underrepresentedness, or overachievement) of subgroups within each lumpy category—as in a report, for example, that 50.5 percent of "Asian-Americans" ages twenty-five to twenty-nine completed college (Holmes 1998), which occludes the absence of Hmong or other groups typically not attending college. It implicitly encourages stereotyping of "all" Blacks or "all" Whites or "all" any group, attributing to all subgroups the modal traits assumed to be characteristic of the group as a whole.

The changed mode of "accounting" established by the OMB and being implemented in Census 2000 has moved us toward rethinking, particularly in the provision for an identity narrative based on multiplicity. This is an implicit recognition *in practice* of the nonscientific character of race, ethnicity, and their categories. As it has been and continues to be treated in the media and in school discussions, it has already and will continue to alter public perceptions. The change will also have a profound impact on programs and services. As agencies grapple with this change and its reporting requirements, it will subvert the taken-for-granted character of race-ethnicity and the categories and presuppositions concerning their scientific nature. The standard operating procedure, autopilot character of policy and program design will be challenged as new reporting mechanisms are developed—even though OMB Directive 15 stipulates that its race-ethnic standards are not to be used for program eligibility determinations. As Martha Feldman (1995, p. 52) has noted, category structures not only limit what we see, but they privilege their own characteristics (Is this a that?) over those of their individual members. In expanding, changing, and even dismantling them, even if only analytically, we stop confounding the artifactual reality of categories with the lived realities of individuals.

This rethinking and framing will not be easy. Part of the problem may be located in legislators making laws for others, not for themselves, or for imagined others based on themselves. On the one hand, the problem is one of limited experience. On the other, the widespread understanding of the existing race-ethnic categories is largely not based on "local knowledge"— the collective self-understanding of members of these various groups, rooted in their lived experiences. One implication of this analysis is that if race-ethnic-based categories are retained for some programs, the five (or six) lumpy categories should be abandoned, and program personnel—police, for example—should be trained in the differences internal to Whites, Blacks, Indians, Asians, and Hispanics, as well as the importance for self-identification of mixed-race identities. Self-identification is also differentiation, but of a different quality: it is self-proclaimed difference, rather than difference imposed from without. It retains a sense of autonomy and agency. Identity is some complex interaction among who I think I am, who you think I am, and how I want you to see me. When I cannot answer clearly who I am, but I have a clearer sense of who you are and how you see me, it helps me answer who I am. This is why the ability to self-identify is so important.

Proliferating Boxes, Prejudice, and Difference

The federal task force studying proposed changes to Census 2000 and OMB Directive 15 warned in 1997 that the proliferation of multiple possible identifications, such as in a "multiracial" category, would exacerbate racial tensions and fragmentation. The task force, made up of thirty federal agencies, made judgments that appear to have been based on outdated understandings of "race." It was reported to believe that using "multiracial" would "cause confusion since it would, for example, lump together those who are the product of a black-white relationship with those who are the offspring of Asian and white parents" (Holmes 1997a, p. A12). It is not clear for whom this would cause confusion: presumably, those so-identifying are not confused at all. The continuation of the article suggests that the confusion would be for agency statisticians having to figure out how to report out these data: the task force thinks that people answering questionnaires testing the new format did not understand what "multiracial" meant, as it was checked off both by children of Chinese-Korean unions and by those of Jewish–non-Jewish parentage. This is a misunderstanding only from the perspective that "Jew" denotes a religion alone; but given the usage of "race" in the census to mean culture as well as color and country of origin, there is no confusion here, except on the part of the task force members. Similarly, Ruth McKay, a statistician at the Bureau of Labor Statistics, noted that people who were part Irish and part Italian, or German and white, or black Deutsch (referring to a particular Dutch dialect) were all claiming multiracial status, "mixing ethnicities, nationalities, and what we have until now used as racial groups," creating "problems in collecting good data" (Kalfus 1996). Once again, these individuals are, in fact, following the operative use of race-ethnicity in the census, which in practice mixes all these meanings.

However, precisely the opposite development could also occur: with an increase in possible boxes and individual membership in several of them, it becomes more difficult to identify people for discriminatory purposes. An increased variety of race-ethnic classifications opens the door to consider economic and other factors in identity and in discrimination.

The mixed race designation poses some of the same problems for social justice as eliminating the categories altogether. In one example, "lawyers in employment discrimination suits will at times try to prove that a company is racially biased by comparing the number of blacks in particular jobs with the proportion of African-Americans in the local population. Such litigation could be greatly affected if a significant number of blacks list themselves as being of more than one race, and the Government counts them as something other than black" (Holmes 1997b, p. A19). However, the statistical count is already problematic, in that some people of "mixed" heritage self-identify in different ways at different times, depending on the situation. The possibility for multiple self-identification may, in fact, increase group counts.

What do you know about me if you "know" that I'm American Indian or White? asks Armstrong (2001, p. 6C). Does it change if you know I'm Leech Lake Chippewa of the Pillager band and Loon clan? Which of us is less likely to go to college, get a well-paying job, not be afraid to drive home at night? Those answers depend—on where we grew up, the quality of the schools we attended, the shade of our skin and shape of our noses and facial bone structure. Here is where we need some concept other than class or gender or sexuality—and "race" has become the polite term for "color," for looking, speaking, and acting differently. But this is the second problem with using the five (or six) categories, and it is not a problem of counting. Redistribution is a problem of wealth, of class, of entry into the power and decision-making structures of American society; discrimination is a problem of skin color, accent, and cultural practices such as dress or diet. The two interact, and they are conflated in our categories as they are used, as well as in much of our public discourse. This is one of the things that makes the problem so intractable. The undifferentiated lumpiness of the categories is what creates stereotypes that all Blacks are poor, all Asians are smart, and so on. How are we to address the brutalities of prejudice, without a language to name those against whom prejudice is levied? How are we to address "racism" without the language of "race"? Arab-Americans and other Moslems cannot claim federal protections against discrimination without everyday language and policy categories for anti-Arab or anti-Moslem hate crimes. If Middle Eastern–North African Moslems and Arabs are disappeared into "White," as the OMB definition does, there is no language for talking about race-ethnically-based discrimination of that variety. This is an even harder problem to solve than the counting problem.

It is possible that moving toward a more varied, multiple account of race-ethnicity will help undermine racism, itself, and make inroads against the injustices imposed upon certain people because of their "differences," whatever those are perceived to be, including skin color and facial structure. It is much easier with only five or six "race-ethnic" categories to label one as mainstream, as "American," and the others as "different." With sixty-three varieties and more, it becomes much more difficult. How much more so, when all groups—including "Whites"—are publicly understood to be, and seen as, "mixed." Without a public discourse based on the concepts of "race" and "ethnicity," and with a concerted educational effort to show that they lack scientific basis, perhaps discrimination itself will eventually disappear (although I suspect that it would be unduly unrealistic to hope for an end to prejudices and hate crimes).

If "race-ethnicity" is a socially constructed concept, then it (or they) can be deconstructed. We cannot pretend that discrimination and prejudice against darker skin shades, accents, or certain eye, nose, and hair types have miraculously disappeared since the spread of the Civil Rights movement in the 1960s or since *Brown* v. *the Board of Education* in 1954. Although much has changed—increasing numbers of non–European-Americans are prominent in government, business, education, the arts—there is still a long way to go. The promise of the multiplicity of identity categories from Census 2000 is that it has the potential to alter, conceptually, the power relations among groups—and changing conceptions may well, in this case, lead to changing attitudes and actions. It seems to me that a "color"-conscious strategy for dismantling "race-ethnicity" can serve only to reinforce it: the banal mundanity of repetitive enactments—whether in school classrooms in which teachers send students off to their "integration groups," "integration teachers," and "integration classrooms" (Stein 2001) or in hospitals where parents of newborns check off "race-ethnicity" boxes according to which an administrator or statistician later assigns the infant's race-ethnic identity—conveys a reality to race, ethnicity, and the categories that is powerfully persuasive. The list itself, the very language, the act of instructing and being instructed to check a box, and the physical act of marking the appropriate one (or refusing to, or marking "Other") communicate that these entities are real—that they capture or reflect something of essence in the social world. The debates over educational access, health care availability, economic power, and other (in)equalities of opportunity—so vivid at the level of policy discourse—are lost, submerged, and silenced at the level of daily implementation. Race-ethnicity *does* matter—discrimination and prejudice are experienced social realities—enough for me to want to do away with the categories that serve to perpetuate its discriminatory aspects, while retaining the ability to move toward a more just society and to tell our "Heinz" 63—or more—variety stories.

The argument in favor of rethinking and even dropping the categories we use is not, then, an argument against affirmative action per se. We are not a race-blind country. Race-ethnic practices infiltrate all of our lives, in myriad, often discriminatory or even degrading ways. At times, perhaps strategic essentialism is in order: perhaps, as Christine Di Stefano (quoted in Theodoulou and O'Brien 1999, p. 66) has suggested in the context of gender, there are times when we should approach race-ethnicity as simultaneously real and false—as a human creation that has real impacts on people's lives. As Bickford (1997, p. 2) notes in a similar vein, at times we may need the "fiction" of category-based identity. At the same time, as Henry Louis Gates, Jr. (1995) points out, "The stronger a sense you nurture of the contingent nature of all such identities, the less likely you will be harmed by them, or in their name inflict harm on others." Moreover, an appreciation for the contingent character of these categories can encourage us to change them: there is no need, as I have said before, for us to restrict ourselves to the existing patterns of race-ethnic categorization for all policy issues (or for any of them)—unless we choose to accept an evaluative set driven by the simplifying needs of statistical analysis.

Might it be possible to stop counting ourselves in race-ethnic terms and yet retain the storytelling features of these categories? Can we lose the sense that we are saying anything meaningful about race-ethnicity, and yet retain the sense that we are narrating something of importance about family and community histories? I am not "just" an American, but a Jewish American, as I know when I walk through San Francisco's Chinatown or any city center or neighborhood in December. And I am not "just" an Eastern European Jew; I am an American Jew—something amply in evidence when I live in Israel or attend a Passover seder in The Hague. If I had not the experience of growing up in a family that celebrated its own community's holiday, food, dress, and other rituals in that community's languages, perhaps I would argue for giving up all categories altogether, in favor of proclaiming that we are all "just" Americans. In light of that experience—with all its complexity of feeling, many, many times, like a marginalized stranger in this country—the idea of hyphenation pleases me, and the more hyphens, the better: they allow each of us to tell a fuller story about our rich heritage, without feeling that we have to deny any part of it.

The anthropologist Orvar Löfgren (1993) notes that nation-states should be considered equal to one another, but that national cultures "should be as different as possible" (p. 166). Similarly, the proliferated race-ethnic categories should be considered equal—and I think universal hyphenization accomplishes this, at least in linguistic structure; but they should enable the telling of stories that are as different from one another as history and experience can be. In universalizing and celebrating our hyphenated identities, we will, I hope, succeed in moving beyond the hierarchical gradations of the species chain of being. Such equal valuation of different American identities will, in time, lead to a more equal allocation of national resources. As naïve as this may sound, the telling of collective identity stories is both conceptually and politically powerful: it distributes hyphenated differentiation equally across all Americans, detoxifying the stigma attached historically to "mixed" identities. It unites and differentiates at the same time: we will all have stories as Americans whose ancestors contributed to the *pluribus* out of which the *unum* has been built, and in which *pluribus* and *unum* coexist. We need positive rituals and other symbols to cement this equalization through both memorialization and celebration: national museums and other holy public spaces that commemorate the history of slavery, the incarceration of Japanese-Americans during World War II, the decimation of American Indians, and other marker events that emblemize the historic inequalities of dominant-subdominant group relations, as well as national festivals that celebrate the strengths and contributions of various groups.

I am convinced that we must stop giving accounts of ourselves in terms of the five gross, lumpy race-ethnic categories: they create, impose, and maintain identities that are, by and large, not embracing of individuals' lived experiences and, because of the baggage of meaning that they carry, detrimental to human dignity. And yet, as convinced as I am of that position, I am equally convinced of the fact that we need modes of storytelling for collective and individual identity purposes, including a story of national origins. We need conceptual language to tell such stories to articulate our own identities as members of an entity—a community—larger than ourselves and our individual existences. We also need to be able to tell personal collective-identity stories, because without a grounding in one's own story, it is difficult to grasp another's. And yet (again), there is nothing that requires us to continue to use the five, or six, now-common categories for these narratives. Personally, I narrate myself as a Jew, with Polish-Russian-Carpatho-Rus, Bostonian, Bayonne (New Jersey), Bronx (New York), and S'faradi-liturgical ancestry; and I would like to hear others' Chilean and Andalucian and Xi'an and Lakota and Atlanta-Chicago stories. This does not confound a "faith" story with an "ethnic" one, except in narrow Protestant conceptions of religion: when Amina Chaudary says, "'I define myself as a Muslim. . . . To me that's what dominates my life'" (Schmitt 2001a, p. A12), she is not necessarily defining herself "in religious rather than racial or ethnic terms," nor is race necessarily "tak[ing] a back seat to faith," as both newspaper editor and reporter wrote. Even Jew and Moslem, as they are used, are race-ethnic designations, not just "religious" ones (which narrows the understanding of religion to faith, rather than seeing it, as these two religions do, as a way of life, including ritual, food, dress, and acts).

If "American" comes to mean people who have particularistic stories of family origins in many different elsewheres together with a national story of rerootedness here, the strangeness of and tensions between distinct cultures—the culture of the house versus the culture of external society—and ensuing estrangement from one or the other will be increasingly diminished. "Difference" will increasingly be seen as a commonplace aspect of American identity and as an attribute of the "good" citizen, rather than as marked, lesser membership. The alternative mode of compressed racialization into membership in one of the five or six categories instead offers a coercive model, albeit a relatively benign one, akin to enforced identification with dominant groups, such as the Arabization of Assyrians in Iraq through bans on teaching the Syriac language, the loss of their group name from census categories, the nationalization of their schools, forced migration, and other modes of ethnic cleansing. American ethnogenesis may be less physically violent, but it remains an erosion of identity, with a concomitant sense of loss.

As Haney López (1994, pp. 52–53) writes, "Racial structures are pervasive, not permanent. Deconstructing race reveals its human origins, thus exposing race's baneful power, but also confirming our ability to contest it. . . . Accepting the possibility that we can remake ourselves through our choices, we must also accept some of the responsibility for choosing to trap ourselves." Contesting racism does not require us to limit ourselves to a discourse of five or six lumpy categories.

Policy Judgments and Administrative Action

Policy and administrative judgments require achieving a balance between the group and the individual, or creating possibilities for case-by-case judgment. This is clearly seen in the case of the census categories for race-ethnic identity. Focusing on race-ethnic categories denies the individual other sources of identity. The parable at the front of the book stands as a warning to category builders: don't assume you know who I am because you have a category for me. The assumption that you can only know whether fish are happy if you are a fish privileges physical resemblance as the criterion for inclusion in the category; in so doing, it elevates the designated criteria for category membership and disqualifies the individual who appears not to match the image of those criteria. Emphasizing visible criteria denies other possible courses of action and judgment. Emphasizing the boundedness of group identity denies the possibility of human empathy that allows a nonfish to understand fish: maybe there's something in my background that allows me to understand fish, even if I look to you like I'm not a fish, or even if I am not a fish. Or, "fishness" may not be the most salient characteristic on which to build categories. The parable points to the tensions between individual identity and group membership and between self-identification and other-identification.

If we who wish to change practices in regard to social justice issues do not grasp both how race-ethnicity is commonly understood and practiced and how this practice is at odds with the understanding of most contemporary biological and social science, our idealism and efforts will, I have sadly concluded, be for naught. Today, race-ethnic categories appear to be proxies for social status and class. But since we have inherited a national mythology of classlessness, alluding to class through race-ethnic labels elevates the importance of racial discourse while it silences public discourse concerning economic, geographic, and other possible bases of status. "What we do with difference, and whether we acknowledge our own participation in the meanings of the differences we assign to others, are choices that remain" (Minow 1990, p. 390). Race, ethnicity, and the categories are a system for managing difference. Surely we can find other ways to appreciate difference and to bridge it. We—social scientists and Americans alike—must be more direct in confronting and challenging the choices that we continue to make in maintaining reliance on race-ethnic categories that embody and mask cultural, class, and other differences.

In the discussion of the 1997 revisions to Directive No. 15, the OMB noted that agency decision makers were constantly reminded "that there are real people represented by the data on race and ethnicity . . ." (U.S. Office of Management and Budget 1997). This does not sit well with a drive to keep the number of standard categories "to a manageable size, *determined by statistical concerns and data needs*" (idem., emphasis added). We need to return to some central questions driven by human concerns, and ask, again, publicly: How do we get to where we wish to be without reinforcing the very thing we want to get rid of? What is wrong? How might we fix it? Does the present system work? Is there a better way of repair? There is a very real social experience of continuously being viewed as different and being treated as different, given the American predilection to see "different" as "lesser." Through the proliferation of American identity tales, on the one hand, and the softening, if not outright elimination, of the race-ethnic discourse that takes place through common, everyday policy and administrative category practices, on the other, we may eradicate that punishing sense of difference along these insidious lines. We might, then, no longer need a race-ethnic discourse, except in a celebratory sense.

Notes

1. Though Anderson (1988, p. 205) dates this to the early 1960s.

2. Apparently, income categories tabulated by the Census Bureau have served a similar function as indicators of "class." But, according to Lenneal Henderson (comment, ASPA panel, July 20, 1993), these indicators are often contradicted by data on housing conditions. Because disposable income is not as great as it used to be, the Census Bureau needs a different measure to "read" class information out of its data (such as net wealth).

3. See, for example, Carter (1991), Gates (1986), Guinier (2001), Marable (1995), Steele (1990), P.J. Williams (1991), Wilson (1978). Delgado and Stefancic (2000) include several essays on both sides of the issue. That this list of individual works is exclusively of African-American scholars may be indicative of the strength of their voices in this debate, or it may reflect my reading practices. See also the argument in Zuberi (2001), informed by his reading of the history and use of statistics.

4. See Zack (1993, pp. 121–126).

5. I thank Nicole McClenden for bringing this to my attention.

6. The scientization of the census was led by Census Office Superintendent (1870 and 1880) Francis Amasa Walker, who developed population maps later linked to the U.S. Geographic Service and who became president of MIT in 1881 (Anderson 1988, pp. 86–100).

7. See also Edelman (1985, Afterword) on language. I elaborate on these points in Yanow (1996).

8. Quite aside from this are questions of the bases for statistics' claims to legitimacy. See McClure (1999) on the establishment of the Royal Society for Statistics and the problematic grounds of its claims.

9. He continued: "In order to get beyond racism, we must first take account of race" (quoted in Lustig 1997, p. 9).

References

Abma, Tineke, ed. 1999. *Telling Tales: On Narrative and Evaluation.* Advances in Program Evaluation, vol. 6. Stamford, CT: JAI Press.

"Advertisement for Workforce 2000." 1992. *Public Management* 74 (December): 17.

The American Heritage Dictionary of the English Language. [1975] 1992. Palo Alto, CA: Houghton Mifflin.

Amselle, Jean-Loup. 1995. Seminar. Center for the Comparative Study of Race and Ethnicity, Stanford University, February 13.

Anderson, Margo J. 1988. *The American Census: A Social History.* New Haven, CT: Yale University Press.

Anderson, Margo J., and Fienberg, Stephen E. 1999. *Who Counts?* New York: Russell Sage Foundation.

Angier, Natalie. 2000. "Do Races Differ? Not Really, Genes Show." *New York Times* (August 22): C1, 3.

Anthony, Ted. 1998. "Melungeon Awakening." *San Jose Mercury News* (July 12): 27A.

Armstrong, Travis. 2001. "Just a Chippewa Guy." *San Jose Mercury News* (April 1): 6C.

Arrillaga, Pauline. 2001. "Mexican Indians Aim to Reclaim Identity amid 'Hispanic' Labels." *San Jose Mercury News* (January 1): 19A.

Bahloul, Joelle. 1994. "The Sephardic Jew as Mediterranean: A View from Kinship and Gender." *Journal of Mediterranean Studies* 4(2): 197-207.

Beals, Ralph L., and Hoijer, Harry. [1953] 1965. *An Introduction to Anthropology.* 3d ed. London: Macmillan.

Bean, Robert Bennett. 1935. *The Races of Man.* New York: The University Society.

Behar, Ruth. 1992. "Arroz con MacArthur." *Chronicle of Higher Education* (November 4): A4.

Bell, Catherine. 1997. *Ritual.* New York: Oxford University Press.

Bell, Claudia. 1996. *Inventing New Zealand: Everyday Myths of Pakeha Identity.* Auckland: Penguin Books.

Benest, Frank. 1991. "Marketing Multiethnic Communities." *Public Management* 73(12): 4–8, 11.

Berger, Peter L., and Luckmann, Thomas. 1966. *The Social Construction of Reality.* New York: Anchor Books.

Bickford, Susan. 1997. "Reconfiguring Pluralism." Paper presented at the annual meeting of the Western Political Science Association, Los Angeles, March.

Borges, Jorge Luis. 1966. *Other Inquisitions.* New York: Washington Square Press.

Bowker, Geoffrey C., and Star, Susan Leigh. 1999. *Sorting Things Out.* Cambridge: MIT Press.

Bradshaw, Carla K. 1992. "Beauty and the Beast: On Racial Ambiguity." In *Racially Mixed People in America,* ed. Maria P.P. Root, chap 7. Newbury Park, CA: Sage.

Brainard, Jeffrey. 2000. "Federal Support Grows for Research on the Role of Race in Public-Health Problems." *Chronicle of Higher Education* (November 24): A25.

Bronner, Ethan. 1998. "Inventing the Notion of Race." *New York Times* (January 10): A13, 15.

Buker, Eloise. 1987. *Politics Through a Looking-Glass.* New York: Greenwood.

Bulkin, Elly. 1984. "Hard Ground." In *Yours in Struggle,* ed. Elly Bulkin, Minnie Bruce Pratt, and Barbara Smith. Brooklyn: Long Haul Press.

Burrell, Gibson, and Morgan, Gareth. 1979. *Sociological Paradigms and Organisational Analysis.* Portsmouth, NH: Heinemann.

California State Senate. 1995. Chapter 415, Section 4, Article 5, ¶ 102900 (Bill 1360).

Cannizzo, Jeanne, and Parry, David. 1994. "Museum Theatre in the 1990s." *Museums and the Appropriation of Culture,* ed. Susan Pearce, 43-64. London: Athlone Press.

Carson, Clayborne. 1995. "Multiracial Democracy Will Require Changes in Behavior, Political Practices." *Campus Report* (August 30): 5–6.

Carter, Stephen L. 1991. *Reflections of an Affirmative Action Baby.* New York: Basic Books.

Cavalli-Sforza, L. Luca; Menozzi, Paolo; and Piazza, Alberto. 1994. *The History and Geography of Human Genes.* Princeton: Princeton University Press.

Chang, Jack. 1999. "2000 Census to Contain 63 Racial Groups." *San Francisco Chronicle* (October 12): B1.

Chin, Steven A. 1988. "Reagan's Census Bill Veto Criticized." *San Francisco Examiner* (November 12): A1, 16.

Chock, Phyllis Pease. 1989. "The Landscape of Enchantment: Redaction in a Theory of Ethnicity." *Cultural Anthropology* 4: 163–181.

———. 1991. "'Illegal Aliens' and 'Opportunity': Myth-Making in Congressional Testimony." *American Ethnologist* 18: 279–294.

———. 1995a. "Ambiguity in Policy Discourse: Congressional Talk about Immigration." *Policy Sciences* 18(2): 165–184.

———. 1995b. "Culturalism: Pluralism, Culture, and Race in the Harvard Encyclopedia of American Ethnic Groups." *Identities* 1(4): 301–323.

Choudhury, Enamul H. 1995. "Exploring Questions on Cultural Diversity and Public Administration." Paper presented at the annual meeting of the Public Administration Theory Network, Hayward, CA, June.

Clifford, James. 1988. "Identity in Mashpee." In *The Predicament of Culture,* chap.12. Cambridge: Harvard University Press.

Cohen, Roger. 1998. "The German 'Volk' Seem Set to Let Outsiders In." *New York Times* (October 16): A4.

Coleman, Troy L. 1990. "Managing Diversity at Work." *Public Management* 72(10): 2–5.

Collins, Gail. 1999. "Hillary's Rootlessness." *New York Times* (November 26): A31.

Collison, Michele N-K. 1993. "A Twist on Affirmative Action." *Chronicle of Higher Education* (November 24): A13–14.

Cook, Scott, and Yanow, Dvora. 1993. "Culture and Organizational Learning." *Journal of Management Inquiry* 2: 373–390.

Copeland, Lennie. 1988. "Valuing Diversity II: Pioneers and Champions of Change." *HR Focus* (July): 44–49.

———. 1989a. "Four by Four: How Do You Manage a Diverse Workforce?" *Training & Development Journal* (February): 17–20.

———. 1989b. "Learning to Manage a Multicultural Workforce." *League of California Cities* (February): 8–12, 36.

Cordes, Colleen. 1995. "NSF Re-examines Preferences Based on Race and Gender." *Chronicle of Higher Education* (November 10): A31.

Coughlin, Ellen K. 1991. "Political Survey Notes Differences among Latinos." *Chronicle of Higher Education* (September 11): A12.

Cowell, Alan. 1997. "Like It or Not, Germany Becomes a Melting Pot." *New York Times* (November 30): 1, 3.

Cox, Taylor, Jr. 1990. "Problems with Research by Organizational Scholars on Issues of Race and Ethnicity." *Journal of Applied Behavioral Science* 26: 5–23.

Cox, Taylor, Jr., and Blake, Stacy. 1991. "Managing Cultural Diversity." *Academy of Management Executive* 5: 45–56.

Cox, Taylor, Jr., and Nkomo, Stella M. 1990. "Invisible Men and Women: A Status Report on Race as a Variable in Organization Behavior Research." *Journal of Organizational Behavior* 11: 419–431.

Cox, Taylor; Lobel, Sharon A.; and McLeod, Poppy Lauretta. 1991. "Effects of Ethnic Group Cultural Differences on Cooperative and Competitive Behavior on a Group Task." *Academy of Management Journal* 34: 827–847.

Crispell, Diane. 1991. "How to Avoid Big Mistakes." *American Demographics* (March): 48–50.

Crossette, Barbara. 1996. "Citizenship Is a Malleable Concept." *New York Times* (August 18): E3.

Dallmayr, Fred R., and McCarthy, Thomas A., eds. 1977. *Understanding and Social Inquiry.* Notre Dame, IN: University of Notre Dame Press.

Dang, Nghiem Van. n.d. " Ethnic Identification in Vietnam." Unpublished manuscript.

Daniel, G. Reginald. 1992. "Passers and Pluralists." In *Racially Mixed People in America*, ed. Maria P.P. Root, chap. 8. Newbury Park, CA: Sage.

Davis, F. James. 1991. *Who Is Black?* University Park: Pennsylvania State University Press.

de la Garza, Rodolfo. 1993. "Researchers Must Heed New Realities When They Study Latinos in the U.S." *Chronicle of Higher Education* (June 2): B1–3.

de Leon, Peter. 1998. "The Evidentiary Basis for Policy Analysis: Empiricist Versus Postpositivist Positions." *Policy Studies Journal* 26: 109–113.

Delgado, Gary, and Sen, Rinku. 1988. "Shades of Race." Review of Michael Omi and Howard Winant, *Racial Formation in the United States from the 1960s to the 1980s. Socialist Review* 18(3): 143–148.

Delgado, Richard, and Stefancic, Jean. 2000. *Critical Race Theory*, 2d ed. Philadelphia: Temple University Press.

De Vito, Bill. 1992. "Workforce Diversity Policies in New Zealand." *Public Management* 74(11): 16, 20.

Dobbins, James E., and Skillings, Judith H. 1991. "The Utility of Race Labeling in Understanding Cultural Identity." *Journal of Counseling & Development* 70 (September/October): 37–44.

Dominguez, Cari M. 1991–1992. "The Challenge of Workforce 2000." *Bureaucrat/ Public Manager* (Winter): 15–18.

Dorgan, Michael. 1997. "Malaysia: Affirmative Action—with Muscle." *San Jose Mercury News* (September 3): 15A.

Douglas, Mary. 1966. *Purity and Danger.* London: Routledge & Kegan Paul.

———. 1975. *Implicit Meanings.* London: Routledge & Kegan Paul.

———. 1979. "World View and the Core." In *Philosophical Disputes in the Social Sciences,* ed. Stuart C. Brown, 177-187. Atlantic Highlands, NJ: Humanities Press.

———. [1973] 1982. *Natural Symbols.* New York: Pantheon.

———. 1986. *How Institutions Think.* New York: Syracuse University Press.

Dubinskas, Frank A. 1992. "Culture, Work, and Diversity: The Practical Construction of Cultural Differences." Paper presented at the annual meeting of the Academy of Management, Las Vegas, Nevada, August.

Durkheim, Emile, and Mauss, Marcel. [1903] 1963. *Systems of Primitive Classification.* Trans. R. Needham. Chicago: University of Chicago.

Duster, Troy. 1991. "Understanding Self-Segregation on the Campus." *Chronicle of Higher Education* (September 25).

Edelman, Murray. [1964] 1985. *The Symbolic Uses of Politics.* Chicago: University of Illinois.

———. 1977. *Political Language.* New York: Academic Press.

———. 1995. *From Art to Politics: How Artistic Creations Shape Political Conceptions.* Chicago: University of Chicago Press.

Egan, Timothy. 1993. "A Cultural Gap May Swallow a Child." *New York Times* (October 12): A8.

Ehrenreich, Barbara. 1992. "Cultural Baggage." *New York Times Magazine* (April 7): 16, 18.

Erikson, Erik. 1963. *Childhood and Society,* 261, 270. Quoted in Hoover 1993, 3.

———. 1959. *Identity and the Life Cycle,* 102. Quoted in Hoover 1993, 12.

Fan, Maureen. 1999. "Census' Multiple Choice Puzzle." *San Jose Mercury News* (October 31): A1, 10.

Fausto-Sterling, Anne. 2000. *Sexing the Body: Gender Politics and the Construction of Sexuality.* New York: Basic Books.

Feldman, Martha S. 1995. *Some Interpretive Techniques for Analyzing Qualitative Data.* Beverly Hills, CA: Sage.

Ferber, Abby L. 1995. "Exploring the Social Construction of Race." In *American Mixed Race,* ed. Naomi Zack, chap. 11. Lanham, MD: Rowman & Littlefield.

Fine, Marlene G.; Johnson, Fern L.; and Ryan, M. Sallyanne. 1990. "Cultural Diversity in the Workplace." *Public Personnel Management* 19: 305–319.

Fischer, Frank. 1998. "Policy Inquiry in Postpositivist Perspective." *Policy Studies Journal* 26: 129–146.

Fischer, Frank, and Forester, John. 1993. *The Argumentative Turn in Planning and Public Policy.* Durham, NC: Duke University Press.

Fischer, Michael M. J. 1986. "Appendix: Work in Progress—Ethnicity as Text and Model." In *Anthropology as Cultural Critique,* George E. Marcus and Michael M. J. Fischer, 173–177. Chicago: University of Chicago Press.

Foster, Badi G.; Jackson, Gerald; Cross, William E.; Jackson, Bailey; and Hardiman, Rita. 1988. "Workforce Diversity and Business." *Training & Development Journal* (April): 38–42.

Foucault, Michel. 1971. *The Order of Things.* New York: Pantheon.

Fox, Charles. 1990. "Implementation Research: Why and How to Transcend Positivist

Methodologies." In *Implementation and the Policy Process,* ed. Dennis J. Palumbo and Donald J. Calista, 199–212. New York: Greenwood.

Foxman, Loretta, and Walter L. Polsky. 1989. "Cross-Cultural Understanding." *Personnel Journal* 68(11): 12–14.

Frankel, Max. 1998. "Let's Be Chromatically Correct." *New York Times Magazine* (December 6): 46, 48.

Frazier, E. Franklin. [1939] 1966. *The Negro Family in the United States,* rev. ed. Chicago: University of Chicago Press.

Freire, Paulo. 1973. *Education for Critical Consciousness.* New York: Seabury.

Friedman, Raymond A. 1991. "The Balanced Workforce at Xerox Corporation" (Case No. 9-491-049), Harvard Business School, Cambridge.

Fuchs, Lawrence. 1990. *The American Kaleidoscope.* Hanover, NH: Wesleyan University Press.

———. 1993. "An Agenda for Tomorrow: Immigration Policy and Ethnic Policies." *Annals of the American Academy of Political Social Science* 530 (November): 171–186.

Galagan, Patricia A. 1993. "Trading Places at Monsanto." *Training & Development Journal* (April): 45–49.

Garn, Stanley. 1968. *Readings on Race,* 2d ed. Springfield, IL: Charles C. Thomas.

Gasiorowicz, Mari; Chiang, Lifang; Parker Alison; Wolf, Heather; Burnside-Mora, Libby; and Deamer, Kathy. 1993. "Alameda County: Profile of Ethnic and Immigrant Populations." International Institute of the East Bay, Newcomer Information Clearinghouse, Oakland, CA.

Gates, Henry Louis, Jr., ed. 1986. *"Race," Writing, and Difference.* Chicago: University of Chicago Press.

———. 1995. Untitled excerpt from graduation address at Emory University. *New York Times* (May 29).

———. 1996. "White Like Me." *The New Yorker* (June 17): 66-72, 74-81.

Geertz, Clifford. 1972. "Deep Play: Notes on the Balinese Cockfight." *Daedalus* 101 (Winter): 1–38.

———. 1973. *The Interpretation of Cultures.* New York: Basic Books.

———. 1983a. "Common Sense as a Cultural System." *Local Knowledge,* chap. 4. New York: Basic Books.

———. 1983b. "From the Native's Point of View." *Local Knowledge*, chap. 3. New York: Basic Books.

Gershon, Ilana. n.d.a. "Funding Samoanness in the U.S. and New Zealand." Unpublished manuscript.

———. n.d.b. "The Sense of the Colonial Census: Populating Papua New Guinea." Unpublished manuscript.

Gilligan, Carol. 1982. *In a Different Voice.* Cambridge: Harvard University Press.

Gillum, Richard F.; Gomez-Marin, Orlando; and Prineas, Ronald J. 1988. "Discrepancies in Racial Designations of School Children in Minneapolis." *Public Health Reports* 103: 485–488.

Glazer, Nathan, and Moynihan, Daniel P. 1963. *Beyond the Melting Pot.* Cambridge: MIT Press.

Goldberg, David Theo. 1992. "The Semantics of Race." *Ethnic and Racial Studies* 15: 543–569.

———. 1995. "Made in the USA: Racial Mixing 'n Matching." In *American Mixed*

Race, ed. Naomi Zack, chap. 18. Lanham, MD: Rowman & Littlefield.

Golden-Biddle, Karen, and Locke, Karen. 1993. "Appealing Work: An Investigation in How Ethnographic Texts Convince." *Organization Science* 4: 595–616.

———. 1997. *Composing Qualitative Research.* Thousand Oaks, CA: Sage.

Goldstein, Jeffrey, and Leopold, Marjorie. 1990. "Corporate Culture vs. Ethnic Culture." *Personnel Journal* 69(11): 83–92.

Gordon, Mary. 1996. *The Shadow Man.* New York: Random House.

Grant, Nancy K. 1993. "Adapting Fire Protection to Multicultural Constituencies." Paper presented at annual meeting of the American Society for Public Administration, San Francisco, July 17–21.

Graves, Joseph L., Jr. 2001. *The Emperor's New Clothes: Biological Theories of Race at the Millennium.* New Brunswick, NJ: Rutgers University Press.

Gray, John. 1996. *Isaiah Berlin.* Princeton, NJ: Princeton University Press.

Greenblatt, Stephen. 1996. "An English Obsession." Review of James Shapiro, *Shakespeare and the Jews. New York Times Book Review* (August 11): 12–13.

Greenhaus, Jeffrey H., Parasuraman, Saroj, and Wormley, Wayne M. 1990. "Effects of Race on Organizational Experiences, Job Performance Evaluations, and Career Outcomes." *Academy of Management Journal* 33(1): 64–86.

Greenhouse, Carol J., ed. 1998. *Democracy and Ethnography.* Albany, NY: SUNY Press.

Greenhouse, Carol J., and Greenwood, Davydd J. 1994. "Introduction: The Ethnography of Democracy and Difference." Working paper.

Greenwood, Davydd J. 1984. *The Taming of Evolution.* Ithaca, NY: Cornell University Press.

———. 1985. "Castilians, Basques, and Andalusians: An Historical Comparison of Nationalism, 'True' Ethnicity, and 'False' Ethnicity." In *Ethnic Groups and the State*, ed. Paul Brass, chap. 6. London: Croom Helm.

———. 1989. "The Anthropologies of Spain." Working paper 2, Spanish Studies Round Table, University of Illinois at Chicago.

Griffin, John Howard. [1960] 1977. *Black Like Me*, 2d ed. Boston: Houghton Mifflin.

Grimes, Barbara F., ed. 1992. *Ethnologue,* 12th ed. Dallas: Summer Institute of Linguistics.

Guinier, Lani. 2001. "Colleges Should Take 'Confirmative Action' in Admissions." *Chronicle of Higher Education* (December 14): B10–12.

Gusfield, Joseph. 1963. *Symbolic Crusade.* Chicago: Illini Books.

———. 1976. "The Literary Rhetoric of Science." *American Sociological Review* 41: 16–34.

———. 1981. *The Culture of Public Problems.* Chicago: University of Chicago Press.

Haller, Mark H. 1963. *Eugenics.* New Brunswick, NJ: Rutgers University Press.

Hanamura, Steve. 1989. "Working with People Who Are Different." *Training & Development Journal* (June): 110–114.

Haney López, Ian F. 1993. "Community Ties and Law School Faculty Hiring: The Case for Professors Who Don't Think White." In *Beyond a Dream Deferred: Multicultural Education and the Politics of Excellence,* ed. Becky Thompson and Sangeeta Tyagi, 100–130. Minneapolis: University of Minnesota Press.

———. 1994. "The Social Construction of Race." *Harvard Civil Rights Civil Liberties Law Review* 29: 1–62.

———. 1995. *White by Law.* New York: New York University Press.

Harding, Sandra. 1991. *Whose Science? Whose Knowledge?* Ithaca, NY: Cornell University Press.

Hawkesworth, M. E. 1988. *Theoretical Issues in Policy Analysis.* Albany, NY: SUNY Press.

Hawkins, Robert. 1992. "Diversity and Municipal Openness." *Public Management* 74: 33–35.

Healey, Jon. 1992. "Lumbees Don't Get Status of Tribe." *Wall Street Journal* (February 29).

Healy, Paul. 1986. "Interpretive Policy Inquiry." *Policy Sciences* 19: 381–396.

Herrnstein, Richard, and Murray, C. 1994. *The Bell Curve.* New York: Free Press.

Ho, Robert. 1990. "Multiculturalism in Australia." *Human Relations* 43(3): 259–272.

Hodder, Harbour Fraser. 1998. "Minority Wannabes." *Harvard Magazine* (November-December): 23–24.

Hodgkinson, Harold L. 2000. "What Should We Call People? Race, Class, and the Census for 2000." *Phi Delta Kappan* 77: 173–176, 178–179.

Holmes, Steven A. 1997a. "Panel Balks at Multiracial Census Category." *New York Times* (July 9): A12.

———. 1997b. "People Can Claim More than 1 Race on Federal Forms." *New York Times* (October 30): A1.

———. 1998. "Women Surpass Men in Educational Achievement, Census Reports." *New York Times* (June 30), A18.

Holt, W. Stull. 1929. *The Bureau of the Census.* Washington, DC: The Brookings Institute.

Hoover, Kenneth. 1993. "Identity: The Politics of a Concept." Presented to the Western Political Science Association, Pasadena, CA, March.

———. 1997. *The Power of Identity.* Chatham, NJ: Chatham House Press.

Hughes, Grace Flores. 1991–1992. "A Categorized Workforce." *The Bureaucrat/Public Manager* (Winter): 23–26.

Hull, Gloria T.; Scott, Patricia Bell; and Smith, Barbara, eds. 1981. *All the Women Are White, All the Blacks Are Men, but Some of Us Are Brave.* New York: Feminist Press.

Hymowitz, Kay S. 1993. "Multiculturalism Is Anti-Culture." *New York Times* (March 25): Op-ed page.

Ibarra, Herminia. 1993. "Personal Networks of Women and Minorities in Management." *Academy of Management Review* 18: 56–87.

Isaacs, Asher D. 1995. "Interracial Adoption: Permanent Placement and Racial Identity—An Adoptee's Perspective." *National Black Law Journal* 14: 126 ff.

"Italian-Americans Air W.W. II Loss of Liberties." 1999. *San Jose Mercury News* (October 27): 3B.

Jaimes, M. Annette. 1995. "Some Kind of Indian." In *American Mixed Race*, ed. Naomi Zack, chap. 10. Lanham, MD: Rowman & Littlefield.

Jefferson, Margo. 1999. "Revisions: Labels Change, Carrying Different Emotional Baggage." *New York Times* (November 15): E2.

Jennings, Bruce. 1983. "Interpretive Social Science and Policy Analysis." In *Ethics, the Social Sciences, and Policy Analysis*, ed. Daniel Callahan and Bruce Jennings, chap. 1. New York: Plenum Press.

———. 1987. "Interpretation and the Practice of Policy Analysis." In *Confronting Values in Policy Analysis*, ed. Frank Fischer and John Forester, 128–152. Newbury Park, CA: Sage.

Johnson, Deborah. 1992. "Developmental Pathways." In *Racially Mixed People in America*, ed. Maria P.P. Root, chap 4. Newbury Park, CA: Sage.

Jones, Camara Phyllis; LaVeist, Thomas A.; and Lillie-Blanton, Marsha. 1991. " 'Race' in the Epidemiological Literature." *American Journal of Epidemiology* 134: 1079–1084.

Kalfus, Marilyn. 1996. "People of Mixed Race Seek Own Label." *Orange County Register* (August 12).

Kan, Sergei. 1995. "Friendship, Family, and Fieldwork." Paper presented at the annual meeting of the American Anthropological Association, Washington, DC, November 15.

Kang, Peter. 1996. Letter to the editor. *New York Times* (June 3).

Kavanaugh, Paul, and Retish, Paul. 1993. "The Mexican American Employee." *Public Personnel Management* 22: 421–432.

Kellough, J. Edward. 1990. "Integration in the Public Workplace." *Public Administration Review*: 557–566.

Kennedy, Jim, and Everest, Anna. 1991. "Put Diversity in Context." *Personnel Journal* 70(9): 50–54.

Kenner, Hugh. 1997. "The Silent Majority." Review of Douglas C. Baynton, *Forbidden Signs: American Culture and the Campaign Against Sign Language. New York Times Book Review* (January 26): 30.

King, Michael. 1985. *Being Pakeha*. Auckland: Hodder and Stoughton.

———, ed. 1991. *Pakeha: The Quest for Identity in New Zealand*. Auckland: Penguin Books.

Kirnan, Jean Powell; Farley, John A.; and Geisinger, Kurt F. 1989. "The Relationship Between Recruiting Source, Applicant Quality, and Hire Performance: An Analysis by Sex, Ethnicity, and Age." *Personnel Psychology* 42: 293–308.

Kopelman, Elizabeth. 1994. "Enemies—A Love Story: The Prisoner's Dilemma and the Construction of Enemies in Legal and International Negotiations." Seminar presentation, Stanford Law School, Spring.

Kroeber, Alfred Louis. [1923] 1948. *Anthropology,* rev. ed. New York: Harcourt, Brace.

Kuhn, Thomas S. 1970. *The Structure of Scientific Revolutions*. 2d ed. Chicago: University of Chicago Press.

Kusmer, Kenneth L. 1996. "Xenophobia, Racial Violence and Social Change in the United States and Germany, 1830–1940." Paper presented at the Seminar on Comparative Race and Ethnicity, Stanford University, April.

Lakoff, George. 1987. *Women, Fire, and Dangerous Things*. Chicago: University of Chicago Press.

———. 1996. *Moral Politics*. Chicago: University of Chicago Press.

Lakoff, George, and Johnson, Mark. 1980. *Metaphors We Live By*. Chicago: University of Chicago Press.

Latour, Bruno. 1987. *Science in Action*. Cambridge: Harvard University Press.

Levitt, Barbara, and Nass, Clifford. 1994. "Organizational Narratives and the Person/ Identity Distinction." *Communication Yearbook* 17: 236-246.

Lewis, Neil A. 2000. "Searching Only in Profiles Can Hide a Spy's Face." *New York Times* (September 17): 4, 6.

Linder, Stephen H. 1995. "Contending Discourses in the Electromagnetic Fields Controversy." *Policy Sciences* 18: 209–230.

Lipsky, Michael. 1979. *Street-Level Bureaucracy*. New York: Russell Sage Foundation.

Litvin, Deborah R. 1997. "The Discourse of Diversity." *Organization* 4: 187–209.

Loden, Marilyn, and Loeser, Ronnie Hoffman. 1991. "Working Diversity: Managing the Differences." *Bureaucrat/Public Manager* (Spring): 21–25.

Löfgren, Orvar. 1993. "Materializing the Nation in Sweden and America." *ethnos.* Folkens Museum-Etnografiska (Stockholm) 3–4: 163–196.

Longino, Helen E. 1990. *Science as Social Knowledge.* Princeton: Princeton University Press.

Lott, Tommy L. 1992–1993. "Du Bois on the Invention of Race." *The Philosophical Forum* 24: 166–187.

Lustig, R. Jeffrey. 1997. "Race, Class and Politics: Universalism in the Shadow of Identity." Paper presented at the annual meeting of the Western Political Science Association, Tucson, March 13–15.

McBride, James. 1996. *The Color of Water.* New York: Riverhead Books.

McCloskey, Donald. 1985. *The Rhetoric of Economics.* Madison: University of Wisconsin Press.

McClure, Kirstie. 1999. "Figuring Authority: Statistics, Liberal Narrative, and the Vanishing Subject." *Theory & Event* 3: 1 (June): (electronic journal: Johns Hopkins University Press and Project Muse; www.muse.jhu.edu/journals/theory_&_event/).

McCulloch, Anne Merline, and Wilkins, David E. 1995. "'Constructing' Nations within States: The Quest for Federal Recognition by the Catawba and Lumbee Tribes." *American Indian Quarterly* 19: 361–388.

McDonald, Kim A. 1998. "Genetically Speaking, Race Doesn't Exist." *Chronicle of Higher Education* (October 30): A19.

McGrath, Charles. 2000. "Interview: Zuckerman's Alter Brain [Philip Roth]." *New York Times Book Review* (May 7): 8.

McNeil, Donald G., Jr. 1998. "Like Politics, All Political Correctness Is Local." *New York Times* (October 11): E11.

Magner, Denise K. 1993. "Colleges Faulted for Not Considering Differences in Asian-American Groups." *Chronicle of Higher Education* (February 10): A32, 34.

Marable, Manning. 1995. "Black Studies, Multiculturalism, and the Future of American Education." *Items* (Social Science Research Council Newsletter) 49(2/3): 49–56.

Marks, Jonathan. 1995. *Human Biodiversity: Genes, Race, and History.* Hawthorne, NY: Aldine de Gruyter.

Markus, Hazel Rose; Mullally, Patricia R.; Kitayama, Shinobu. 1996. "Selfways: Diversity in Modes of Cultural Participation." Chapter of manuscript prepared for *The Conceptual Self in Context,* ed. Ulric Neisser and David Jopling.

Martinez, Maurice M. 1995. Letter to the editor. *New York Times* (February 23).

Matthes, Karen. 1992. "Attracting and Retaining Hispanic Employees." *Personnel/HR Focus* (August): 7.

Maynard-Moody, Steven, and Stull, Donald. 1987. "The Symbolic Side of Policy Analysis." In *Confronting Values in Policy Analysis,* ed. Frank Fischer and John Forester, chap. 11. Newbury Park, CA: Sage.

Miller, Donald F. 1982. "Metaphor, Thinking, and Thought." *Et cetera* 39: 134–150.
———. 1985. "Social Policy: An Exercise in Metaphor." *Knowledge* 7: 191–215.

Minow, Martha. 1990. *Making All the Difference.* Ithaca, NY: Cornell University Press.

Montagu, Ashley. [1942] 1997. *Man's Most Dangerous Myth,* 6th ed. Walnut Creek, CA: Altamira Press.

Moore, Zena. 1995. "Check the Box that Best Describes You." In *American Mixed Race,* ed. Naomi Zack, chap. 4. Lanham, MD: Rowman & Littlefield.

Morello, Carol. 2001. "Census Finds that More Are Claiming Tribal Roots." *San Jose Mercury News* (April 10): 13A.

Navarro, Mireya. 1997. "Black and Cuban-American: Bias in 2 Worlds." *New York Times* (September 13): 7.

Nemetz, Patricia, and Christensen, Sandra. 1995. "A Theory of Multiple Interpretations of Multiculturalism in Personal, Societal, and Organizational Settings." In *Proceedings of the Academy of Management Annual Meeting*: 324–328.

Ni Bhrolchain, Maire. 1990. "The Ethnicity Question for the 1991 Census." *Ethnic and Racial Studies* 13: 542–567.

Nicholls, Richard E. 1995. "Henry Roth, Who Wrote of an Immigrant Child's Life in 'Call It Sleep,' Dies at 89." *New York Times* (October 15): A19.

Nobile, Robert J. 1991. "Can There Be Too Much Diversity?" *HR Focus* (August): 11.

Nobles, Melissa. 2000. *Shades of Citizenship.* Stanford, CA: Stanford University Press.

Noguchi, Sharon. 1993. "The Wrong Rice." *San Jose Mercury News* (December 8).

Omi, Michael, and Winant, Howard. 1994. *Racial Formation in the United States*, 2d ed. New York: Routledge.

O'Neill, William L. 1998. "Toil and Trouble." Review of Jacqueline Jones, *American Work: Four Centuries of Black and White Labor. New York Times Book Review* (February 15).

Ortony, Andrew, ed. 1979. *Metaphor and Thought.* Cambridge: Cambridge University Press.

Ossolinski, Rita Soler. 1992. "The Richness of Diversity." *Public Management* 74(12): 15–17.

The Oxford English Dictionary. [1971] 1991. Oxford: Clarendon.

Paley, Julia. 2000. "Making Democracy Count." *Cultural Anthropology* 16(2): 135–164.

Petersen, William. 1987. "Politics and the Measurement of Ethnicity." In *The Politics of Numbers*, ed. William Alonso and Paul Starr, chap. 5. New York: Russell Sage Foundation.

Petrini, Catherine M. 1993a. "The Language of Diversity." *Training & Development Journal* (April): 35–37.

———, ed. 1993b. "Training in the Kaleidoscope." *Training & Development Journal* (April): 15–24.

Phillips, Margaret E., and Sonja A. Sackmann. 1991. "Mapping the Cultural Terrain in Organizational Settings." Working paper.

Polanyi, Michael. 1966. *The Tacit Dimension.* New York: Doubleday.

Polkinghorne, Donald. 1983. *Methodology for the Human Sciences.* Albany, NY: SUNY Press.

"Population of Interracial Couples Has Doubled." 1993. *San Jose Mercury News* (February 12).

Potter, Elizabeth. 1989. "Modeling the Gender Politics in Science." In *Feminism and Science*, ed. Nancy Tuana, 132–146. Bloomington: Indiana University Press.

Pressman, Jeffrey L., and Wildavsky, Aaron. 1973. *Implementation.* Berkeley: University of California Press.

Rabinow, Paul, and Sullivan, William M., eds. 1979. *Interpretive Social Science.* Berkeley: University of California Press.

Rein, Martin, and Schön, Donald A. 1977. "Problem Setting in Policy Research." In *Using Social Research in Policy Making*, ed. Carol Weiss, 235-251. Lexington, MA: Lexington Books.

Reynolds, Larry. 1992. "Companies Will Work Together on Workforce Diversity." *HR Focus* (December): 17.

Rich, Wilbur C. 1989. "Minorities and the Public Service." *International Journal of Public Administration* 4:651–670.

Ricoeur, Paul. 1971. "The Model of the Text: Meaningful Action Considered as Text." *Social Research* 38: 529–562.

Riessman, Catherine Kohler. 1993. *Narrative Analysis.* Newbury Park, CA: Sage.

Roberts, Sam. 1995. "An Integrationist to This Day, Believing All Else Has Failed." Conversations/Kenneth B. Clark. *New York Times* (May 7): 4, 7.

Robbin, Alice. 1998a. "The Problematics and Potency of the Official Classification of Race and Ethnicity." Draft manuscript. (April 30).

———. 1998b. "Contested Terrain: The Social Construction of Race and Ethnicity." Draft manuscript. (July 10).

Rodriguez, Roberto. 1990a. ". . . And Here at Home." *Washington Post* (April 29): D1.

———. 1990b. "Census Figures Help Group Clout, Hardly Count the Minority of One." *Los Angeles Times* (April 1): M3.

Roe, Emery. 1994. *Narrative Policy Analysis.* Durham, NC: Duke University Press.

Rogers, Reuel. 1997. "Race, Ethnicity, and the Politics of National Belonging: Interrogating Afro-Caribbean Ethnic Consciousness." Paper presented at the annual meeting of the Western Political Science Association, Tucson, AZ, March 13–15.

Root, Maria P. P. 1992. *Racially Mixed People in America.* Newbury Park, CA: Sage.

Rosenbloom, David H. 1980. "The Federal Affirmative-Action Policy." In *The Practice of Policy Evaluation,* ed. D. Nachmias, 169–186. New York: St. Martin's Press.

Rosenhan, David L. 1973. "On Being Sane in Insane Places." *Science* 179: 250–258.

———. 1975. "The Contextual Nature of Psychiatric Diagnosis." *Journal of Abnormal Psychology* 84: 462–474.

Ross, L. 1977. "The Intuitive Psychologist and His Shortcomings." In *Advances in Experimental Social Psychology,* ed. L. Berkowitz, vol. 10: 174–187. New York: Academic Press.

Russell, Kathy; Wilson, Midge; and Hall, Ronald. 1992. *The Color Complex.* New York: Harcourt Brace Jovanovich.

Sachs, Susan. 2001. "Ellis Island Opens a Web Door to Let Families Trace Roots." *New York Times* (April 17): A19.

Safire, William. 1999. "On Language: One Guojia?" *New York Times Magazine* (August 15): 27–28.

———. 2001. "On Language: Judge Fights." *New York Times Magazine* (May 27): 12.

Said, Edward W. 1978. *Orientalism.* New York: Pantheon.

Samhan, Helen. 1993. Arab American Institute Statement to the House Subcommittee on Census, Statistics and Postal Personnel, Hearing on the 2000 Census, June 30.

Sante, Luc. 1996. "Living in Tongues." *New York Times Magazine* (May 12): 31–34.

Satris, Stephen. 1995. "What Are They?" In *American Mixed Race*, ed. Naomi Zack, chap 5. Lanham, MD: Rowman & Littlefield.

Scales-Trent, Judith. 1995. *Notes of a White Black Woman.* University Park, Pennsylvania State University Press.

Schachter, Jim. 1988. "Firms Begin to Embrace Diversity." *Los Angeles Times* (April 17): Section 1, 1.

Schmidt, Ronald J. 1988. "Cultural Pluralism and Public Administration: The Role of Community-Based Organizations." *American Review of Public Administration* 18: 189–202.

Schmidt, Ronald, Sr. 1999. "Is an English-Only Language Policy 'Racist'?—An Exploratory Analysis." Paper presented at the annual meeting of the Western Political Science Association, Seattle, March.

———. 2000. *Language Policy and Identity Politics in the United States.* Philadelphia: Temple University Press.

Schmitt, Eric. 2001a. "Broader Palette Allows for Subtler Census Portrait." *New York Times* (March 12): A12.

———. 2001b. "Blacks Split on Disclosing Multiracial Roots." *New York Times* (March 31): A1, A10.

———. 2001c. "Portrait of a Nation." *New York Times* (April 1): A18.

Schön, Donald A. 1979. "Generative Metaphor." In *Metaphor and Thought*, ed. Andrew Ortony, pp. 254–283. Cambridge: Cambridge University Press.

Schön, Donald A., and Rein, Martin. 1994. *Frame Reflection.* New York: Basic Books.

Schram, Sanford F., and Neisser, Philip T., eds. 1997. *Tales of the State.* New York: Rowman & Littlefield.

Scott, James C. 1998. *Seeing Like a State.* New Haven, CT: Yale University Press.

Segal, Daniel A. 1991. "The European." *Anthropology Today* 7(5): 7–9.

———. 1998. "The Hyper-Visible and the Masked: Some Thoughts on 'Race' and 'Class' in the United States Now." In *Democracy and Ethnography*, ed. Carol J. Greenhouse, pp. 50–60. Albany: State University of New York Press.

Segal, Daniel,and Handler, Richard. n.d. "American Multiculturalism and the Concept of Culture." Paper presented at the conference on "Defining the National," Bjarsjolagard, Sweden, April 27.

Sengupta, Somini. 1997. "Asians' Advances Found to Obscure a Need." *New York Times* (November 9): 1, 17.

Shea, Christophter. 1994. "Application from 'White African American' Causes Coast-to-Coast Stir." *Chronicle of Higher Education* (July 20).

Sheldon, William, with Stevens, S. S. and Tucker, W. B. [1940] 1970. *The Varieties of Human Physique (*2d reprint with corrections). Darien, CT: Hafner.

Shenhav, Yehouda. 1992. "Entrance of Blacks and Women into Managerial Positions in Scientific and Engineering Occupations." *Academy of Management Journal* 35: 889–901.

Short, John Rennie. 1996. *The Urban Order.* Cambridge, UK: Blackwell.

Simpson, J.A., and Weiner, E.S.C., eds. [1971] 1991. *The Oxford English Dictionary.* Oxford: Clarendon.

Singer, Rena. 1997. "China Takes Aim at Ethnic Inequality." *San Jose Mercury News.* (September 3): A15.

Sisneros, Antonio. 1993. "Hispanics in the Public Service in the Late 20th Century." *Public Administration Review* 53: 1–6.

Skinner, Samuel K. 1991. "Workforce Diversity." *The Bureaucrat/Public Manager* (Summer): 29–31.

Slavin, Seymour. 1993. "Multiculturalism: The Next Stage Implications for the Public Services and Public Administration." Paper presented at the annual meeting of the American Society for Public Administration, San Francisco, July 17–21.

Sollors, Werner, ed. 1989. *The Invention of Ethnicity.* New York: Oxford University Press.

Solomon, Charlene Marmer. 1991. "Are White Males Being Left Out?" *Personnel Journal* 70(11): 88–94.

Sontag, Deborah, and Dugger, Celia W. 1998. "The New Immigrant Tide: A Shuttle between Worlds." *New York Times* (July 19): A1, A12–14.

Spickard, Paul R. 1992. "The Illogic of American Racial Categories." In *Racially Mixed People in America*, ed. Maria P.P. Root, chap. 2. Newbury Park, CA: Sage.

Squire-Hakey, Mariella. 1995. "Yankee Imperialism and Imperialist Nostalgia." In *American Mixed Race*, ed. Naomi Zack, chap. 16. Lanham, MD: Rowman & Littlefield.

Staples, Brent. 1998. "Editorial Observer: The Shifting Meanings of 'Black' and 'White.'" *New York Times* (November 15): A14.

———. 1999. "Editorial Observer: Why Some Get Busted—and Some Go Free." *New York Times* (May 10): A22.

Star, Alexander. 1997. "Don't Look Back: A Proposal for Our Roots-Obsessed Culture." *The New Yorker* (February 3): 81–83.

Starr, Paul. 1987. "The Sociology of Official Statistics." In *The Politics of Numbers,* ed. William Alonso and Paul Starr, 7–57. New York: Russell Sage Foundation.

Steele, Shelby. 1990. *The Content of Our Character.* New York: St. Martin's Press.

———. 1997. "Op-ed: Indoctrination Isn't Teaching." *New York Times* (January 10).

Stein, Sandra J. 2001. "'These Are Your Title I Students': Policy Language in Educational Practice." *Policy Sciences* 34: 135–156.

Steinberg, Stephen. 1989. *The Ethnic Myth.* Boston: Beacon Press.

Stephan, Cookie-White. 1992. "Mixed-heritage Individuals." In *Racially Mixed People in America*, ed. Maria P.P. Root, chap. 5. Newbury Park, CA: Sage.

Stone, Deborah A. 1988. *Policy Paradox and Political Reason.* Boston: Little, Brown.

———. 1997. *Policy Paradox.* New York: Norton.

Swanigan, Pamela. 1993. "'Both' or 'Other'? It's Not as Clear as Black and White." *Chicago Tribune* (January 17).

Tafoya, Sonya M. 2000. "Check One or More. . . . Mixed Race and Ethnicity in California." In *California Counts: Population Trends and Profiles,* vol. 1(2). San Francisco: Public Policy Institute of California.

Taylor, Charles. 1971. "Interpretation and the Sciences of Man." *Review of Metaphysics* 25: 3–51.

———. 1988. Lecture, NEH Summer Seminar on Interpretation, University of California, Santa Cruz. July 5.

———. 1989. *Sources of the Self: The Making of Modern Identity.* Cambridge: Harvard University Press.

Theodoulou, Stella Z., and O'Brien, Rory. 1999. *Methods for Political Inquiry.* Upper Saddle River, NJ: Prentice-Hall.

Thernstrom, Stephen; Orlov, Ann; and Handlin, Oscar. 1980. *Harvard Encyclopedia of American Ethnic Groups.* Cambridge: Harvard University Press.

Thomas, R. Roosevelt, Jr. 1991–1992. "The Concept of Managing Diversity." *Bureaucrat/Public Manager* (Winter): 19–22.

Tucker, William H. 1994. *The Science and Politics of Race Research.* Chicago: University of Illinois Press.

U.S. Bureau of the Census. 1989. *200 Years of U.S. Census Taking: Population and Housing Questions, 1790–1990.* Washington, DC: U.S. Government Printing Office.

———. 1997. *Results of the 1996 R and A T T.* Working paper no. 18, Population

Division, Economics and Statistics Administration, U.S. Department of Commerce, Washington, DC.

U.S. Congressional Information Service. 1988. *American Statistical Index, 1988.* Washington, DC: U.S. Government Printing Office.

U.S. Department of Health, Education, and Welfare. 1978. *Characteristics of Births, U.S., 1973–1975* (PHS 78-1908). Appendix: Technical notes. Hyattsville, MD: U.S. Government Printing Office.

U.S. Department of Health and Human Services. 1990. *Birth and Fertility Rates by Education: 1980 and 1985.* Hyattsville, MD: U.S. Government Printing Office.

———. 1992a. *Vital Statistics of the U.S., 1988.* Volume 1, Section 4, Technical appendix, 4–5. Hyattsville, MD: U.S. Government Printing Office.

———. 1992b. *Prevention Profile, 1991.* Hyattsville, MD: U.S. Government Printing Office.

———. 1993. *Vital Statistics of the U.S., 1989.* Volume 1, Section 4, Technical appendix, 5–6. Hyattsville, MD: U.S. Government Printing Office.

———. 1994a. "Effect on Mortality Rates of the 1989 Change in Tabulating Race." In *Vital and Health Statistics,* Series 20, No. 25. Hyattsville, MD: U.S. Government Printing Office.

———. 1994b. *Vital Statistics of the U.S., 1990.* Volume 1, Section 4, Technical appendix, 5–6. Hyattsville, MD: U.S. Government Printing Office.

U.S. Equal Employment Opportunity Commission. 1968. *Legislative History of Titles VII and XI of the Civil Rights Act of 1964.* Washington, DC: U.S. Government Printing Office.

U.S. Office of Management and Budget. 1997. "Revisions to the Standards for the Classification of Federal Data on Race and Ethnicity." *Federal Register* (October 30). Available at http://www.whitehouse.gov/OMB/fedreg/ombdir15.html.

Varenne, Hervé. 1998. "Diversity as an American Cultural Category." In *Democracy and Ethnography,* ed. Carol J. Greenhouse, pp. 27–49. Albany: State University of New York Press.

Veres, John G., III; Green, Samuel, B.; and Boyles, Wiley R. 1991. "Racial Differences on Job Analysis Questionnaires." *Public Personnel Management* 20: 135–144.

Washington, Charles W. 1987. "Acculturation of Minorities in Large Organizations." *The Bureaucrat* (Spring): 29–34.

Wasserman, Paul, and Morgan, Jean, eds. 1976. *Ethnic Information Sources of the United States.* Detroit: Gale Research Company.

Waters, Mary C. 1990. *Ethnic Options.* Berkeley: University of California Press.

Watson, Warren E.; Kumar, Kamalesh; and Michaelsen, Larry K. 1993. "Cultural Diversity's Impact on Interaction Process and Performance." *Academy of Management Journal* 36: 590–602.

Webster's II New Riverside University Dictionary. 1984. Boston: Houghton Mifflin.

Wheatcroft, Geoffrey. 2000. "Where the Historical Is Political." Review of Bernard Lewis, *The Multiple Identities of the Middle East. New York Times Book Review* (January 2): 8.

Williams, Gregory Howard. 1995. *Life on the Color Line.* New York: Dutton.

Williams, Patricia J. 1991. *The Alchemy of Race and Rights.* Cambridge: Harvard University Press.

Williams, Richard. 1990. *Hierarchical Structures and Social Value: The Creation of Black and Irish Identities in the United States.* New York: Cambridge University Press.

Wilson, Terry P. 1992. "Blood Quantum." In *Racially Mixed People in America*, ed. Maria P.P. Root, chap. 9, Newbury Park, CA: Sage.

Wilson, William Julius. 1978. *The Declining Significance of Race.* Chicago: University of Chicago Press.

Wuthnow, Robert; Hunter, James Davison; Bergesen, Albert; and Kurzweil, Edith. 1984. "The Cultural Anthropology of Mary Douglas." In *Cultural Analysis,* chap. 3. New York: Routledge and Kegan Paul.

Wypijewski, JoAnn. 1999. "Sweet Home Arizona." Review of Linda Gordon, *The Great Arizona Orphan Abduction. Lingua Franca* (Fall): B12–15.

Yanow, Dvora. 1992a. "Silences in Public Policy Discourse: Policy and Organizational Myths." *Journal of Public Administration Research and Theory* 2: 399–423.

———. 1992b. "The Social Construction of Affirmative Action and Other Categories." Paper presented at the Fifth National Symposium on Public Administration Theory, Chicago, April 9–10.

———. 1993. "The Communication of Policy Meanings: Implementation as Interpretation and Text." *Policy Sciences* 26: 41–61.

———. 1995. "Policy Interpretations." *Policy Sciences* 28: 111–126.

———. 1996. *How Does a Policy Mean? Interpreting Policy and Organizational Actions.* Washington: Georgetown University Press.

———. 1999a. "From What *Edah* Are You? Israeli and American Meanings of 'Race/Ethnicity' in Social Policy Practices." *Israel Affairs* (Winter-Spring): 183–199.

———. 1999b. "The State, Science, and the Production of Difference: The Case of Jewish Israeli 'Ethnicity.' Paper presented at the annual meeting of the American Anthropological Association, Chicago, November 17–21.

———. 2000a. *Conducting Interpretive Policy Analysis.* Newbury Park, CA: Sage.

———. 2000b. "Seeing Organizational Learning: A 'Cultural' View." In *Organization* (Special Issue: "Knowing in Practice"), ed. Silvia Gherardi, 7: 247–268.

Yinger, J. Milton. 1985. "Ethnicity." *Annual Review of Sociology* 11: 151–180.

Young, Iris Marion. 1990. "Polity and Group Difference." In *Throwing Like a Girl and Other Essays in Feminist Philosophy and Social Theory*, chap. 7. Bloomington: Indiana University Press.

Zack, Naomi. 1992. "An Autobiographical View of Mixed Race and Deracination." *American Philosophical Association Newsletter on Philosophy and the Black Experience* 91(1): 6–10.

———. 1993. *Race and Mixed Race.* Philadelphia: Temple University Press.

———, ed. 1995. *American Mixed Race.* Lanham, MD: Rowman and Littlefield.

Zuberi, Tukufu. 2001. *Thicker than Blood: How Racial Statistics Lie.* Minneapolis: University of Minnesota Press.

Newspaper and magazine articles provided primary data in showing how "race," "ethnicity," and their categories were being perceived and treated by Americans generally, as well as by reporters and editors. Sources included the following: *The Chicago Tribune, The Chronicle of Higher Education, The Herndon Observer* (Virginia), *The Los Angeles Times, The New Republic, The New York Times, The New Yorker, Newsweek, The Oakland Tribune, The Orange County Register* (California), *The San Francisco Chronicle, The San Francisco Examiner, The San Jose Mercury News, Time, The Wall Street Journal, and The Washington Post.*

Index

About the Author

Dvora Yanow is professor and chair of the Department of Public Administration, California State University, Hayward. Her research focus is shaped by an overall interest in the communication of meaning in organizational and policy settings. Her publications include articles on organizational learning from an interpretive-cultural perspective, the role of built space in communicating meaning, and local knowledge in organizational and policy contexts. She is the author of *How Does a Policy Mean? Interpreting Policy and Organizational Actions* (1996) and *Conducting Interpretive Policy Analysis* (2000). Her articles have been published in such journals as *Policy Sciences, Administration & Society,* the *Journal of Public Administration Research and Theory, Organization, Organization Science,* and the *Journal of Management Inquiry.* In her nonacademic life, she reads mysteries; practices the piano, violin, and doumbek; folk dances and sings; grows tomatoes and herbs; and walks a fourteen-minute mile.